Chronicles of an Ordinary Boomer

Paul D. Riley

27th November 1955 - 18th October 2023

*Working Title: It's All About Me
.....or is it?*

Copyright: Paul D. Riley 2022

All Rights Reserved

Published by Path Head Press 2024

Cover Design: Andrew McCann

ISBN: 9798884653924

Path Head Press
An imprint of Val Scully Books
Raising Funds for Charity

8 Summerhill
Blaydon on Tyne
NE21 4JS

https://www.valscully.co.uk/path-head-press

PATH HEAD · PRESS ·

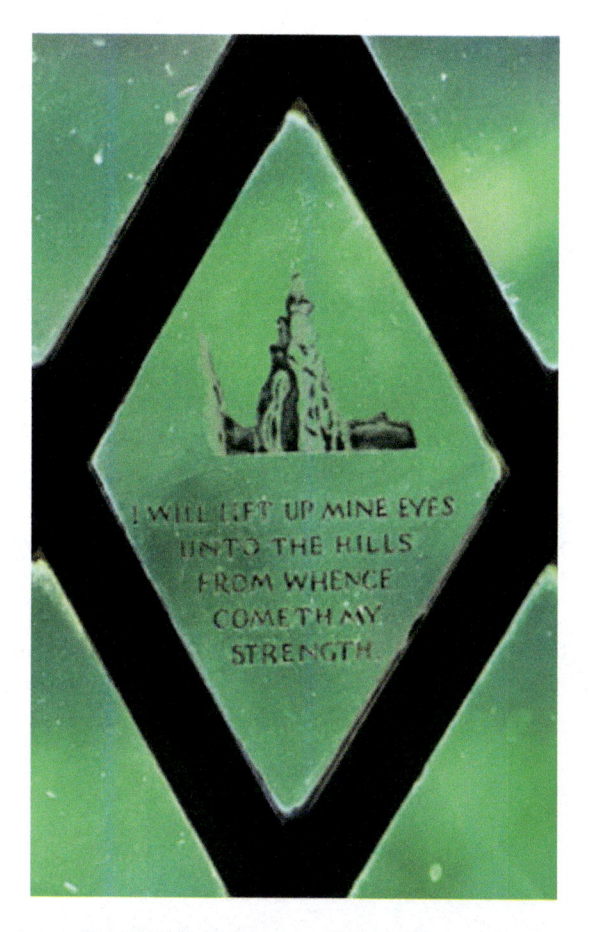

"I will lift up mine eyes unto the hills
From whence cometh my strength"
Wasdale Church, Lake District, UK

'Vivendo Discimus'
By living we learn......Patrick Geddes

FOREWORD

Paul always wanted to understand everything! At first it was the physical word, through science and chemistry in particular. During our travels, his desire to understand expanded into the world of ideas, so he started his PPE Degree with the Open University.

In 2017, when he completed it (with a First!) he decided he wanted to explore his own life and place in it all, and as he had always loved keeping records and lists, writing up his adventures and thoughts happily evolved into this 'Diary of an Ordinary Boomer'. Because of the tragedy of losing his son Chis, and then his cancer diagnosis, he became determined to finish his writing, and throughout his treatments, whenever he felt strong enough, he added to his story... thankfully it was mostly a happy place for him to revisit! A life well lived...

He loved so many people and hoped that each one of us would find something in his life story to enjoy and share and learn from... However, he was nothing if not a realist and often laughed that not everyone would want to read everything he had written, so do feel free to dip in and out!!
I owe a huge debt of gratitude to Val for all her kindness and patience and hard work in changing Paul's notes into a real book.

Candy Giaquinto

NOTE FROM THE 'EDITOR'

When Candy asked me to help her to get this book into print so that it could be read by his family and friends, I gladly accepted the challenge, astonished that Paul had found the time, courage and motivation to produce this work in addition to everything else he achieved! I have interfered with nothing, edited nothing: my role was simply to take Paul's words and images and collate them into book form to the best of my ability. We hope you enjoy it!

Val Scully

CONTENTS

Part 1: Autobiography

P.1	Introduction
P.2	A Child is Born
P.10	Moving House and Going to School
P.23	My Family & Other Animals; Early Years
P.30	Aireborough Grammar School & Huddersfield
P.42	Moving to Rawdon & Back to AGS
P.64	University & College
P.72	Starting Work
P.75	South Craven School
P.87	Marriage, Home and Family; Middle Years
P.107	Airebronians & Other Rugby Adventures
P.116	Mountains on my Mind
P.173	Upper Wharfedale Fell Rescue Association
P.188	Moving East; Qatar, China & Singapore
P.217	Family and France; The Aunat Years
P.245	Christopher Richard Martin Riley

Part 2: Philosophy

P.254	The Unexamined Life is not Worth Living'… Socrates
P.278	'The Sages' and My Foundations
P.290	Ethics & Morals
P.301	Politics, Economics & the Existential Life
P.307	Philosophical Thoughts: Causation, Consciousness & Free Will

Appendices: P.333 – 352
1 - Horsforth, 2 - Stoney Croft, 3 - AGS Letter,
4 - Autographs, 5 - Coins, 6 - Grant,
7 - Student Union Cards, 8 - Cars,
9 - Mountains & Caves,

Introduction

It is April 2020, as I start writing in the veranda of my old house in a sparsely populated village high in the Eastern French Pyrenees. The sky is azure blue on this beautiful spring morning and sparrows and tits are feeding in the pine tree of our small 'jardin anglais'. Close by, though it may as well be a thousand kilometres away, still with traces of snow on its high peak, is my favourite mountain, The Pic d'Ourtiset, whose peak at 1934m I have visited 32 times........so far! Around the world a pandemic, COVID-19, is bringing much of life to a halt, a strange phenomenon which may yet change society forever?

Born in 1955, I am of the post—WW2 generation, often called the Baby Boomers. As it turns out a lucky generation, at least in the Western World but current events may put an end to that, more of that later. I am not special in any real sense, being neither rich nor famous, poor nor infamous, genius nor idiot, handsome nor ugly, witty nor dull; though some if not many of my students, relatives and friends may disagree on these points. My contributions to the world have been neither significant nor trivial........in short I am both unique and yet just an Ordinary Boomer!

These Chronicles are an attempt to set down for my descendants a very subjective and often personal view of an ordinary life in the latter half of the 20th and the first half of the 21st century. To bring into focus not only some of the incredible changes that have affected humanity, but also to express a unique perspective of day to day lives and events, alongside hopes & fears. They follow, in the main, the arrow of time with some deviations as areas of my life developed. Obviously they are subject to the vagaries of a memory which has been foreshortened by time, increased by familiarity and dulled by ageing. In short, there has been no attempt made to make this account either comprehensive or historically accurate, errors and oversights abound, the recent is clearer than the past; it is my story as it sits with me now.

I am hoping by the end to also have covered some of my thinking about the world around me. Wishing to stimulate thoughts in other minds about what Scottish philosopher David Hume called the problem of 'what is and what ought to be'.

To those who I already know, I hope I have the skill not to offend while still remaining honest. I have left other people's stories mainly up to them to elucidate. To those not yet born, I hope I can inform, educate and perhaps occasionally entertain.

Paul David Riley, B.Ed,B.Ed(HC),B.A(Hons),M.Ed. IML. Aunat, April 2020

A child is born.

I arrived in the world on the 27th of November 1955 at the Four Gables nursing home, Clarence Rd., Horsforth, about tea time! (Appendix 1, Map of Horsforth). I know this because my mum Patricia, 24 and always Pat, used to remind me she missed her tea. Allegedly a bonny bouncing baby boy......well bouncing! My dad Peter, usually Pete and 25, was born and bred in Horsforth and worked for the Leeds Co-Operative Society, known to everyone as 'The Co-Op', as a warehouseman. Mum was a shorthand typist from Farsley, working for English Electric Co. in Bradford, in their typing pool. Both had left school at 14, having lived through WW2 as children. They had met at a Friday dance at Broadway Hall in Horsforth, close to where we would live for a while, marrying in January of 1955. To save you the maths, that is 10 months before me!.......

Arthur, Linda, Peter, Pat, Doris, Nellie and Joe Sr.
21 st. January 1955

In the early days we lived at 15 Bank Gardens, Horsforth with my dad's parents: Arthur, Grandad Riley and Linda, Grandma Riley. Bank Gardens was a nice three bedroomed Council house, what we would now call social housing, with both front and rear gardens. Grandad R. loved his garden, especially growing prize winning Chrysanthemums. He always gardened in an old shop coat, shirt and tie, not unusual at the time!

Grandad R. also had an 'outhouse' in which he bred and showed budgerigars. He won many certificates, some of which I still have.

Some of Arthurs many certificates for flowers and budgerigars, which I keep in an old tea caddy in France.

Grandad R. had spent all his life working for the Co-Op and had risen from shop boy to shop manager in Rodley by the time I was born. Living through WW1 as a child, his only career deviation had been caused by volunteering for the RAF at the outbreak of WW2 in 1939. They trained him as a cook and then sent him overseas for the next five years. First to live in the deserts of North Africa, cooking alongside Monty and the 8th Army. Then off to Sicily and finally to Italy, visiting Rome, Sorento, Naples and Florence.

He was blown up, in Tunisia I think, and an American Hospital saved his arm. His row of campaign medals included an American Purple Heart for being wounded in combat, presented in hospital by an American General.

Arthur, Santa Maria, Italy, 1944

He wore this Royal Flying Corps cap badge, from a family member I don't recall, throughout the war.......nobody noticed!

As a small boy I would sit on his knee and he would weave fantastic stories about his time in the desert. Often, I see now, a combination of real experiences and his enjoyment of historic adventures such as One Thousand and One Nights. He would tell me of his adventures on his Arabian stallion called, of all things, Tony? Grandma R. was a lunch time supervisor or 'dinner lady' at a local junior school but when I started school she left to help look after me.

My mum returned to work soon after I was born. Quite a progressive step for a young mother in the 50s. I was looked after for a while by her mum Doris, Grandma Wood, in Farsley and sometimes Grandma R. in Horsforth. Grandma W. had two children, my mum Pat and her younger sibling, Uncle Joe. She often called him Young Joe and I will use that term here. Young Joe was named after his father, my grandfather, Grandad Wood.

The elder Joe was something of an athlete, he had played cricket at a good level with Pudsey St. Lawrence and football for Farsley Celtic. He had been taken on as a semi-professional footballer by Leicester City just before the war. Volunteering for WW2 he was judged to have flat feet and so ineligible for the forces. Our family's best athlete, Joe spent his war making munitions at The Avro in Yeadon, his football career was ended. I still have a hand grenade, not live, and an aircraft cannon shell, that I found in one of his shed drawers!

To deviate slightly, I once had a phone call at work from my youngest son Alasdair. As a teenager he and his friend Tom had removed the pin from the grenade and couldn't get it back in. They were stood in the house 'shitting' themselves and holding on to the spring for all they were worth.

A very rare view of the AVRO works 1940 painted in camouflage to deceive German aircraft, on the roof are false farm buildings. School boys were employed to go on the roof every day to move the animals around.

Before the war Grandad W. had met Grandma W. while working in the same wool mill, at the bottom of Richard Shaw Lane, or 'Rikitsher Lane' as they called it, in Stanningley. After the war he worked for British Rail on track maintenance. His Mother Nellie was also still alive and lived near them, my only remaining Great Grandparent. Like my dad's parents, these grandparents lived in a three bedroomed Council House on Cotefields Avenue, Farsley, with front and rear gardens, curtesy of a post war Labour government.

I believe I have a few memories of those early days before school, but they may be stories:

I remember my mum running up the road happily waving a confirmation letter from the council offices in Horsforth. The letter gave us our first family home, a three bedroomed council house at 40 King George Road, Horsforth. By then my dad had moved up in the world and become a company Sales Representative or 'Rep'. I think it was for a company selling fluorescent lighting to the wool mills of Yorkshire and the cotton mills of Lancashire........the job included a car!

I remember dad washing the back of the car, out on the street. It started to move and I have an image of him in his wellies, chasing it down the road. Another couple of car anecdotes of the same time come to mind, though I don't recall either directly, they became family folk law. One was of an old car we owned at some stage. It just kept stopping! Then my mum discovered that this was linked to a switch I had discovered under the dashboard. In those days there was no such thing as seat belts or child seats. As a small child I just sat on my mum's knee in the front seat. The other story was travelling to West End village, near Blubberhouses. This was a deserted village about to be covered by flooding to make the West End Reservoir. A steep hill leads up to it and on the way up the boot flew open and the spare tyre rolled out, down the hill. I also remember I had a stick-on steering wheel, so I could help to drive.

Oh, that brings another story to mind, I can't place it in time, all I know is that I was there and young. We had all been to Blackpool with Grandad and Grandma R. Approaching Skipton on the A6069 Grandad wanted to pee. The road was dark and we stopped by a wall. He jumped over and landed in the canal, thinking the dark band over the wall was another road. He had to travel home in his undies, with a blanket around his legs.

My first bike had stabilisers, the day the stabilisers were taken off I was away. Soon after I came off, no helmets in those days, and badly cut my knee on the gravel path. I still have the scar 65 years on. Another memory of King George Road was of a tortoise I had which died. We buried it in the garden, said a prayer and my mum told me it would go to heaven. Several days later I arrived in the kitchen with said tortoise, to tell my much distressed mother that she lied! Thus began, I think, my lifelong scepticism about religion, but more of that later. My final memory of that house is vague, dad trying to make me think that Santa had been, by ringing some bells down stairs.
….I was not convinced, ringing the bells myself to check my theory, empirically…..what a precocious child, even at 3 or 4, I must have been.

I remember watching: Watch With Mother, The Wooden Tops and Andy Pandy (available now on U-Tube) with Grandma W.

The Wooden Tops

Bill and Ben, Andy Pandy, Looby Loo & Teddy

This was of course in Black and White at a time when there were only two channels: BBC and ITV. There was very little daytime TV and most of the time you could just watch the Test Card.

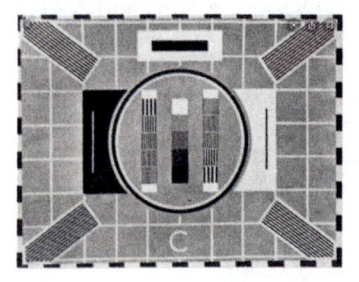

An early example of the Test Card, compulsive watching for most of the day.

There was also another compulsive thing to watch on TV, the 'dot'. The picture on old TVs, which had a large back on them to hold the valves and tubes, would shrink to a dot in the middle of the scree when switched off. It would take several seconds for this dot to vanish. We got our first TV while still in King George Road, a 12" screen(1958), as my dad always liked to keep up with the neighbours.

Grandma W. and I would sometimes take the bus from Farsley through Stanningley and up to Horsforth, as Grandma took me home. I always loved to sit at the front of the top deck. Sometimes we would have a treat and ride to Bradford on the Trolly Bus, a double decker buses with no track, but attached to electric cables overhead. Yes, an e-bus! Once or twice I can remember walking out of Cotefields Avenue, over the fields which now contain the Ring Road (A6120) joining the road at Rodley, then up the road to Horsforth. About 4km and a long way for a pre-schooler. Maybe this is where I got my love of walking?

Neither Grandma nor Grandad Wood could drive. They went on holiday on coach trips, often run by Wallace Arnold's. I can remember being taken to Belle Vue Zoo, Manchester, by my grand parents on a Wallace Arnold's day trip. The Zoo closed in 1977.

A Bradford Trolly Bus

I had a happy childhood and never seemed to get bored with my own company. As the only child of a large group of adults, I felt well loved by everyone.

Moving house and going to school

Mum and dad must have been doing quite well. After only a couple of years at King George Road they bought a new build dormer-bungalow at 12 Stoney Croft, Horsforth (Appendix 2). Like most houses of the time, Stoney Croft had no central heating or double glazing. This meant that in winter the bedroom windows would freeze.......on the inside. I remember writing my name in the ice on a number of occasions. At the same time I was enrolled into Featherbank County Primary (Infant) school.

Our new house was at the top of a cul-de-sac, on the turning circle. It had three 'dormer' bedrooms and a built in garage under the kitchen. The back garden was large and it had a small front garden and drive. My parents were the first that I know of in our extended family to have bought their own home. At the time, everybody else seemed to live in a council house.

The new street had many young families. Around the turning circle was Alison Barr a pleasant girl of my age who I hardly dare speak to. Next door was my best friend through junior school, Stephen Buseden, aka 'Busby', also my age, and his younger sister Mandy. On the other side was Gina, a younger girl who often played with Mandy. Then Stephen's mum's parents and finally two younger boys Stephen and Glen Taylor. I ended up playing rugby with this second Stephen, many years later. His dad was a maths teacher and gave me some maths tuition for a while, when I started secondary school.

Gina, Mandy, Stephen('Busby'), Me, Gina's sister, Glen, Stephen

At the bottom of the street was another boy of my age, I think his name was Anthony Broomhead. We sometimes played together, but he went to a different school, along with Alison. He comes to mind not because he was my first death but because he was my first encounter with dying. He was knocked of his bike at about aged 10 or 11 on the junction between Stoney Lane and Broadway. We crossed there for school every morning. We heard about the accident and went to see. I can, to this day see him laying in the road, with blood on his head. Then being put into the ambulance.......we never saw him again! Shortly after his family moved away.

The accident happened just across the road from another school friend Alan Wade, aka 'Alf', who lived at the top of Featherbank Lane. I played rugby with Alf for many years, both at school and for our club Airebronians RUFC, now Aireborough RUFC. I still see him from time to time. He is my oldest continuous friend and the person in the world I have known continuously for the longest time. Alan's mum was the Crossing Warden for Broadway.

I digress, I've moved forward quickly in time and need to return to my early years.

I started Featherbank School at about 4.5yrs. The same school buildings that my dad had been in for his whole school life. It's most famous pupils are Marc Almond of Soft Cell fame, who was in the year below me and for a short while after I had left, Labour Leader Ed Milliband. The school still had a large air raid shelter in the middle of the playground, when I arrived.

Years 1 and 2 were spent in the infant school, my first teacher being Mrs Crooks, she was nice. The toilets were in the playground and had no roof, so you got wet when peeing in the rain. We would have competitions to see how far we could wee up the wall. The sit down toilets had wooden half-seats and always smelled......I can't ever remember going to them.

I don't remember much about those early days. Though I do remember being taunted on my first days by an older boy, as I stood around at 'play time' not knowing who to talk to. This was my only incidence of bullying throughout my school career. I must have made friends quickly, though I have no idea how, as I am by nature quite shy. I loved those early days of learning, something which has stuck with me for the whole of my life. I once remember, in Year 1 apropos nothing, telling the teacher if she put a 'T' on the end of the 'We' she had on the blackboard it would make 'wet'.....

I got a sweet from the sweety box. In those days and for much of my own later career, teachers wrote in chalk on a blackboard. On a visit from the fire brigade a bee stung me on the ear as we waited to look around the engine. I remember the fireman was pleased to show off his first aid.

At break time……'play time'……we would get a third of a pint of milk to drink. This was free and lasted until 1968 in secondary schools. It was withdrawn by a Labour government under Harold Wilson. It was withdrawn for children under 7 in 1971 by the Conservative Education Secretary, 'Margaret Thatcher, the 'milk snatcher', under PM Edward Heath.

Each lunchtime Grandma R. would pick me up from school and walk me to her house for lunch, then walk me back to school. At the end of school, 15.00(infants), 15:30(juniors), she would pick me up again and walk me to her house. It became a tradition that we walk home via Rose Terrace and the Rose Stores, now a private house. I would get 6d(2.5p), six old pence, for sweets. I loved sherbet fountains, but often bought football or other cards with an awful piece of chewing gum in them. We would walk home and I would watch black and white TV, or 'play out' while she cooked my tea.

My mum and dad must have had some sort of arrangement with her. They would arrive from work together at about 17.30 and stay for tea, before we all went home. Grandad R., who had a driving licence but couldn't drive, would get in about 18.30. He got a driving licence for a motorbike he had before the war. This enabled him to drive anything, without ever having to take a test, but he always took the bus.

I got to know some of the kids in Bank Gardens, quite well, I spent a lot of time there. The house was on a crescent opposite the roundabout, with a little unkept shrub area in front. This was ideal for all sorts of hiding and climbing games. It had two trees, but because I was heavy I always struggled to climb them. Susan Warmsley, two doors up was our leader, she was four years older than me and the epitome of a Tom Boy. David Marsden next door, a couple of years younger than me and his elder sister, Anne, were part of our gang. Stuart from the house on the end, a year or two older than me, sometimes joined us. Susan was my friend, she knew everything!

As I got older I was allowed to move between home and my Grandma's without supervision. Dad had a telephone installed at Stoney Croft and persuaded my grandparents to be attached as an extension line. They had not had a telephone until then. This meant I could call as soon as I arrived home, at no cost.

My mum and dad were party animals. Though it's probably not an accurate record I remember them going out almost every Friday and Saturday night. When I was very young my Grandma R. would walk me home from her house and stay until they got back. That soon changed and I spent many weekend nights with my grandparents.

Our extension phone at Stoney Croft Horsforth 4063 looked exactly like this.

My 'Aunties' Joan and Minnie Farrar, of whom more later, lived together on Stanhope Drive. They had a much older phone.

Joan and Minnie's phone was an old Bakelite model, without the curly plastic connection wire to the handset.

13

We have 35+ years to go before mobile phones, so out and about we used a public telephone, run by the GPO (General Post Office). You may have seen one?

An old telephone 'kiosk'

Buttons A & B: Put your coins in the slot and dial. If someone answers, press A to talk, if not, press B to get your money back

The only other thing which strikes me about those first years is 'play time' in the rain. Why was it that us infants had to go inside, while the big boys and girls in the junior school played out in their coats? The sheer injustice of it!

Moving up to juniors we moved into the big building. Every morning we would line up in the central hall for assembly. Some sort of religious lesson would be read, usually by the Headmaster, Mr Heselgrave. Then one of the teachers would play the piano, while we all sang along from a big hymn sheet on the wall. I can still sing along with many popular hymns because of that indoctrination. My favourite was always 'Onward Christian Soldiers'. I wanted it at my first wedding, but it was vetoed by my prospective mother-in-law, Joyce Helliwell! I also remember a boy in the class above us peeing his shorts in assembly, all over the floor! Our first teacher was Miss Brown who was rather severe and quite old. Then Mrs Cuthbertson, across the road in what must have been an old Nissen Hut left over from the war. She was nice and friendly, I liked her.

Featherbank, circa 1970

Featherbank Junior School, hardly different from when I was there. We always used the 'Boys' entrance on the right, which lead to the cloakrooms and boys toilets and staff kitchen. This went into a central hall, surrounded by classrooms. My dad did all his schooling there (1934-1945)

The finally two years were with Mr Dobson, first sharing half the class with the bottom half of the year above and then as the 'Top Class'. Mr Dobson had a partly bald head and was in his 50s. He was strict, but a nice man, and I liked him too.

From Mr Dobson's class I remember a couple of things. We sat at single desks, lined up in pairs. All our books were in our desk, which flipped open. At the top of the desk was a slot to stop your pen from rolling off and next to it was an ink well.

In our last year we used these and an ink pen to write in our 'best books'. This worked alongside a piece of blotting paper or 'blotter', to dry up the ink so it didn't smudge. The worst job was ink monitor, filling ink wells. After a day of that your hands were blue for a week.

School desk with inkwell and storage for books.

Simple pen and ink that we used in the 'top class' for working in our 'best books'.

A couple of other jobs came our way as 'senior' in School. One was a rota for making staff tea an coffee at breaks. Can you imagine being allowed to do that these days! We worked unsupervised in pairs in the small kitchen next to the boys cloak room. We had to boil a large kettle on an old gas ring, then make pots of tea and coffee. We put out biscuits and rolled the whole lot into the central hall. You also got the honour of washing up after break. The best bit of this was missing a short piece of the lessons, before or after break.

We also had bell ringing duty. A large hand bell kept in the Head's office. This could be in the morning, at the finish of breaks and lunch and at the end of school. I also came in early to unlock store cupboards in the hall. Like the bell duty I had to arrive early, this time taking the keys from a board in the Head's office, unlock the cupboards and return the keys.

The only school work I remember was writing out our times tables, 2s to 12s, every Friday morning, followed by a spot test and more maths stuff. There wasn't much in the way of homework in those days. Perhaps spellings 10 or 15 words for a spelling test, so we had lots of time to play out. I joined the 9th Airedale 'Grove' Cubs for about a year. This was OK except for Sunday Parade at the local Methodist chapel, once a month........I never made it into scouts. In my final year the school had a project, to build a swimming pool over the road, where my old classroom had been. This involved collecting, bundling and selling old newspapers. A whole classroom was set aside and we set about the task of filling it. I never did know if it got built?

In the 'top class' we went swimming for a whole morning, once a week. The reason that it was a whole morning was that we had to travel by coach 8km each way to Pudsey baths. I hated swimming, I was shiny white and pudgy and, like my dad, I couldn't swim. The single thing that comes back to me from swimming was the very last lesson. A girl called Jackie Dunning, a good swimmer, persuade me to let her pull me into the deep end. Me, being held by a girl, in just my trunks.......whatever next! I did go round to her house for tea once too, but there was no further touching.

Dad went out 'for a drink' on Thursday night and Sunday lunchtimes with his long time mate, my 'Uncle' Derek Baldwin. Mum and dad would also meet up with Derek and his wife Brenda on Friday and Saturday nights. Having said that I very rarely saw either my mum or dad more than happily tipsy. Though my dad built a bar in the lounge which always had plenty of bottles, drink was never in any way a problem in the house and the bottles were rarely touched.

Derek and Brenda, my mum and dad's best friends for many years. They had an argument about their children going to my mum and dad's 25th Wedding Anniversary. After that, I didn't see them again until my dad's funeral...now that is holding a grudge!

I'm fairly sure that my mum didn't really like Brenda, but put up with her for my dad's sake. My recollection is that Pat was a very duty-full wife, though mum and dad would argue often. Rather unusually, my dad did all the important cooking, as he too was a cook, like his father, in the RAF during his 2 years of National Service.

It was in these last two years at junior school that I developed an interest in sport. I had always played cricket and kicked a football around with Grandad Wood. Neither my dad nor his dad had the slightest interest in either of these two sports. Though Grandad R. was rather a good Crown Green Bowler and taught me how to play. I often went to watch him, playing in his trilby, and I was a sort of mascot for the Horsforth Cons. (Conservative Club) team for a while. I still have his very distinctive bowls here in France.

Arthur, Grandad Riley, playing Crown Green Bowls

Summers were for cricket, we would play in the school yard at every opportunity. I played cricket for the school team for two seasons, being the captain in the last season and winning the Airedale and Wharfedale trophy. I could bat quite well and fielded close in, at Silly Mid-Off, or in the Slips.
At football I was not so good......though in the winter we played every day in the school yard I was usually the fat lad in goals, often towards the last to be picked. Never the less I played a few times for the school team, until I was dropped for Patrick Magee, a much better goalie..... I hated Patrick! I needed a sport more in tune with my stature, roll on secondary school and rugby!

One of my friends was called Michael Pullford. I remember he was very clever and lived on Broadway. I often went to his house. Michael's parents moved to Cottingham in Hull. We exchanged letters for a while, then lost touch.

The 'Leavers' (Year 6) at Featherbank in 1967, just before we separated to go to different secondary schools. I am in the back row, 4th from the left. My friend Stephen is on the front row, far right and Alan is front row second from the left.

In our final year a few students had to take some tests. We were part of a new system to replace the 'Eleven Plus' called the Thorne Scheme. I wasn't asked to do the test. Later that year we received a letter in the post to say that I was eligible to move up to Aireborough Grammar School (Appendix 3). Busby, next door, and Alf were going too. Unfortunately Alison from our group wasn't selected and her parents sent her to Priesthorpe, a secondary Modern School in Farsley.

I was surprised that a number of my friends also didn't make the cut. In particular Andrew Alanach, who lived at an amazing address, 20 Park Drive.....a cigarette brand. His dad was a football Ref. and would sometimes take us to run touch.......Patrick didn't make it either lol! Most of those who didn't make it to the Grammar School went to the local Secondary Modern, Benton Park.

My Dad did try to get me into Leeds Boys Grammar School, which was fee paying. I did an initial test in school, along with a girl called Janice Hardisty. Janice was applying for the Girls Grammar School. I had another test later, at the school and both I and my parents had interviews. I didn't get a place.

Mr Heselgrave later told my dad and my dad told me, that he thought that they, not me, must have failed the interview. Who knows, I was pleased to be going to Aireborough with some of my mates!

Shortly after I started school mum got a new job, as the Personal Assistant to Arthur Green, the Group's Secretary to Joint Promotions. This was an umbrella company for those organising All-in-Wrestling contests. Wrestling was a very popular spectator sport on TV and could be watched most Saturday afternoons.

Quite a few times I was allowed in the office for a day, to 'work' with my mum. My main job was to use the printer to make sure there were enough addressed envelopes for each wrestler in their files. I also got to meet a lot of the men who I saw on TV on a Saturday. Those in the office also got to meet other 'famous' sports stars, as my Autograph Book shows. (Appendix 5, for other examples)

Harold Sakata was Oddjob in the 1964 James Bond movie, Goldfinger. He came into the office once and put his famous steel rimmed hat on my head.

My mum and dad were not poor, so I always had good quality school clothes and never went short of toys. Though I wouldn't say they spoiled me.

I always had a bike to ride and they bought me a 10 speed racing bike for being selected for AGS. I would get knocked off it cycling to Guiseley from Horsforth when I was about 12. It was my fault and luckily, even without a helmet, I was unhurt!

My favourite toys were Scalextric and Action Man.

This was the sort of Action Man kit I would buy in the 60s

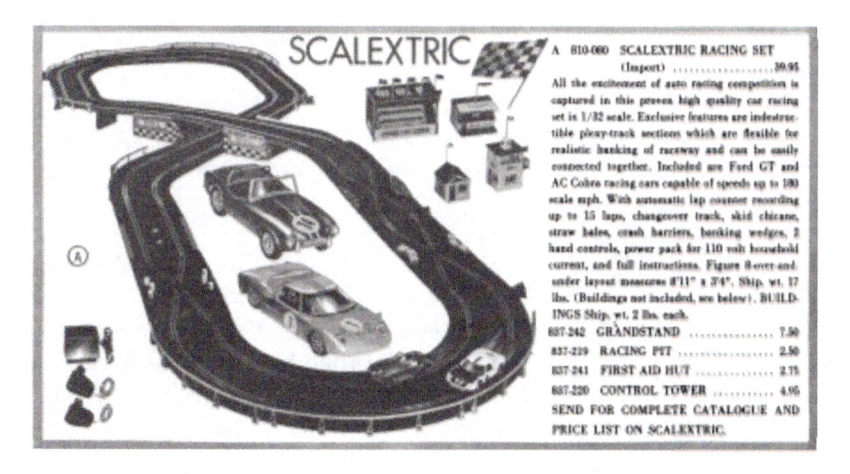

The Scalextric set above has the same cars I had: AC Cobra(green) & Ford GT (light blue). I also had the bridge, grandstand & chicanes.

I also enjoyed playing a table football game called Subbuteo. I would go to Alf's house after school, often for an hour or so to play. Alf was an expert! I also had Subbuteo Cricket, but that wasn't nearly as good.

As I got a little older I was allowed further afield. By the age of 10 I could go to Horsforth Hall Park and play on the swings with my friends, walk to Cubs, shops on Town Street or ride my bike to Aunty Minnies. Kids were allowed more freedom in the 60s & 70s. Society didn't expect parents always to act as 'dads taxi'. I don't know if this is better or worse for a child's development? It didn't seem to do me or my friends any harm, but maybe we were just lucky.

My family and other animals, early years.

We have met my closest family: Peter, Pat, Arthur, Linda, Joe, Doris and Nellie. There were a few others on the scene in those early years that need a short introduction, if only because they are interesting in different ways.

First on the list must be my 'Aunty' Joan, she was a Farrar, Grandma R's maiden name, but not my real Aunt. My dad always called her 'cousin Joan' even though she was some 10 years older than him. She was a buyer for the Leeds Co-op and very much into Amateur Dramatics. As I sit here I can see on my shelf sets of Dickens novels and a couple of copies of Shakespeare's complete works, which were left to me by her. Upstairs is a reproduction Chippendale desk and in the study the matching chair, also left to me..........Joan was my favourite aunt.

Unfortunately she died of breast cancer when I was about 7 or 8, my first experience of a family death. I never really understood why God had taken away my favourite Aunt. Everyone had a different explanation or excuse for it, but all seemed to be made up.....this only encouraged my life long scepticism. By the time I was 11 it had turned into outright disbelief.

Over the last few months a friend of my step-daughter Bea has been researching my family tree. Strangely Joan could not be found. Though Grandma R. had a number of brothers and sisters, Joan was not the child of any that we could find. Further research on Joan has produced a small family tree for her, which as yet has no connection to mine. This is most intriguing, as Joan lived with one of Linda's unmarried elder sisters, my Great-Aunt Minnie.

Photo opposite, about 1912+ : back right is probably my Great Grandma, Clara Farrar(b.1867), Front Right is my Grandmother, Linda(b.1901). The others are more of a guess. Back L to R: Mary Emma (b.1887) Maud (b.1895) Middle L to R: Minnie(b.1891), Clara(b.1895). Front L to R: Arthur(b. 1897), ?

23

Minnie and Joan lived in another Council House, this time in Stanhope Drive. Once again it had three bedrooms and front and rear gardens. When Joan was alive it always struck me as rather 'posh'.

Minnie, like her sister Maud, could not walk without walking sticks. Her legs, particularly her shins were both very bent, which meant she sort of moved like a crab. I never did find out what was wrong with them, though some early photos I have suggest they were both OK as teenagers. Perhaps they had severe Rickets, Blount's or Padget's Disease or Osteomalacia?

Minnie outlived Joan by quite a few years. I used to visit her as a late teenager. By this time she was quite old, well into her 80's, her sight was fading, but she loved to bake. She always added too many eggs and her buns would be shaped like volcanoes. I arrived one day to find her sat crying at the kitchen table "I've been burgled" she said. "When? How?" I replied, the house looked fine! "Somebody has sneaked in and stolen my buns from the oven" she sobbed. That was very unlikely, so I went to the oven to investigate. She was old, maybe she had never actually made the buns? But no, they were there, in a burned heap at the bottom of the oven, mixed with the plastic tray she use by mistake.

Just opposite to where Minnie lived was Salmon Crescent and the War Memorial Rock. Behind the rock was a Youth Centre, long since demolished for housing. It was there that I was a St John's Ambulance Brigade Cadet, for perhaps a year.

First certificate and cap/lapel badge

Our uniform was a grey St. John's Shirt with a white platted lanyard, a white shoulder bag to carry our first aid kit, black tie, black beret and badge and a special belt and buckle.

Great aunt Maud Farrar was another of Linda's sisters. She lived in Beeston, Leeds. My dad would bring her quite often to Bank Gardens on a Friday evening. When I was small we would share Linda's spare room. Her favourite phrase was "Its time to go to the blanket market". Maud taught me how to play Whist and Dominos.

A kitchen range, similar to Aunt Maud's

It was a strange experience going to Maud's house. It was like going back in time. She lived on a cobbled street, in a back to back house. It only had one door, one room at ground level, a scary coal cellar and one bedroom upstairs. It had no electricity, the lighting was gaslights on the wall. In the centre of one wall was a huge black 'range', for cooking and baking and the bath was a zinc tub which was hung behind the cellar door. Most remarkable of all was the toilet. A key hung behind the front door and the toilet was in a block about 5 doors down the street. Maud used to cut up squares of newsprint, tied on a string, for toilet paper. At night time, she had a porcelain 'po', chamber pot or 'guzunder', because it guzunder the bed!. I remember feeling uncomfortable with the kids next door, who all seemed to have two streams of grey snot running from their noses. Maude was moved out into a new flat, sheltered accommodation, when I was about 12. The old street she lived in was pulled down.

Maud had been a seamstress and made my school shorts all through infant and junior school. I hated them and wanted bought shorts like all the other kids. Like most of the lads of my age, my first pair of 'long trousers' was for Secondary school. Thankfully they were bought from the school suppliers, Rawcliffe's in Rawdon.

Like my dad, Young Joe Wood had done National Service after the war. This involved two years in one of the armed services. Also like Arthur and my dad he had become a cook/baker in the RAF. As I grew up Young Joe had left the RAF and become a bread baker in a local bakery in either Farsley or Stanningley. I remember his uniform hanging in a plastic bag in Doris's home. The RAF had posted him to Germany and his spoken German was good.

Young Joe was different, to me as a child, as he lived with another man. Ray Pearson became 'Uncle Ray' and they lived together for over 50 years. Nobody ever spoke, in my hearing, about them being a 'gay couple'. Young Joe and Ray ended up running a bed and breakfast place in Bournemouth. I never had much to do with them over the years, mainly because they lived so far away. They did give me a solid gold Rotary watch for my 18th Birthday, which I still have.

We: Ruth, Christopher, Alasdair and I, did stay with Young Joe and Ray a couple of times on our way to France in the summer. Once Young Joe took us all swimming and Chris was stung by a Weaver Fish. His foot and then leg started to go red and swell. We had an interesting evening in the local hospital, just immersing it in hot water. Some years later Alasdair and I went to Young Joe's funeral, Ray had died some months earlier but I was not informed.
They were obviously both well liked by the gay community in Bournemouth.

Ray, me, Pat and Young Joe (circa 1957)

Finally a quick mention about Nellie, my Great Grandma. Her name was actually Sarah Ellen (Blades) (b.1885 in Hawes). She was married to my Great Grandfather William(b.1884, in Pudsey) who I never knew. Nellie lived in a downstairs flat on Thorp Road in Pudsey and was often to be found at the Derby and Joan Club. Grandad & Grandma W. moved to an upstairs flat on the corner of Thorp Road and Lodge Road, sometime in the late 60s, to be close to her.

Nellie, my Great Grandma Wood, probably taken in the early 70s at a Christmas gathering of the Rileys and Woods. She would have been in her late 80s.

WW1 medallion from Joe's father, my great grandfather, William. As yet I have not been able to find out exactly where it came from...

There is one family member who has not yet had a mention, my dog, Tiger. So called because as a puppy, apart from colour, he looked just like a young tiger cub.

He was Welsh. When I was both 10 and 11 we spent our summer holiday on a farm in Wales, along with Derek & Brenda and their three children, Julie, John and Vanessa. The farm was just outside a small village called St. Florence 7km outside Tenby, Pembrokeshire.

A short aside. The farmer's wife would often put me to bed with a 'butterfly kiss' good night. For this we brushed eyelashes.

Tiger was born to the farmers sheepdog. A pure bred Welsh Collie, which was a 'blue merle', with a 'wall eye'. His father was a Labrador. Luckily my puppy had a blue merle coat and a partial 'Wall' or white eye. He was my soul mate throughout my teenage years.

We went on holidays over the years, but never 'abroad'. My only flight was to Jersey, possibly when I was 9. We travelled round Scotland one summer with my Grandad and Grandma R., staying in small hotels and bed and breakfast places. My Grandad loved castles and history and we would stop often so that he and I could have adventures. His joke was "Look, no parking! I'm not stopping there, I like Parkin"...you had to be there !

Tiger, my dog and best friend throughout my teenage years.

I remember staying in pubs in North Wales and Bridlington. We were at a Guest House in Blackpool when Neil Armstrong stepped onto the Moon, 3:56am, July 21, 1969, and watched it the next morning on TV. By the time I was in my early teens my mum and dad had taken to caravanning holidays. I wasn't that keen, but particularly loved staying at Port William in Scotland and having adventures on the Isle of Whithorn. I was about 17 before I travelled onto the Continent, on a ski trip from school. I never travelled abroad with my parents.

Thus I grew up as the only child in a secure and loving environment. The centre of attention of quite a large group of adults. I had plenty of friends of my own age outside of the family but grew up lacking confidence in social settings, being shy, self-aware, desiring of approval, while still being somewhat independently minded with my friends and family. I suspect my family setting accounts for some of my psychological glitches, which have taken me a lifetime of work to attempt to circumvent.

Aireborough Grammar School & a sojourn in Huddersfield.

In September 1967 I started at Aireborough Grammar School (AGS).

Yeadon and Guiseley Secondary School, 1910

AGS, my form room in Year 7, then called the 'First Form' or 1 Fairfax, was in the room on the bottom floor, far right. My form room in Years 10 & 11, 4G & 5G, was above it. AGS closed in 1991 and houses were built on the site.

To identify your 'House', in my case Fairfax, our school blazer badge was in the house colours.

Fairfax was 'Greens'. The other houses were Coverley (Yellow), Cavendish (Red) and Foster (Blue)

30

To get to school I had to travel by bus from Horsforth (6km). We had a bus pass which gave us free travel. I remember the first morning well, dressed in my new uniform, with long dark grey trousers, a black blazer and school tie. I had a school scarf too! I also had on a school cap, which I only wore twice! The next time was 7 years later, on the day I left. All my new school kit: fountain pen, ink, pencils and a geometry set, were in my brand new leather school satchel. I had always enjoyed school, was quite academic and so looked forward to this next life stage. We didn't get a visit to the school before our first day, so everything was brand new to us!

A school satchel, for all your stuff.

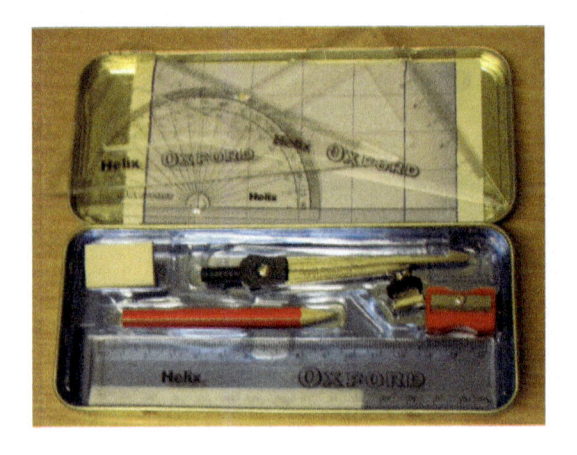

Geometry set, with all the essentials for Maths and Science diagrams.

I walked down to the bus stop with 'Busby' and we met 'Alf'. It was packed with students from all years. We caught the bus and it picked up more students along the route. I remember being excited and quite scared. On arrival the bus pulled into Dibb Lane, school gates on one side and the 'Tuck Shop' on the other. New students were told to wait in the playground until all the others had gone to their classrooms. We gathered around those we knew from junior school, then were led into the main hall. Names were read out and we had to follow our new form tutor to the classroom. There we were sat in alphabetical order, boys then girls. There weren't many people from my old school, but I did see Alf two seats behind me & Denise Carter at the other side of the room. Three of what were to become long standing friends were also in 1 Fx: Keith Parker(Piggy), Martin Cooke(Smart Mart) and Chris Briggs (Briggsy).

Unlike primary school, all the boys were always called by their surnames by staff and we all had to stand up whenever a member of staff came into the room. We sat at individual desks, in alphabetical order, by surname. As with most secondary schools we often moved to the teacher rather than the teacher coming to us, so we got to know the school quickly. There were Year 13 or '6th Formers' who had responsibilities at breaks and lunch to look after students. At AGS they formed the 'School Council' and sat on the stage with the Head, Deputy and Senior Teacher: Mr MacDonald or 'Mac', Miss Kent and Mr Wickham, during assembly. They were called 'Councillors'. Councillors didn't wear a school uniform, just smart 'office' clothes. Some wore a blazer with their school 'Colours'. For many years I converted one of those badges!

In those early days I loved: Science, Maths, Geography, History and of course PE. I liked rather less: RE, English, French, Art and Woodwork. Some of the comments from my report reflect this view:

> *French: Variable. He has not been consistently determined. Could try harder.*
> *English: Disappointing exam result. Written work needs a great deal more care. 32/34.*

It's interesting that my arrogance held me up in French. My attitude was "the French teach English well, so a French person who can't speak English must be dim. Who wants to speak to a dim French person". As it turns out, I was wrong! I missed a great opportunity which, to say the least, I regret every single day of my life here in France!

The other two things which stand out about those first couple of years at AGS are Rugby and Swimming. Swimming first; I learned to swim in the little pool in the bowels of AGS. I can remember the moment distinctly. It was the end of a lesson, boys PE, about half way through the year. I was in the shallow end with the non swimmers, one was Alf. The teacher, Geoff Thompson, said its time to get out and I thought 'here goes'. I pushed off from the side and swam a breadth. I shouted up to Geoff, or Dan as he was called by the boys, as he looked somewhat like Desperate Dan, "I swam". "Very good" he replied, "Now out and get changed!". I had to wait a week to see if I could do it again, and sure enough I could.

Desperate Dan, 'Dan' Thompson, from the popular comic, The Dandy

I never struggled with swimming after that, though I was never good at 'crawl' or 'butterfly' I was competent in the water. I gained my Bronze Personal Survival at the end of the year. It took me a further two years to get my Gold, but that was due to a change of school which didn't do swimming, more of that later.

ASA Bronze (1968) and Gold (1970) Personal Survival badges.

I was also a member of Aireborough Swimming Club for about a year, from when we moved to Guiseley in 1968. (Appendix 5, some swimming certs.)

In early 1968 my mum and dad decided to change their occupation, they took over the New Inn, Towngate, Guiseley and we moved house.

This is a picture of the New Inn from 1912, it hadn't changed much. In our day the section to the right of the drain pipe, the old shop, had recently closed. Our living room was the upper right bay, to the left was the kitchen window and left of that was mum and dads bedroom. Downstairs the right bay was the 'music room' and the left bay was the 'tap room'. The lounge bar was to the rear.

My dad, always the showman, a trait which embarrassed me no end, ran it as the 'Texan Bar". The Lounge Bar had imitation 'cowboy' hats, rifles guns etc. Dad would put on his cowboy hat and holster and do tricks with his imitation gun, for the customers. A first in 'theme pubs'.

Illegal at the time, but not as illegal as now, he also had a Smith & Wesson, Webley or Enfield '38 revolver. We shot it a couple of times in the 'bottle store' located behind the pub. Dad handed it in to the police when we left the pub. At that time there were no questions asked, as I believe there were still quite a lot of handguns out there from WW2.

The bottle store behind the New Inn, being converted into the Parish Centre.
We fired the gun a couple of times on the top floor. It made a lot of noise.

I learned to play rugby at AGS, and for quite a few years it would be a big part of my life. We started playing as a team in Year 8, Under 13's and I was a bit of a star! I was quite a big boy at this stage, maybe 5'7" (1.7m) and 10+ st. (63.5kg). I played at No.8, as anywhere else I would have unbalanced the scrum.

UNDER 13's. PLAYED 10, WON 9, LOST 1, POINTS FOR 134, AGAINST 44.
The fine playing record of the team speaks for itself and, when it is added that they were very unlucky to lose 9-13 at Bingley G.S., it can be appreciated how quickly they established themselves as a reliable team with good forwards and really fast, quick-handling backs. Graham Peel's solidity at full-back did much to establish the defensive record. Only Bingley G.S. scored more than 8 points. Nicholas Wood, the captain, led the forwards very ably, and alongside Glen Hirst, a fine hooker, and Geoff Stone, a very promising prop, formed a formidable front row. With good second row support from Keith Parker, a ball-handling forward, and Chris Brigg, good possession was always assured. When the opposition did obtain possession, the back row of David Kirk, Paul Riley and Jeremy Collier were quick to spot and quench any danger. The backs always looked dangerous with the ball, and with good passing, they proved capable of splitting any defence.
Mark Heaton's service as scrum-half developed tremendously from game to game, and Terry Hardwick, the vice-captain, and stand-off, always looked likely to produce tries in possession and tackled with great determination. The threequarters, Graham Kemp, Kevin Boyle, Bryn Griffith, Paul Haigh and Alan Wade improved throughout the season, but really ran riot with any weaknesses in the opposition defence.
Even after the departure of Paul Riley, a fine prospect who scored 13 tries in 6 games, the team played well together, and the fact that the backs scored eighty points against 12 by the rest of the forwards, bears witness to the attractive rugby produced.

A couple of friends came round to the pub to play. One was Kevin Boyle, and I often see him and his wife Val when we go over to the UK for a visit. He lived with his Mum, Christine, his Dad Charlie and his sister Julie at 1 Queensway, Guiseley. We would sometimes play darts in the Tap Room when the pub was shut, or pinch drinks from behind the bar. The other friend who visited was Tony Hair. his father Grenville had played football for Leeds United, with 474 appearances and was now the coach at Bradford City. One day the Head came into our classroom with his mother and Tony was taken out. We found out later that his dad had collapsed and died while training. I never saw Tony again!

By Christmas of 1968 mum and dad had decided to quit the pub. They bought a fish & chip shop in Huddersfield and that involve me moving school. My dad went to ask the Head at AGS, 'Mac' where I should go. 'Mac' had an old army friend who was the Head at King James Grammar School, Almondbury, Huddersfield.......so that is where I went........I wasn't a happy chappy!

King James's was a very old, selective Grammar School of about 350 boys from all over Huddersfield. I found it very strange and never really made friends or settled in.

The school dates from 1547 and got a royal charter in 1608. Many of the buildings were very old. My first classroom was called 'Dorm.2' and had been a dormitory, in the past, for resident students.

King James's was very different from AGS. They had 6th Formers (Year 13), some of whom were 'Prefects'. These could give you work or even keep you in detention at breaks, lunch or after school. Their favourite punishment was a 'Green Paper'. a sheet of green paper on which you had to complete a given task by the next day. The most common was: cube 13, easy 2197!, Then take away 13s until you get back to zero. If you didn't, start again!......very time consuming without a calculator. They also made you line up outside every break, to be allowed into school. If you didn't behave they would bring all of you back after school and you would miss the bus!

King James school badge: interestingly the date is wrong!

We lived a long way from Almondbury! I needed to get up at 6:30 to get the 7:15 bus into Huddersfield. From there, often after a wait in the rain, the 8:00 bus went to Almondbury centre. Then fifteen minute walk down to school. I loved the mornings my dad drove me in!

Our house/shop was 338 Blackmoorfoot Road, Crossland Moor, Huddersfield. The shop front has changed, but the building is the same. The centre building of a row of three. The fish shop was on the centre left and the centre right was a small 'wet fish and frozen food' shop. My mum and dad's bedroom was over the fish shop and mine was over the wet fish shop. On the ground floor, behind the shop was a living room and kitchen.
We had a garage and driveway at the back, but no garden.

The Huddersfield chip shop. The front looked much less flash in those days and there were no 'roof lights'. My bedroom was on the right

Being so far from school I didn't have any school mates who lived close. This was a good thing in a couple of ways: My schoolwork improved, as I spent a lot of time doing homework. I was also able to work in the F&C shop when I was on school holidays and at weekends. When I wasn't doing sport I ran the Wet Fish shop on a Saturday morning.

I have a couple of stories of working in the F&C shop. One was on a day that it got so hot that the 'pop' bottles started to explode on the shelving. The second was 'stealing' a chip from the 'range' behind me, getting in the wrong place and putting my fingers in the hot fat.....Ewww! Oh yes! Huddersfield people call salt & pepper 'seasoning' and 'scraps' are 'bits'.

The Wet Fish shop involved me in cutting, and skinning pieces of fish. I became very adept at the weight of a piece of fish being able to cut it very accurately. We also sold loose frozen food from a large chest freezer. This enable people to buy, say, 4oz of frozen peas etc. a fairly novel idea at the time. This was how I earned my spending money.

Some Saturday mornings I did sport. I was able to play for the school cricket team straight away, as we arrived at Easter. Unlike most things sporting at King James we were quite good, winning the Huddersfield Cup. The report in the school magazine: The Almondburian stated:

> **JUNIOR CRICKET**
> Pride of place this season must go to the U13 XI who, by their victory in the Huddersfield Schools Cup Final, completed their fullest and most successful season. Of six matches played five were won and one was a very narrow defeat. The team blended experience in the shape of Smallwood, White and Boothroyd, with youth and enthusiasm, Lawton, Marshall, Riley, Evans and Farnsworth with Kent, Medley, Rothery and Fawthrop combining to make an efficient unit.
> v Mirfield G.S. Won.
> v Holmfirth (Cup) Won.
> v Almondbury (Cup). Won.
> v St. Gregory's G.S. Lost.
> v Deighton (Cup) Won.
> v Rawthorpe (Cup). Won.

In the summer I did athletics and won both the Junior (Y7 & 8) and Intermediate (Y9 & 10) shot put in the school competition. I also came 2nd representing the school at the shot put in the Huddersfield Schools athletics competition.

In winter we played football....whoopee. I'm not that great at football, so getting in the team tells you something of the standard. Fortunately they had a goalie so I played at right back. My main skill was stopping people getting past me with my shear bulk and a bit of speed. The end of term Almondburian had this to say

> The Under-14s too have had a disappointing season, winning only one match in a season marred by postponements and cancellations. Lawton, however, has shown some fearless goalkeeping under pressure, while Riley, the Colossus of the team's defence, has inflicted a number of bone-shaking tackles.

You can take the boy out of rugby, but you can't take rugby out of the boy.......apparently!

We had a holiday to Whitby, I think, and my dad bought me some old pennies in a case. I still have them.

This started me on Numismatics; coin collecting. when my dad went to the bank he would pick me up a £5 bag of old pennies: £1 =240 old pence (1d) in those days. Other coins: Half-penny or Ha'penny(1/2d), Threepenny bit (3d), Sixpence(6d), Shilling(1/-), Two Shillings(2/-), Half-crown(2/6) (and Crown(5/-), these were never used in circulation in my time). There were also paper notes, Ten Shillings(10/-), Pound(£1) and Five Pounds(£5). The farthing (1/4d) had gone out of use in 1956.

I was particularly interested in old pennies minted since 1900, as these were still in circulation to be sorted and collected. (Appendix 6, for some examples). I joined the Huddersfield Numismatic Society, which was mostly old men ....and a boy!

One outstanding fact about this time in Huddersfield was that I read my first proper book. I was off school ill and the daytime TV was very poor, if non existent. There was no Video Cassette, or DVD, and we were many years away from the Internet and Netflix. I chose to read Charles Dickens, A Christmas Carol. I didn't really read another proper book, cover to cover, for another six years! I never finished my O-Level text, Cider with Rosie and still don't now how it ends!

In 1969 we got our first Colour TV, which looked something like this. Three stations, very little daytime TV & no remote!

I really didn't enjoy Huddersfield and my favourite times were going to visit G & G Riley in Horsforth. We kept spare clothes there, which didn't smell of F&C. I could meet up and play with those people I knew. For a long time I struggled to make new friends in any social setting.

We sold the F&C Shop in March of 1970 and moved into a house in Rawdon. Mum had been having breathing problems and the doctor had put it down to the fat vapour from the friers. I was able to get back into AGS, even though it was full! The Head remembered I had been good at rugby and squeezed me into one of the lower forms 3SL(Year 9)..I was a happy chappy again.

February 1971 also saw the introduction of Decimal Coins, or New Pennies. This put 100 New Pence to £1 (instead of 240d). Some coins remained, 1/- = 5p, 2/- = 10p and 10/- = 50p (now a coin, not a note)

41

Moving to Rawdon and back to AGS.

We moved into 142 Harrogate Road, Rawdon about Easter Time of 1970. School was a 4.8km round trip walk each day. With 'Piggy' & 'Mini Parker'

142 Harrogate Rd. I lived here until I got married in 1982. My bedroom was at the back. The 'best room', which we rarely used, was at the front with mum & dad's bedroom above it.

It was great to be back at AGS, but I found the class I was in was very unchallenging after King James. It became my aim to work hard for a term to get promoted to one of the top forms in September. I made it into 4G, which ran in parallel with 4A as the top form........I was truly back!

My return to rugby was not quite an anti-climax. Though I hadn't gained much height or weight since I left, I was still reasonably mobile. I played in the Second Row all season, and to be fair it wasn't my favourite position. I did manage to score 17 tries, the most of any forward. We had a great season and were worthy of pictures in the local papers.

Back: N.Wood, G.Kemp, K.Parker, C.Briggs, G.Heap, P.Riley, M.Cooke, S.Claughton, G.Stone, A.Wade, G.Hirst.
Front: P.Haigh, K.Boyle, G.Peel, T.Hardwick, S.Harrison, M.Heaton, D.Hall,
Seated: D.Kirk, B.Griffiths. Coach: G.Thompson

COLTS (UNDER 15's) NOV. 1971
PLAYED 20. WON 20. POINTS FOR 540. POINTS AGAINST 63.

This team was undoubtedly the finest Colts XV ever produced at the school. Under the captaincy of T. Hardwick, the side played some extremely attractive rugby.

A feature of the season was the fact that only 9 tries were conceded.

The team performed admirably in the Halifax Schools " Sevens." After defeating Whitcliffe Mount G.S., Roundhay School and Castleford G.S., we were narrowly defeated in the final by Q.E.G.S. (Wakefield).

The following boys were members of the team :- T. Hardwick (capt.), G. Peel, K. Boyle, S. Harrison, P. Haigh, A. Wade, M. Heaton, G. Stone, G. Hirst, N. Wood, M. Cooke, P. Riley, G. Heap, K. Parker, C. Briggs, D. Kirk, B. Griffith, D. Hall, S. Claughton.

37

From 'The Bridge' AGS magazine. Played 20, won 20!

43

The cricket team that summer was no less successful

> **UNDER-15**
> PLAYED 7. WON 7.   NOV.1977
>
> THE UNDER-15 CRICKET TEAM are to be congratulated on achieving a one hundred per cent record over the season. The average number of runs scored over the seven games was 83 per game and the average victory margin was 36 runs. The top scorers were Paul Haigh (vice-capt.), 149 runs, Andrew Robinson, 92 runs, Paul Riley, 87 runs, and Keith Parker, 61 runs.
>
> The bowling was shared mainly between Alan Wade (capt.) and Keith Parker, the former taking 20 wickets for an average of 5 runs, and the latter taking 19 for an average of 4 runs.
>
> Haigh, Heap, Parker, Wade and Riley (reserve) are to be congratulated on their selection for the Airedale and Wharfedale District team.
>
> The team was selected from :—P. Haigh, G. Heap, A. Robinson, P. Riley, G. Peel, A. Wade (capt.), K. Parker, P. Lane, G. Jennings, K. Hardcastle, R. Megson, L. Hobson, G. Stone, M. Cooke, C. Briggs, P. Hewitt and G. Dennison.

Socially the 4th form (Year 10) was an interesting time. My close group of friends were in Horsforth: Briggsy, Alf, Busby, Graham Heap, David Kirk aka 'Goliath'. We spent hours hanging around in Horsforth Hall Park, playing cricket or drinking cider. We also had season tickets for Leeds Rugby League, so would go on a Saturday to watch the home games and sneak a pint or two in the Headingley bar. Thanks to Graham Peel, from my form-4G, I became 'Mal', named after a RL player, Mal Reilly.

Alf was the drummer in a trio which played mostly things typified by Jimmy Hendrix. The lead guitarist, Bob Westmorland, had been at Featherbank with us. He had a great ear for picking up a tune. It was at that time I lost some of my self-consciousness about dancing to the band. I was never really into that sort of guitar based music and secretly preferred the more pop style of bands like 'Slade', 10cc, Blondie, Roxy Music and Dire Straits. But I also liked Deep Purple, Led Zeppelin and Black Sabbath. It was around this time that Briggsy and I got a taste for old Rock & Roll music, and Kung Fu films. Much to the consternation of many of our friends.

Many of my friends wore old Army or Airforce Great coats, possibly a tie-dyed 'Grandad vest' and Levi jeans patched and old. My favourite jacket at the time was a fake brown sued jacket with tassels on the sleeves and back........fortunately I don't think there is any photographic evidence.

Mine was a bit darker and a lot more 'faux'........but this gives the idea. We also had long hair, this was me contemporary to the jacket, in Year 10.

We would play table-tennis in the Baptist Church Hall at weekends. It has to be said that it was during this time that we started to visit pubs, just sneaking in for a 'pint or two' of Tetley's Bitter. Sometimes we would get turned away, but not often. There was no such thing as ID. It was easier for some than others, but honestly things were a lot more relaxed regarding under age drinking in the early '70s. We heard of people being fined, but I never actually met anyone who had been.......we were 15!

We also started on the Duke of Edinburgh bronze award. Though I never finished it.......which I regret. Honestly, I was influenced by my friends who also gave up. It was another group in our year who went on eventually to get their Gold. We did however experience Youth Hostelling. A few of us walked the Skipton, Linton, Grassington, Kettlewell, Malham route, which I was to lead a number of times, many years later, as a teacher. We also walked Whitby to Scarborough, Youth Hostelling again. Today we can laugh at the gear!

My first rucksack was like this old A-frame army sac, but in blue.

The tweed breeches were all the rage in the 70s and early 80s, kit really hadn't changes in over 50 years. Many people used ex-WW2 Army kit. Boots were big, heavy and leather, or old army boots. The materials revolution was not to come until the mid 80s.

Drugs were not a problem with the group I was in, or in the area in general. A few kids smoked pot, but not my group. I do remember someone in a higher form, when I was in about Year 9 being caught. It turned out he was selling Smarties with the colour sucked off!

About that time too there was an IRA bomb scare, and we had to stand outside for a couple of hours. Again that was eventually found to be a pupil. Then there was a boy who took a shot at the Head in his study with an Air Rifle, it cracked the window!

In maths we didn't have calculators, my first was at University(1974)! For multiplications we used Logarithmic Tables, these came in a booklet alongside tables for square roots and Sin and Cosin for trigonometry.

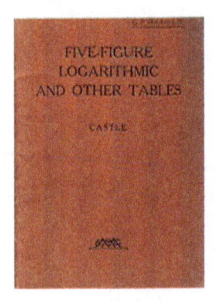

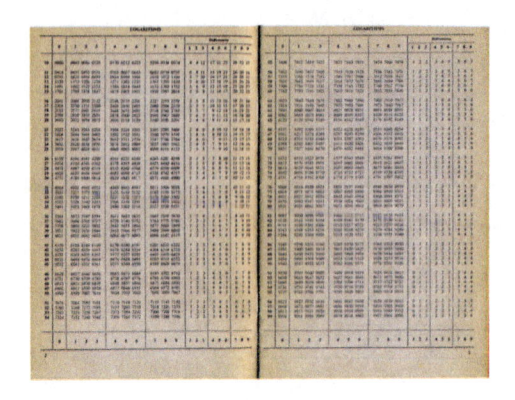

Log Tables allowed you to do complex multiplications by simple addition.......how do you use them? I have no idea now!

    Academically I had made my subject choices for O-level, a qualification which pre-dated GCSEs, but only covered the top grades(4-9, in 2021). I had to do: English Language and English Literature, Maths (Group 2), French and PE and chose: Chemistry(Group 1), Physics(Group 1), Geography and History. I passes O-level maths in Year 10(at something like a 6 in the new system, 2020) and so went on to do Pure Maths & Mechanics (Group 1) in year 11 or the 5th Form.

    The 5th Form was just more freedom really. I went out with a girl that I had met in Horsforth Park, called Karen Hendy. It wasn't for a long time but it did help me to get over at least some of my shyness. I spent a lot of time in Horsforth and would sleep at Grandma & Grandad R's most weekends. We would roam the streets and go to people's houses and the park.

    Briggsy had a French pen pal over to stay and that was my first association with anyone 'foreign'. J.P. was a year older than us and spoke really good English. We did find that if we spoke really fast we could say things in front of him and he didn't understand.......but that was just being lads!

On the subject of French we had a great teacher in Mrs Varco. She was blond and petite and always wore tight fitting short knitted dresses. Briggsy, Heap(or Bone) and I sat on the front row. This didn't do me any good, as after a very poor mock exam we discussed not taking the O-level. She made it very clear that it was my choice. I spent the rest of the year working in the library. Looking back what an idiot I was. Five years of French, 4 or 5 hours a week and nothing to show for it! How it would have served me well at this time in my life, here in France!

"The opportunity of a lifetime only lasts for the lifetime of the opportunity"

I also took to staying in Horsforth when my mum and dad went on their caravan holidays........I really didn't like caravanning with them!

Possibly my last holiday with my parents, at Port William. I loved going on the rocks at the Isle of Whithorn. It was this holiday that we were approached in our tiny 9ft. dinghy by a 10m basking shark........fin out of the water, holy shit!

January '72 saw one of the miners strikes and a coal shortage. This was used to make both gas and electricity in those days, so much had to come to an end. People went onto a 3 day working week and schools lost their heating. Kids came in on a rota, except Years 11 & 13, who were to do O and A-levels. As that was us, we spent a lot of time in a our coats in cold classrooms. Little did I know this wouldn't be my last time doing this, I would be doing it again teaching in China. During the day and at evenings there would be power cuts for a few hours at a time, though we did get warnings in advance.

Rugby continued and I was selected for the school 1st XV, moving to open side Prop. The mainstays of the team were Year 13, with virtually no Year 12. Then perhaps 8 or so of us, mostly forwards, from Year 11. This meant that we had quite a weak team overall. Playing with lads a couple of years older was also not great fun at the start. I was 'dropped' for only 1 match, then scored 4 tries in a 98-0 victory over Otley Prince Henry's for the 2nd XV. I also miss a couple of games with a knee injury from Skiing.

Played 17, Won 7. Actually not that bad for a team with 8 Year 11s, 1 Year 12 and 8 Year 13s.

49

It was at this stage that I started to feel that the coach, Terry Lazenby, didn't much like me! As it turns out, he was to hassle my playing 'career' for much longer than I expected.

> **Inter-School Rugby**
>
> 1st XV
>
> With a young inexperienced side the first XV did well to win seven of its seventeen matches and although the playing record is not good it should be remembered that the first XV fixture list has never been stronger. Once again A.G.S. players figured in the Bradford and District XV which played against Wharfedale as part of the Yorkshire trials.
>
> Colours were awarded to R. Butchart, P. Morse, G. Stone, M. Heap, D. Joliffe and J. Rees-Jones.
>
> Half colours were awarded to J. Doyle, K. Denison and N. Wood. R. Butchart (full back), J. Doyle (centre) and J. Rees-Jones (flanker) were selected to play for Bradford and District XV against Wharfedale.

Short and to the point. Not even a mention for a number of us!

The Skiing holiday to Fieberbrunn in Austria, with school, was my first trip abroad. I had flown with my parents to Jersey years before, but this was, though exotic to me, quite English. I remember being with Boylie and Goliath on the trip & Boylie's younger sister Julie. Looking back Julie spent a lot of time with me, even giving up a days skiing to be with me when I couldn't walk.......I didn't notice the attraction! The injury had come on about day 3, skis going one way and me another. Knee twisting and.......whiteout. The staff didn't think it was serious enough for the doctor, but I hobbled to the end of the holiday with a knee the size of a balloon! We had an interesting return journey too. We had flown into Innsbruck, but the weather had closed it down. To get us home they drove us through the night to Nurnberg in Germany, some 300km. I remember the coach had no heating, we were frozen as we sped along the Autobahns.

AGS was always at the front of changes. We did a two week work experience and I chose a local Junior School in Rawdon. I really enjoyed my time there and the idea of becoming a secondary school PE teacher seemed to be something I might look at in the future. Certainly the idea of teaching, with its short days and long holidays was very attractive!

I remember the summer of '72 was good for revision, and cricket in the park. My revision was usually the day before an exam. I remember trying to read my whole History text book in a day. A bit of advice from a slow learner. Plan well ahead for an exam, perhaps even months! Revise bits at a time and go over it regularly. You may be able to rely on your 'native' intelligence to get a pass, but one or two days revision for a major exam will never give you the best results you can get......and I know, it took me 60 years of experience to finally get this right!!!The exams passed, I passed and we passed onto the summer holidays. My dad and Briggsy's dad drove us and the caravan up to Berwick and we had a week there: Me, Briggsy, Busby, Piggy & Alf. We had a great time, Briggs, as always, meeting a Scottish girl called Maggie! I was mortified when Busby broke the large front window while opening it.........mum and dad were not too pleased either and we all chipped in to pay for it. The most disgusting part of the trip was emptying the chemical toilet. Alf volunteered to do it in order to use it. Then it was too heavy for him! He still owes me for the help!

Busby, Me, Alf and Briggsy

Toilet duty, me & Alf

At the end of the summer the O-Level results were published and I passed all seven. I already had Maths, but the sketchy revision took a toll on the grades. In modern parlance I got 5 at grade 6: Maths, Pure/Applied Maths, Chemistry, Physics and English Language and 4 at grade 5: Geography, History and English Literature, Sociology(Y12) & General Studies(Y12) at grade 4. This changed my choices at A-Level, as I had intended to do Physics, Maths with Mechanics and Geography. The Geography got changed for Chemistry. Little did I know it then but the next 40 years were influenced in so may ways by that decision! A perfect example of 'The Butterfly Effect"

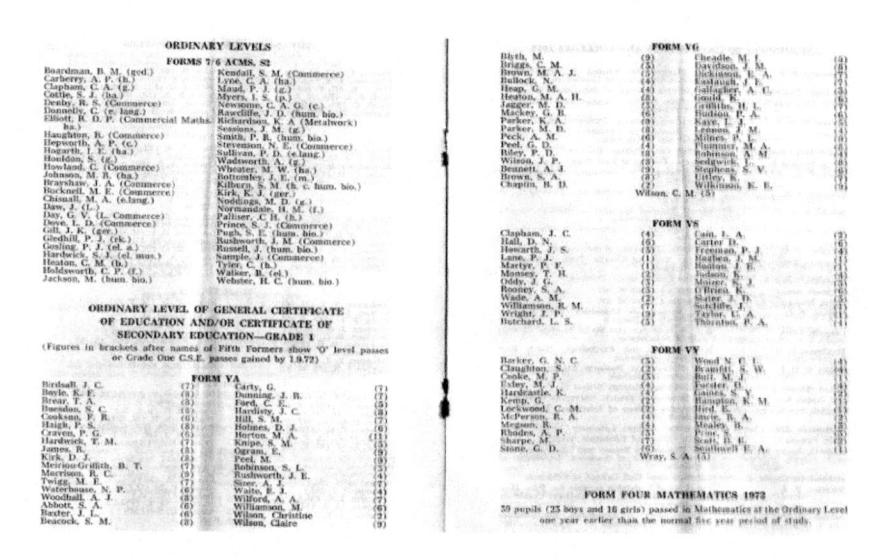

So onto the Sixth Form (Year 12). The classes were changed, depending upon subjects. There were two 'Science' forms, but as everything was taught in 'sets' it really didn't matter which one you were in. I was in 6S2 and then 7S2, with Boylie. I was in the top sets, along with Boylie, for all the subjects I had chosen: Pure Maths with Mechanics, Physics and Chemistry. Kevin did Further Maths instead of Chemistry, with Tez Hardwick and Bryn Griffiths.

In June 1973 I was able to get a part time job. Luckily they had just opened a Morrison's supermarket in Yeadon and they were having a recruitment drive. Quite a few of us went along, including Briggsy and Martin Cooke or 'Smart Mart'. I worked in the supermarket warehouse on Monday and Thursday evenings until I left school. I also worked some full time in Holidays.

52

My main job was 'pricing up'. This was well before bar codes and even before printed price tickets. The job involved getting lists from the shelf stackers on the shop floor, of what was needed. Locating a box of it in the warehouse and finding the price in some large books we had. We then opened the carton with our carton knives and stamped each object with an ink pad & price stamp.

DEPT.	TAX WEEK	TAX CODE	REGULAR HOURS	OVERTIME HOURS	BASIC PAY	OVERTIME PAY	HOLIDAY PAY	OVERALL ALLOWANCE	
01	11	059L W1	6.00	.00	2.25	.00	.00	.00	.00

GROSS PAY	GROSS PAY TO DATE	FREE PAY	TAXABLE PAY	TAX DUE	TAX THIS WEEK	GRAD. PEN. THIS WEEK	GRAD. PEN. TO DATE	EMPLOYEE NAT. INS.
2.25	2.25	11.55	9.40CR	.00	.00	.00	.00	.03

	A.O.E.						NET PAY
.00	.00	.00	.00				2.22

Here some slick maths will lead you to the mind numbing sum of 37.5p for each hour worked. They did manage to get it up to 40p before I left!

These were all loaded onto a pallet which we dragged out into the isles. Later we had a hand held machine which printed a sticky price label. The store closed at 18:00, so we had the shop to ourselves each evening from 18:00 to 21:00. My wages bought my beer, normally 15p a pint.

Life went on in a whirl of school, rugby and socialising. There were regular parties at Nik Wood's house. His mum and dad would let us have the run of the place on a Saturday night. The times can only be described as 'debauched'. We would start off on a Friday going into the Emmot Arms in Rawdon. This was followed by School Rugby on Saturday mornings, then a beer & pie and peas at the Woolpack at the bottom of Henshaw Lane, Yeadon. Then on to watch Leeds RL if they were at home, back home to get changed, back to the Emmot's and on the Nik's for a party. I would often ride to Horsforth on the last bus, with Briggsy and a few others and end up at Grandma's for midnight. My grandparents were always very welcoming. On other occasions it would be F & C and a walk home to Harrogate Road.

It was on one such stopover that my Grandad R. returned from an evening at the Conservative Club ("Con. Club"). He sat in his favourite armchair, as always, and proceeded to try and light a cigarette......with another cigarette! Which he had tried to strike on the side of the cigarette packet. I remember his speech was strange and some words were in the wrong place. I rang the Con. Club to ask "Had he been drinking a lot?". They said "He had played snooker all night, having drunk his usual two halves of bitter". He was never a big drinker. Grandma R. rang for the doctor and I helped him up to bed. When the doctor arrived he said that grandad had had a 'stroke'. It wasn't severe enough to be taken to hospital, but he needed bed rest for quite a few weeks. His motor functions were not affected, and his speech returned to normal after several weeks. Grandad R. was never quite the same after that! They later found a golf ball sized cancer in his lungs and he died within the year.

I lost an unusual number of relatives in the next year. Grandad W., always so big and healthy started to not be able to hold down food. They opened him up from backbone to sternum but found nothing. He really just wasted away, dying soon after Grandad R.

Last picture I have of Grandad Wood, with his wife, Grandma Wood. Taken in the back garden of Harrogate Road, about 1973

Great Grandma Wood went next. At just over 90 years of age I think she saw little point in continuing after my Grandads death. Then my dad found Great Aunt Minnie dead at home on one of his regular visits. She hadn't done badly at about 85. I think Great Aunt Maud went a year or two later?

My Form Tutor, Bernard Thorpe, also one of my chemistry teachers, started to get suspicious at my fourth day off for a cremation, asking "Hasn't that relative died before?"........nice one 'Bernie'!

One interesting bit of family history. Shortly after my Grandad W. died my grandma had a knock on the door. It was her younger sister, who had been given away as a baby and she had not seen since. They remained friends for the rest of their lives.

Rugby continued in the 1st XV during Year 12, with a bit more success than last year. One of our number, Geoff Stone, Ged, had left for work and the Airebronians RUFC. Ged became a great friend of mine both during school and after.......but more of him later. The team had little support from Year 13 and not much from Year 11, which made it another hard season.

G.Heap, Me, C.Briggs, L.Robinson(Y13), K.Parker, M.Cooke, N.Wood,R.Yeadon(Y11).
P.Haigh, G.Peel, A.Wade, J.Rhys-Jones(Y13), G.Wild(Y11), D.Kirk, T.Hardwick.....Coach T. Lazenby

I played cricket in the summer for both the school 1st XI, moving to Wicket Keeper and with Yeadon C.C. Juniors on a Wednesday evening.

We drank at the Emmot's and partied at Nik's. You would, as the song goes 'Always find me in the kitchen at parties' drinking beer, telling rugby stories and generally being a 'lad'. Always invited, always in the 'in crowd' but always too shy to really have a conversation with any girls! All this meant that I didn't do enough work for a chance at taking my A-Level Maths a year early. 35% in the mock exam wasn't considered good enough. I did however pick up two more O-levels, General Studies (grade 4, 2020 equiv.) and Sociology(grade 5, 2020.), giving me a grand total of 10.

It also gave me an almost lifelong disregard for Sociology. The reason for this was that I attended very few lessons and handed in no work. I spent two days reading the assigned text book and passed the exam.........how easy/pointless must that be as a subject!

More maths, we started to use slide-rules for calculations. Again, don't ask me now how to use one!

This was probably towards the end of Year 13, outside the Emmott Arms, Rawdon, so 1974.Top: ?, Susan Stevens, Christine Ford, Katherine Gould, Me, Alf, Heap, Katherine Uttley, Helen Griffiths
Seated: Jane Rishworth, Ann Robinson, Katherine Wilkinson, Melanie Peel.

Skiing again, we went to La Bourboule, near Mont-Dore, in the French Central Massif. We got to know the man in the bar next door so well, that on the last night he gave us a bottle of Pastis! The skiing was fun too, especially watching my two mates learn from scratch. Though my last trip had ended ignominiously it didn't take me long to pick it up again and I did OK!

So Year 13, Rugby, Cricket, Socialising, University Applications and A-Levels.......probably in that order......unfortunately

Me, Briggsy and Smart Mart (1973), France

The Rugby went well. The core of players so outclassed in Year 11 had made it through to Year 13. We were well supported by some young talent fromYear 11. We had a big front five who were never dominated in scrum, ruck or line-out, and some fast backs. Plus, much to my personal relief we had a new coach, Charles Jeremy Hornby Pollard, or 'Dick' as we came to know him. Dick was still playing rugby and had been one of the founder members of the Airebronians in 1971. We respected him as both a coach and a skilful player.

Back: R.Petty(Y11), T.Hardwick, M.Cooke, K.Boyle, C.Briggs, S.Claughton(Y11), C.Marlow(Y12), R.Dodding(Y11)
Front: R.Hodgson(Y11), A.Wade, L.Hobson(Y12), N.Wood, R.Webster(Y11), Me, K.Parker.

For me the best success was against Roundhay G.S, one of the top schools in the county at the time. Sadly three of the team are no longer with us: Dave Hodgson was killed in a car accident, Steve Claughton; 'Cleggs', took his own life and last year Chris Marlow died from a brain haemorrhage.

I almost didn't get my Rugby Colours, to represent a substantial contribution to the team. I was sat with Dick on the coach after the last game of the season and asked him who was getting them. He didn't mention me in the short list! "Oh", I said. "And you and Nik will get re-awards of course" he added. "But I never had them awarded before". "What, incredible! How many appearances have you made?" "Over 60.......I don't think Lazenby liked me?"

In those final couple of years we would play rugby in the morning, then turn out for the Airebronians second team in the afternoon......provided Leeds RL were playing away.

*The Blazer badge I waited so long to get, AGS School Colours.
This one for Rugby, 1974.*

Fairfax (greens) House Badge on an AGS tie, 1974.

In Y13 I was also the Rugby Captain for Fairfax House, winning both the Junior and Senior House Rugby. Piggy was the House Captain and Briggsy was the Swimming Captain. Fairfax did very well in our last year.

At the end of the year the three of us were awarded the highly prize House Badge. Interestingly I was away on the day they were presented. I was presented mine by Dick Pollard in The Stone Trough pub, Rawdon.

*A more informal view of the rugby squad from 1974.
Back: Briggsy & Smart Mart
Front: Alf, Me, Les, Boylie and Nik*

In the summer I played again, without great success for me, for the cricket 1st XI. We had some real talent in Piggy and Alf as bowlers. Peter Williams; Taff, arrived in Year 12 from Wales. He was one of the best batsmen the school had seen for a number of years. Though less good at rugby he was also to become a good rugby mate by the time we got to Airebronians.

G.Heap, P.Williams(stood), R.Petty(Y11), K.Parker, S.Grinham, P.Haigh, A. Wade.

1973 saw a lot of us get our driving license. My dad had given me a few lessons in the Peacock Inn car park, since demolished, over the road from us in Rawdon. I got my provisional licence in December '72, but my first time on the road was not until 25th. I drove down to Leeds to pick up my Great Aunt Maud, there was no traffic, I loved it. During early 1973 I drove loads with my dad, while he worked, during school holidays. So by the time I applied for my test I was an 'old hand' with many bad habits. I booked five lessons in the week prior to the test. At the end of the first lesson the instructor told me that I could drive, but had so many bad habits he didn't know if I could pass. On the last lesson he asked me some Highway Code questions I could not answer. "I'm revising that tonight," I confidently replied.

The next day, 23rd June '72, I passed.......even though at one stage
I turned right instead of left.....oops

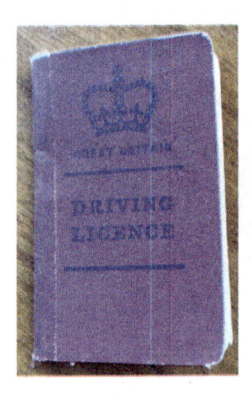

My first driving license was a small booklet, about the dimensions of a modern credit card.

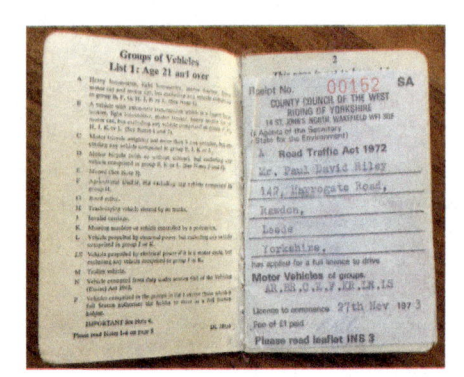

The availability of cars opened up our social lives. I didn't have a car in those early days, but a few of the lads, and some girls, had their mum's car: Smart Mart had a Hillman Imp, Steve Grinham had an enormous Morris 1800, Nik had a convertible Triumph Herald and Charlie Barker had a Mini Pickup.......we were off. We sometimes went to The Harrogate Arms, The Square and Compass and The Smith's Arms at Beckwithshaw. It was very rare to get stopped for drinking and driving, unless you had an accident! Breatherlsisers had only been introduced in 1967.

University had to be sorted. I had decided that I needed a backup to PE teaching so chose a Chemistry Degree. The two top places for me were Durham and York Universities. I had an interview at both. The Durham interview was first, with Faculty and then with College, I had Chosen Van Mildert. I talked rugby at the college interview and they gave me an offer, dependant upon me getting 3 x D at A-level. As it turns out a brilliant offer for Durham. York was just a single interview with the faculty, but I did rather well. York offered me 3 x E, as good as it gets! Unfortunately the pressure was off and in fact I only got 3 x E......lack of preparation again, a pathetic effort, but enough to get me in to York, the first in my family to ever go to University.........another 'butterfly wings'* moment.

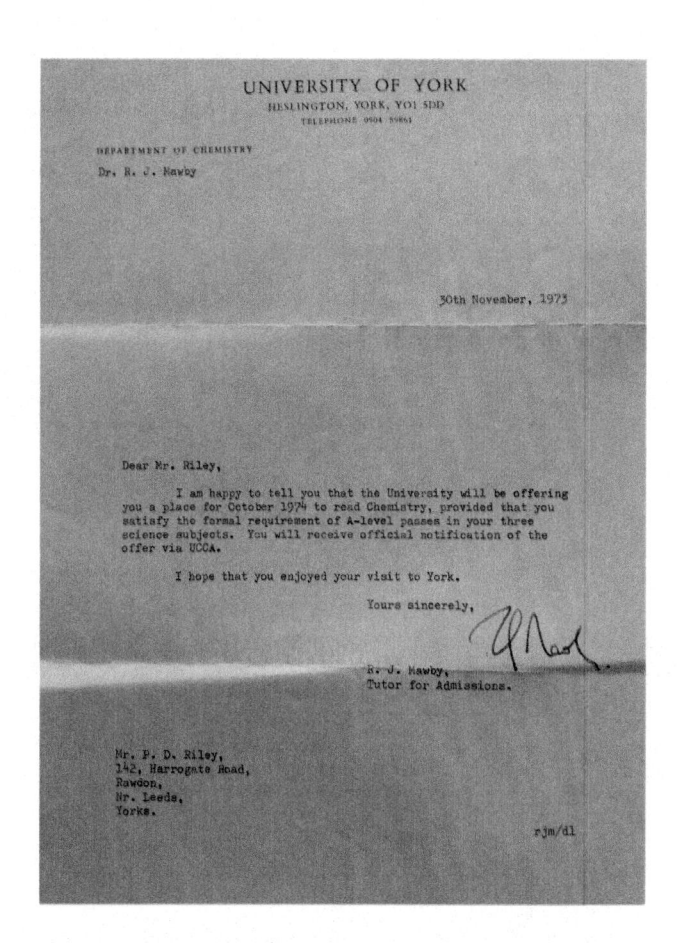

> **UNIVERSITY OF YORK**
> HESLINGTON, YORK, YO1 5DD
> TELEPHONE 0904 59861
>
> DEPARTMENT OF CHEMISTRY
> Dr. R. J. Mawby
>
> 30th November, 1973
>
> Dear Mr. Riley,
>
> I am happy to tell you that the University will be offering you a place for October 1974 to read Chemistry, provided that you satisfy the formal requirement of A-level passes in your three science subjects. You will receive official notification of the offer via UCCA.
>
> I hope that you enjoyed your visit to York.
>
> Yours sincerely,
>
> R. J. Mawby,
> Tutor for Admissions.
>
> Mr. P. D. Riley,
> 142, Harrogate Road,
> Rawdon,
> Nr. Leeds,
> Yorks.
>
> rjm/dl

In the summer of 1974, I started a new job, obtained for me by Boylie's mum and dad. This was at Shires, making baths. I was earning £100 for 40 hours a week, a fortune at the time. When I had earned less than £20 for 56 hours at Morrisons. I was on either the 06:00- 14:00 or the 14:00- 22:00 shifts. In later years I was to be put on the 22:00 - 06:00 shift, which I didn't like because it ran Monday to Saturday, so I missed my Friday night out!

I saved up enough money to buy my first digital watch.

I thought the other type of liquid crystal watch would not catch on. Mine was an LED watch, like this. Most of the time the screen was black, until you pressed a button......I wonder where it went?

Since about the fourth form (Year 10) I had also picked up another important life skill. As I got home from school before my mum & dad I would often prepare tea. This started with my mum leaving things out, to be prepared. Eventually I ended up just raiding the cupboards and fridge and making what I fancied for everyone. My go to dish was a fish in tomato and vegetables sauce. Cooked in a tray on an infra-red grill, often with rice. Though over the years I mastered many dishes, often without a recipe. I have never regretted teaching myself to cook.

University and College

My mum and dad drove me to York in late September '74. I had accommodation in Vanbrugh College, X230. I went up for 'freshers week' to get to meet the Rugby Club and find my way around. The University is quite a way out of town, on its own site. The central feature is a large spaceship of a hall, set next to an artificial lake. It is mostly grey concrete, and quite depressing in the gloom of winter rain.

The meeting of the rugby team was in a pub in Heslington Village. I think it was the Deramore Arms. One of the first to arrive was a big lad who I had played school rugby against. We had bashed heads last season, when playing against Huddersfield New College. A battle royal in the hail of the Huddersfield moor. I can't remember his name, but we recognised each other instantly..... "It's you!". I do recall he had 'come up' to York to read Sociology. We trained twice weekly in the University facilities and I managed to get a place as loose-head prop in their first XV. We would also play twice a week, as Wednesday afternoon was for sport and had no lectures. To be honest, they didn't have a great team and I missed playing for the Airebronians. I had trained with 'Aire' through the summer and got into their first XV at Loose Head Prop before going up to York.

Central hall at York University, usually called The Enterprise by students, due to its resemblance to the USS Enterprise on Star Trek.

Winter was quite bleak and I didn't make any real friends in the chemistry department. We had 2 hours of lectures every day and Labs which lasted from 11.00 - 17.00 on Mondays, Tuesdays and Thursdays. You didn't need to be in the Lab all the time, having certain projects to complete in a given time. Also some experiments could be left to run for a few hours, so could be left bubbling away. We also had a tutorial group of about 4 or 5. This met once a week to discuss a topic which had been prepared during the week. We also had a weekly assignment.

I spent a lot of my time by myself in the first term, it was grey and bleak in the University. I sometimes walked around town, went to the cinema or watched TV in the hall's Junior Common Room. Looking back I was homesick for my mates.

In the labs there was a bank of calculators screwed to a desk. These were the first I had seen and ran at about £175 each. A considerable sum in those days and £1680 in 2020 prices. They were HP-35s, with the characteristic red LED display.

HP-35, 147 mm x 81 mm x 18 mm

Before the end of the year I was able to buy myself a calculator, from money I had saved working at Shires. This was the Sinclair Scientific, small even by today's standards.

Sinclair Scientific, 50 mm x 111mm x 19mm

Because of the way the processor was designed, it used Reverse Polish Notation and was a right pain in the ass for inputting calculations. RPN meant that the difficult implementation of brackets, was offloaded to the user. Instead of an "Equals" button, there is an "Enter" button that tells the calculator when a value has been entered, and then the operators(+,-,x or /) are entered after the operands. For example, to evaluate "(1+2) x 3", the sequence entered would be "3 2 1 + x" Eeeek!

This cost about £50, or £480 at 2020 prices. I was somewhat pleased when about a year later I had my car stolen and the calculator was taken. I could buy a much better one for a far cheaper price.

By about March I was coming home each weekend and had returned to playing rugby for 'Aire'. I would catch the bus from York centre to Leeds, then another from Leeds bus station home. I could be in the Emmot's most Fridays by 19.00. I also started to travel back to University either with a lift from my mum and dad or by bus on Sunday evening. I hadn't settled to new friends or University life.

It was during this time that I decided to change course. My thinking was that I didn't need all the chemistry I was learning, to teach it to A-level, which had become my career aim. So I looked around for other options. My first choice was Leeds Carnegie. I went for an interview, but they would not accept my year of chemistry and allow me to join their second year of BEd.......I would have to start again. I couldn't do this easily, as the BEd was a four year course and I didn't think I could get a 5 year grant.

In those days, all college course fees were payed by the Local Authority, so long as you had the required minimum of 2 x A-levels. You also got a 'grant', the size of which depended upon your parents income. The 'grant' didn't need to be payed back.(Appendix 7, my grant).

I also had an interview at Ripon and York St John's College. They agreed to take me on a special two year Certificate in Education, followed by a one year BEd. This would mean that I could concentrate on the missed 'Education' part of the course. I passed my first year exams at the University and left in the summer of '75. Leeds Local Authority were Ok about the change and I started St. John's in September '75.

The badge from my PE track suit for St. John's College, York

66

In my first year at St. John's I was resident in Heworth Croft. I had a huge room and the science department was on the same site. There were only 9 of us doing mainly chemistry. In addition I did physics, education and PE. I had decided not to take part in their rugby teams, though as the college had a PE 'Wing' their team was better than the University, instead going home each weekend to play for 'Aire'.

It was towards the end of this year that I bought my first car, courtesy of my Auntie Minnie's Will. It was a 1970 Mk1 Ford Escort Van, with side windows an 100 000 miles on the clock! (Appendix 10, Cars). This allowed me to arrange my next two years at St John's based at home. I travelled each day into York, paying for my petrol out of my grant and with money saved from working at Shire's again in the summer holidays I then re-claimed travel expenses and was able to run the van on these. It also gave me a lifelong aversion to car repair. It would often not start after being left out in the rain and broke down a couple of times coming home from York. My advice to all is 'have breakdown cover as soon as you get a car!

One funny incident happened when I got a small rust hole in the petrol tank. I tried to fix it with fibre glass resin, but the resin wouldn't 'go off' due to the petrol. So I made the hole slightly bigger and drained out all the petrol. That night someone stole my car! They didn't get far, I found it at the bottom of the hill near our house......lol, laugh out loud! It did get stolen on another occasion, but as usual it didn't have much petrol in it. This time the thief made it to Ilkley Moor. On the up side I lost an old jacket from the car which had my Sinclair calculator in it. I was happy to recover the cost and buy a much more advanced calculator for a far smaller price.

The two years I spent doing the Cert. Ed. were reasonably easy academically. From being an average chemist at the university I was a bit of a star at college. I had my first long teaching practices at Nunthorp Comprehensive, a very large co-ed in a nice district in Middlesbrough. For this we were paired up in accommodation rather like a boarding house. I enjoyed the practice, the school staff were great, but didn't get on so well with my land lady. It was 5 or 6 weeks and I passed the assessments.

In my second year I had a long teaching practice at The King's Grammar School, Pontefract. This was an all boys school serving the mining town.

I was able to drive from home each day in my van. It was completely different from Nunthorp, but I did enjoy the challenge. I decide here that PE teaching really wasn't for me, though I did do a bit later. I realised that my passion was in doing sport, not watching others. I passed this teaching practice (TP) too (Appendix 9, Assessment of TP).

Kev, myself and Julie somewhere at some unspecified time. possibly towards the middle of 1977, as I had just been doing gymnastics at college?

It was about this time that I started to go out with Kevin's sister Julie. We had something of an on and off relationship for a couple of years.

My most enduring memory of this time with Julie was us both in Nottingham at Kev's end of year University do, in Derby Hall. It was Mungo Jerry who filled the quad. with music. They were shut down by the police at about 1.00am, after complaints from residents in Beeston, some 2 miles away! At the time Kev had started dating Val Scully, who he would later marry.

At the end of this year '77 I had exams. I needed to get 'Commendations' overall in Chemistry and in Education to be eligible for the BEd the following year. Fortunately I didn't find the Cert.Ed. exams too taxing and achieved the grades. This also gave me Qualified Teacher Status (QTS)…….I was a secondary school teacher. When St.John's became a university it rewarded its Cert. Ed. students with a B.Ed (honoris causa) I got a free degree in 2022!

At home I was still playing for 'Aire' and we were on our way to building a clubhouse along with Esholt C.C, just outside Esholt Village. I was particularly keen to get involved with knocking things down!

This is the first Airebronians RUFC 1st XV photo I have. It's unofficial and probably taken by Julie Boyle, somewhere between 1977-79.

Goya, Mackey, Lockwood, Gilroy, Stone, Cottle, Smith, Stead

Black, Daft, Boyle, Riley, Streets, Wade, Marlow

By the start of September '77 I was back at St.John's reading mainly Chemistry in a group of just two. Alongside that I was taking Psychology as my education unit. This involved, at one point, a 5 day residential camping with some disaffected teenagers from Sheffield. There were 4 of us from the Psychology course and a tutor from a centre, in the Peak District. We went walking and camped out. This was my first experience of leading a group outdoors and I quite enjoyed it.

The year went quite fast, travelling to college in York each day in my red van. However I spent too much time training with 'Aire', playing rugby and going out with friends. I was poorly prepared for the 'finals' and came away with an Ordinary BEd Degree. Once again a great disappointment and a salutary warning for you out there! April/May of '78 saw me starting to go for interviews for jobs. I had a couple and finally secured a post at Aireville Secondary Modern School, Skipton. This meant that I didn't need to move accommodation and could keep playing for 'Aire'.

I did learn a useful lesson at this time, 'prepare for an interview as you might for an exam', don't just try and 'wing it'. Find out as much as you can about the job. Prepare questions that they might ask you and formulate answers. Prepare to talk about your own experiences, strengths and weaknesses and how they relate to the job. Have some questions prepared to ask, not only in interview but as you are being shown around. Remember the process starts as you walk through the door! Oh, and be yourself, don't lie, if you don't think they will like you as you are, you may be unhappy in the job. I have chosen to leave more than one interview before the end.

One evening, during my final year at College, I arrived home to find the neighbours waiting for me. They had found my dad unconscious in the garden and he had been taken to Leeds General Infirmary. I rang my mom, as he usually picked her up from work in Leeds, and arranged to pick her up to go to the hospital. It would be some years before we had mobile phones. My mum worked for the Department of Health and Social Security(DHSS), not far from LGI.

When we arrived my dad was in quite a bad way. He had recovered consciousness but his speech was incoherent. He had completely lost the use of his right arm and leg. He had had a massive stroke, a blood vessel in his brain had exploded!.......he was 47 years old.

Dad spent quite a time in hospital, but eventually came home. Through medication and physio, over several months, he regained his speech. Only struggling when he got flustered. He got sufficient use of his right arm to be able to write and drive again, but less use in his right leg. He walked, or the rest of his life with a stick and limp. After a couple of years he was able to drive an automatic car, which my mum bought. Though she never learned to drive.

My dad never went back to work, but became a keen Citizen's Band(CB) radio enthusiast. He also passed his Radio Amateur's(Radio Ham) certificate, allowing him to talk to like-minded folk across much of Europe. His 'handle' was 'Nescafe'. The house became festooned with ariels.

My academic record has been affected by too little work and too much rugby. To much reliance on my natural abilities, already evidenced at A-Level. Through that I missed a place at a very prestigious university, Durham!

Though I did pass the Certificate in Education with Commendations in both Chemistry & Education to attain Qualified Teacher Status, I did far too little work, particularly revision in the following year. I had stayed on at St. John's to do a Bachelor of Education with Honours, mainly in Chemistry. However, the pathetic 'pass' degree I obtained, without Honours, which is a very poor effort, haunted me for some years, both career wise and in my own head.

I knew I was better than this and the cause in the main was lack of preparation for the exams and particularly the exam interview or 'viva'. I finally learned my lesson, that wasn't going to happen again! Luckily I did manage to get a Chemistry teaching job, starting September '78.

Starting Work

A Secondary Modern School is for those students who failed the 11+ exam. They are few and far between these days, as most schools are comprehensive and there is no entrance exam. Skipton is unusual in that it still has selective Grammar Schools, Ermystead's and the Girls High School. Though many schools still retain the title 'Grammar School', such as Ilkley and Otley Prince Henry's, they are in fact Comprehensives.

Aireville School; I started my career in the ground floor laboratory behind the lamp post (centre)

I found the school a complete culture shock in terms of academic ability. I had spent so much of my time over the last 10 years with reasonably smart people, even my final teaching practice had been at a Grammar School. I had not appreciated how low ability can go! As an indication, the total number of O-level passes for the school, in 1979, from 120 students was the same as my personal tally........10!

I taught General Science to the lower forms, Certificate of Secondary Education(CSE) Chemistry and the newly introduced 16+ Physics to the Fourth and Fifth forms (Y10 and Y11). There was no 6th Form, and I soon realised that I would have to apply for other jobs.

Julie and I had stopped going out sometime before she went to university in Manchester. Though I did go over a few times to see her there. After that I dated a few girls, then during the course of my last year of teaching training I met Gillian Gledhill at a party. We were to go out for about 2 years. Gill was heavily into dancing and a regular performer in local amateur dramatics.

Being trained in hotel and catering management she also ran several catering establishments in my time with her. The most outstanding of which was the Ceylon Tea Centre, now closed, on the Headrow in Leeds. I sometimes worked for her in my holidays, in the kitchen and on the front desk/till.

Gill was the first girl I went on a real holiday with. Our first was a week in London, eating out and taking in sites and shows. I remember we stayed at a posh hotel, The Tower, with views of Tower Bridge. I was also to play rugby many times with her younger brother Nick, known to his rugby pals as 'Boot-head', after several hospital visits to be stitched up! I remember once after a game against Skipton arriving back at the clubhouse in Esholt, proudly supporting 6 stitches to my forehead. Only to find Boot-head sat at the bar with 12!

Gill Gledhill outside the Tower Hotel London, 1978

My van was on its last legs when I started work. I bought my dad's car from him, as he could no longer drive it, it was a Vauxhall Victor Estate. However, I found it big and lumpy, so while going out with Gill I bought a sports car, a Triumph Spitfire. I loved that car. (Appendix 10, Cars).

Someone threw a snowball through the rather old plastic roof window. Which meant it needed replacing. I found one cheap in a magazine called 'The Exchange and Mart'. I thought it would arrive and I could just fit it easily. However it needed cutting to size and the press-studs needed to be pop riveted in place. I spent four very cold evenings in my dad's draughty garage. After much swearing and heart ache, I made it fit!

In May I found a job advertised at a large Comprehensive near to Skipton. South Craven School was looking for a chemistry teacher, to teach up to A-Level. I was on a Radiological Protection course at Manchester University on the week of the interview. So I was interviewed early by just the Head Dr Patterson, and the Head of Science, Jim Butterfield. The morning of the interview I went into school for my usual lesson. I left early and had my hair cut short in Skipton and put on my suite. This was the first time I had had short hair since I was 13. The interview was just before lunch, so I could get back to teach in the afternoon.....back at Aireville nobody recognised me! I must have done OK, because when I rang Jim from Manchester the following week, he offered me the job. There was one catch, I wasn't going to be able to start until January 1980........I had to work seven months notice at Aireville!

Some of the things I did while going out with Gill are worthy of historic note. We would eat out fairly regularly at local Wine Bars. These were a relatively new thing, and encouraged me to join with Gill in drinking wine. We both liked, at the time, semi-sweet German wines, such as Piesporter Riesling from Mosel and Niersteiner Gutes Domtal, from the Rhine. Going to restaurants and drinking wine was quite a seed change for me and something I have come to enjoy in life.

South Craven School - The Chalk Face

When I started South Craven in January '80, I didn't realise it would have a significant impact on my life in a number of ways. Not least of which were 2 wives and a girlfriend! It was also through South Craven that I developed a lifetime passion for the outdoors, succeeded in obtaining a Masters Degree, a Certificate in Guidance & Counselling and qualify as a Mountain Leader.

SCS is a modern co-educational 11-18yrs Comprehensive school of about 1800 students. I worked there for 27 of my 33 years teaching.

I found teaching Sixth Formers (Y13/12) quite strange at first. After all, at 18, they were not that far from my own age. Also the first topic I had to teach was a long unit on Biochemistry. I had managed to avoid Biology since Year 9, so the students doing A-Level had a better understanding of the biological aspects than I did. I really enjoyed the experience of being able to teach them the chemistry, while learning basic cell biology from them. A real eye opener for my teaching techniques.

U48, a room in which I have spent a considerable amount of my life. Not looking at its best, as I was in the process of ditching a lifetime's worth of accumulated 'resources'. I believe the total came to 12 large bin bags of stuff going back nearly 30 years!

A Few More Chemistry Tales.

One of the first Y13 group I had was great. They were all very conscientious and ranged from clever to exceptional. I once did a lesson which included the chemistry of ethene (acetylene). Now, ethene is a gas which burns in air. It can easily be made by reacting calcium carbide with water and this is the principle of the old miners lamp and my old caving helmet. So I decided to start the lesson by walking in wearing my caving helmet with the carbide flame on the front.....I thought it might grab their attention! But NO, nobody said anything! So I did the whole lesson without mentioning the helmet I was wearing. Nobody ever mentioned it again, I have no idea what they thought!

I still have the caving helmet, but unfortunately no Carbide.

Another Sixth form lesson was to show how Phosphorus starts to burn as soon as it comes into contact with air. It is normally stored in water and a piece is usually cut in a trough under water, then put on a ceramic mat and left to dry. Eventually it catches fire. This is done in a 'fume cupboard' so the resulting gas is drawn out of the room.

However, I had become 'cocky'. I would take a piece out of the water with tweezers, cut it on the mat, pop the big piece back in the jar, quickly dry the small piece on some paper towels and the leave it on the mat. However, this time, as I cut it the small piece flew onto the pile of paper towels. They caught fire! When I put on the fan for the fume cupboard it sucked the paper towels into the air, filling the cupboard with flaming paper towels.... at that moment my boss walked in, looked at it and walked out saying, "I'll come back later!"

Again with the Sixth Form I was doing an experiment involving liquid Bromine, in the fume cupboard. I hadn't taken the precaution of plastic gloves and spilt some Bromine on my thumb! Bromine burns the skin, but I knew that an antidote was to wash it in sodium thiosulfate, so I did that! However, it looked a bit blistered and I wasn't sure how to treat it next ....so off to hospital! On arrival I was seen by a nurse and she said "I have no idea, I'll get the Doctor" . As the doctor came in I said to the nurse "He has no idea either", "how do you know?" She replied. "Because I taught him Chemistry!" I was right, "Hi Mr Riley, what have you done?" asked Dr Harris. I explained and he replied "I've no idea, I'll go look it up"

Ok, I'm on a roll, memories are flooding back. In my early days they gave me a Y11 group called Science/Maths. In those days Maths was compulsory in Year 10/11, but Science wasn't. However, this bottom maths group was too much for the Maths Department five times a week, so Science had them for a couple of lessons(70mins). There was no syllabus and no exam, it was teach what you want. I have done all sorts with this type of group: First Aid, dredging the canal for creatures, mapping lichen in the woods, paper airplane competitions, building bridges and shaping glass animals. My most dangerous turned out to be hot air balloons! We designed and made tissue paper hot air balloons, powered by 'meths' in a bottle cap. They took several lessons to build and then they needed to be flown on a nice summers day. The balloons were inflated using a hair dryer, then the meths was lit.
The first few were fine, and spectacular, as towards the end they would burst into flames and drop onto the sports field. The last two however suffered from an increase in the wind, drifting quickly over the sports field to the timber yard opposite! I was 'crapping my pants' until luckily they fell short.

Talking of fire on the field. One year our stock check showed we had built up an excess of Sodium over the years. The official way to get rid of it is to dissolve it in ethanol and wash it down the sink. This is expensive and very time consuming. The other way is to have it disposed of by a chemical disposal company, this too is expensive. The third way is put it into water and let it fizz. Jim and I thought the third option might be the cheapest and most fun. So we took the Sixth Form out onto the fields and dug a hole. We put a bucket of water in the hole then dumped the Sodium, less its oil, into the bucket, covered it with a plastic sheet and 'ran'. Nothing happened for a while, then boom! A great white mushroom cloud, a shattered plastic sheet and a spray of unreacted Sodium all over the grass. Students were dispatched to Rural Studies for watering cans. Each time a piece of itinerant sodium was found, it reacted with a puff of smoke!

Alkali metals have caused problems for me in the lab. too. Once, burning a piece of Lithium on my front desk, it exploded. Instead of it hitting my Lab. coat it hit my tie, melting an instant big hole!

Computers in schools began just after I started at SCS. The first one I had access to was a Sinclair ZX81. It was about the size of a piece of A5 paper and 2.5cm deep. It had 1Kb (yes 1Kb!) of RAM memory and and an extension of another 16Kb, about the size of a cigarette packet. Programmes could be typed in or loaded from a tape cassette player and it had to be plugged into a TV.

Sinclair ZX81 with 17Kb of usable memory, including the extension pack on the back. It played through an Ordinary TV. The tapes were to store programs, and played through a standard music tape player.

The next was a Research Machines RM 360Z, about the size of a microwave oven. It had more power, but its main use was that it could be used as a room fan heater in the winter.

RM 360Z, this used a monitor and programs were loaded directly from a '5 inch floppy disc'. This one has a duel disc drive.

An assortment of floppy discs. The most common was the 5 inch. The later 3.5 inch had a hard plastic shell.

Later came the BBC Model B, with its BBC BASIC programming language. This enabled students (and teachers) to write their own programs easily.

A BBC Model B, with monitor and floppy disk drive. I had one of these in my lab from about 1985 until 2000+

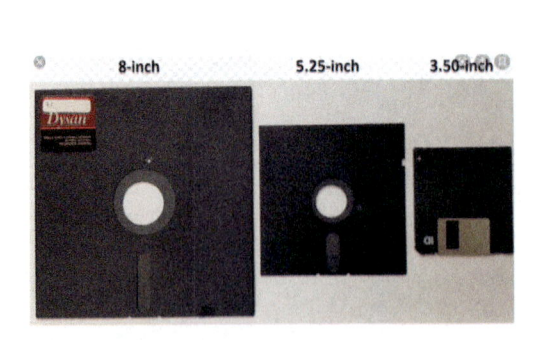

8-inch   5.25-inch   3.50-inch

With the help of some Y12/13 we managed to get this linked to some experiments, such as rates of reaction and acid/base titrations. We were at the leading edge of technology in schools at the time. One of the boys who helped was Jonathan Chapman, my brightest ever student.I entered Jonathan for the International Chemistry Olympiad and he represented the UK, winning a Bronze Medal in Leyden. Jonny became the youngest Professor at Oxford, at the time, when he got the Chair in Mathematics and Its Applications at age 32.

This 'leading edge' didn't last for long, and I had the same BBC computer in my lab. 20 years later! For a little while I also had an Acorn Archimedes, which ran a very basic form of Microsoft Windows.

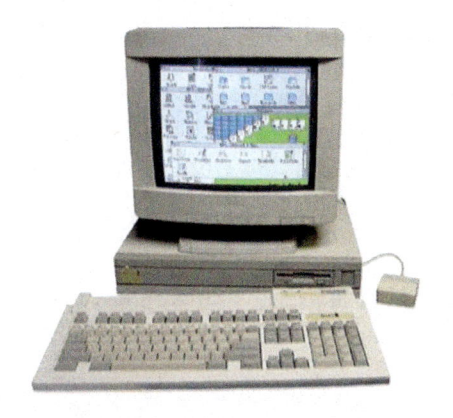

Acorn Archimedes A4000, with a small floppy disc drive and 'mouse'. I used one of these until we got Laptops in the late 1990s

Over my time at SCS we did see a move from reel to reel movies shown in class to Betamax then VHS Video cassettes, then DVDs and finally access to Video via the Internet and school's Intranet. The last of which worked via a digital projector onto a white board. Finally, every member of staff had access to the internet, and the bane of our lives e-mail, via their own 'Laptop'. Typed worksheets and photocopying replaced hand written sheets, duplicated on a 'Banda copier'. It wasn't until I moved to Qatar (2008) and Singapore(2014) that I was finally to work on an interactive whiteboard. I never saw the introduction of pupil's personal iPads in about 2020.

SCS was great, at first, with many opportunities to teach the full range of ability. I was also given Y11 Boys PE, on Friday afternoons. I was in the gym, on a rota, for football, basketball and other sports. We had a good time playing things like 'murder ball', a game which is unfortunately banned now. I also helped with the rugby 1st.XV and managed to get a lot of training in with them. I coached lower teams for a while, but found I hated refereeing, so gave that up fairly soon.

At the end of each year we had 'Project Week'. This was where staff chose an interest and advertised it to students. It varied from chess to art to trips of all kinds. As I arrived at Christmas I sort of missed the details of this, so ended up picking up a group of students who hadn't been bothered to fill out the forms. You can guess what they were like! We did bits of 'school renovation', from painting to gardening and mending paths. I remember one day going to find some sandpaper and coming back to find two lads had painted each other's faces! Luckily they had only been allowed emulsion paint. That taught me a lesson, and the following year I organised a walking/youth hosteling trip on the North Yorkshire Moors. This I did with fellow Science teacher Pam Merrill.

Fairly early on I became involved with the school's Outdoor Club. This ran walks for Y7-9 once a month, to interesting places such as the Dales and the Lake District. They also organised 'School camp', which was a Static Camp in the grounds of Bewerley Park Outdoor Centre, Patley Bridge. It was through this that I got to know my long time mountain buddy, Chris Ainsworth. He taught French & German and had done some outdoor stuff as a student. The club was run by Dave and Di Fuller, assisted by Graham Kirkbride. I will come back to the outdoors later.

Pam and I on the North Yorks Coast, photo by Ruth

At breaks and lunchtimes the Science Department had its own corner of the staff room. Here we were joined by a close friend of Pam's, Ruth Helliwell. Ruth had been a student at SCS, had left to train as a Home Economics teacher and returned there to begin her teaching career. The first SCS student to teach at the school. I was sad to learn that she would be leaving in the summer, as she had a new job on the Isle of Man. It was May 1980, I decided to ask her out!

I started to jog in those early days at SCS and would often run up onto the Billing near my home in Rawdon. One of the Science department at SCS, Doug Lawrence: Head of Biology, asked me if I fancied doing a half-marathon, 21.1km (13.1 miles). It seemed a long way, but I thought I would give it a try. I completed my first, around Otley, in '86 in just under my target time of 2 hrs, with my second target of not stopping or walking also completed. By '88-'89 I was running 5 miles three times a week and had improved my time to around 100 minutes....not bad for a 'well built' lad!

Finishing the Leeds half-marathon ('88?) in good style, while running alongside my friend Doug to 'pace' him in achieving a time of under 2 hours..........what timing! Oh, he sprinted the last 5m so he could say he beat me!

Trips, Clubs and Visits.

I will say more about my main extra-curricular activity DofE, in Chapter 11 and have already mentioned The Outdoor Club. On arriving at SCS I did maybe five years where I organised a London Science trip. This involved something like 65 Year 7 students and half a dozen Y13 students, along with 5 staff. We caught an early morning train from Keighley to Leeds, having booked a whole compartment from Leeds to Kings Cross. The first day was usually split between the Science Museum and the Natural History Museum. Then to a hotel, one such was the massive Regent Palace in Piccadilly Circus. Ok, so they left the keys to the mini-bars on the key rings, we caught that one. But also they put kids on different floors and some staff on floors without kids........go figure! The kids were told not to overuse the lifts and under no circumstances leave the hotel without a member of staff. After eating out, I had booked a burger/pizza restaurant, the staff spent the evening in the bar. The worst part of this particular evening was a call on the PA for a member of staff from SCS, "Some of your children are on the roof!".........fortunately, after a quick trip to the roof, it wasn't our school after all! Also we had to put a couple of of Y13 students to bed........ all in a nights work.

Day 2 was usually a tour of the sights: Buckingham Palace and The Mall, Houses of Parliament and Downing Street, Horse-guards and Changing of the guard. A few times we ended at The Tower, visiting the Crown Jewels. In the early days you could walk down Downing St. and we saw Margret Thatcher(PM) going to PMQs........she waved and some of our kids booed........there goes my OBE!

We crocodile filed, 2x2, the kids through the streets of London, splitting them into groups of 13 with a member of staff to travel on the Underground. Once I lost two students between Whitehall and The Westminster tube station! I found them 'shopping' on route. Another time there was a delay on the Underground and I had to run up to the train station at Kings Cross to ask the Guard to hold the train for a minute or two. He said he couldn't do that, so a threatened to run along the platform opening train doors (before electric doors). He said "you can"t do that"   "watch me!" By the time we had finished arguing my kids were on the train!

I was lucky enough to be asked by Ainsey to help with several school visits to France. First with Y7 to St.Brieuc, on the north coast of Brittany.....or 'Saint Bruik' as the kids called it. Then a couple of times to the coast of Normandy around Granville, with Y9/10. visit with Y10, noted elsewhere. I was also invited on a German visit with a Y8 group.

83

In 2001 the school asked me if I would like to go on an information gathering visit to Albuquerque, New Mexico, USA. Paid for by by the British Council. Four of us: Craig Taylor(Technology), Karen Watson(Maths/Pastoral), Steve Gardiner(IT/ICT) and myself(Science/ICT/Assessment).

Albuquerque is a long way! We had over two weeks, visiting schools, interviewing teachers, watching lessons and interviewing counsellors and school administrators. We visited a new school built by Intel the computer chip company. It had hundreds of computers used as glorified word processors. Nothing for interactive or experimental science.....we were in advance in the UK.

Our assessment systems were also in advance of the those of the school in which we were based. The Principal there picked my brains for over an hour. The main plus I came away with was that the students understood that they were working for themselves, even with homework, and not for the teacher as many UK students have come to believe! Second, the pastoral support system and overall academic monitoring for each student was via trained counsellors and the disciplinary system entirely by non-teaching assistants. Leaving teachers to concentrate on teaching. We were all surprised to find that we could learn little new about the areas we had gone to experience.

We also had some US staff looking after us socially. One of them had a sister with a very large house on the edge of the desert, next to the Indian Reservation. She had two large quad bikes, which she loaned to Craig and I. She told us that the 'reservation' was a great place to ride, but it wasn't exactly legal, don't get caught. We went through the gate and rode by the side of the 'levee', then played with these very powerful bikes on the desert tracks. After a while a car drove up and two guys started to watch us. The red light went on, it was a reservation Police car, we had been warned about, they started to drive towards us. We 'high tailed' it as they pursued us down to the gate and through........they stopped at the gate! Incredibly, we had been chased by Indians off their reservation!

One evening in Albuquerque I decide to walk from the hotel over some open parkland to a bar I could see from my hotel window, less than 1km. I was stopped half way across by a Police Patrol car and asked what I was doing? After explaining the officer said "Ah, that explains it, you are English, most people would get a Taxi". Entering the bar I was asked for ID to get served........at 45! I had to say to the bar man, "we both know that I'm at least 20 years older than you?". He said "Yes, but I still need ID!".....jobsworth!

One of the upsides of dating Candy after 2003 was that I got to go on the Y12/13 Art Trip to New York, twice. These were a great adventure for me, and I was with Candy! In one of the hotels we stayed, the Gershwin Hotel, they had an original Andy Warhol 'Soup Can'. One advantage of NY was that there was also no way the students could get alcohol, as the rules about being 21 and providing ID are very strict. I do remember a student who was autistic who filled in 'yes' to the immigration question "Do you have a mental illness". He was whisked away by immigration and it took all Candy's skill and half an hour to get him back.

On our first trip, my first to NY, we had 32 students. We visited the Statue of Liberty and Ellis Island, where my steel toed boots set off an alarm! We ate at the Stardust Diner, where the staff periodically burst into song/dance and had a very cold and snowy trip to the top of the Empire State Building at night. We experience Chinese New Year in China Town........an experience of things to come.....and we ice skated outside the Rockefeller Centre. Many people, not least myself, were surprised to find that Candy could skate really well. I also booked The Knicks Vs Miami Heat at Madison Square Gardens with Paris Hilton in the audience. I do remember going to the Metropolitan Museum in Central Park and been amazed by the payment method. I was taken into a small office and asked to pay by credit card.......no problem! Then the girl got out a credit card machine that I had not seen in the UK for maybe 10 years. It involved putting my card onto a machine, followed by a double carbonated receipt, filled out with the purchase details. The handle was then pulled left to right and back to 'engrave' the card details and the receipt is then signed by me. I get the copy and they keep the original. Yet another example of the US
being way behind the UK!

The Greasy Poll and the End

My work life was more teaching in the same classroom........U48. I had become first Master in Charge of Chemistry in 1982(Scale 2), then later Charge, then Head of Chemistry. I became Head of Y7 in 1990 and saw that year group through to Y11. I moved from Scale 3 to first 'B' and then a 'C' allowance, dropping my Head of Year role in '95 to take on Whole School responsibilities for Records of Achievement & Assessment. I maintained my Head of Chemistry role throughout and gained responsibility for setting up and running first GNVQ, then AVCE and finally BTEC Science. Interesting times, which always kept me busy at work.

My working life at SCS lasted from January 1st. 1980 until July 2007, nearly 28 years. In that time I taught A-Level Chemistry, GNVQ, AVCE & BTEC(Higher Science) at Advanced Level, Chemistry & Physics at O-Level, Chemistry & Science at GCSE & BTEC(Ordinary Science). I was Head of Chemistry for over 25 years, Head of Year for 5 years & Head of BTEC/AVCE/GNVQ Science for more than 10 years. I also held whole school responsibilities in assessment, and was central to the introduction of, Records of Achievement & Student Planners. I introduced computerised reporting, which lasted for about 3 years and also assisted with the school timetable for several years. This included being responsible for the change from pencil & paper to computerised timetabling. A project which included feeding back directly to the company producing the software, as each 'glitch' came up............In the end, I was pleased to leave!

Oh one final thing, three minutes before I was supposed to leave the school the Head of Sixth Form asked me to write a reference.....cheeky bugger!

Marriage, Home and Family - Middle Years

Things between Gill and I had been stop and start for a few months and I determined to ask Ruth out for a drink before she left. It took me until May to pluck up the courage and after a few hours delay she accepted. I was highly impressed by her parents' place, Hawkcliffe House. Ruth lived in the rather less grand granny cottage attached, Hawkcliffe Ho. Cottage. We had a night out at the pub, I think in Laycock. My trusty Spitfire burst its radiator in the valley and I had to beg a bucket of water to get us back to Ruth's mum and dads house. We decided that the best thing would be for me to stay overnight in her spare room and mend my car in the morning. She popped a note to her parents to let them know. As it turned out she had some Swiss wine and we stayed up all night talking. I met Ruth's dad, a formidable character, Brian, the next morning. Brian was Professor of Engineering Mathematics at Bradford University and Pro Vice-Chancellor. He came out to find my rear end sticking out of my car bonnet, trying to tape up the top hose. As people who know me will vouch, I'm never at my best when my car breaks down.

Ruth and I went out on several more dates, but it was difficult to see how it would continue once she had moved away. I went to Corfu with Gill, as friends, Ruth had OK'd the holiday, but I couldn't wait to get back. Ruth was waiting for me at Leeds Station, we were in a long distance relationship.

The year, with Ruth in the Isle of Man was both long and expensive. We spoke often and for hours on the telephone and I would do weekend jaunts to see her. This period of my life was the first time I had gone overdrawn at the bank, something I would become accustomed to! I could get the overnight ferry from Heysham on a Friday and return on the Sunday overnight ferry. This got me into Heysham at 06.00 and I could get to school in time for registration......most times! Sometimes there would be a delay and I would be a bit late.....oops! Ruth applied for jobs back on the mainland and I tried in the IoM. She was more successful and got a job at Boston Spa Comprehensive for the following September '81.

I don't recall exactly when we got engaged but I do remember the moment. We had agreed to get married in August of '82. We went to Leeds and chose a ring, I think from Ratner's jeweller's in the Merrion Centre. At that time there was a rough car park outside and we became officially engaged in the Spitfire. We returned to Hawkcliffe House to break the news, with some trepidation. Thankfully everyone seemed pleased.

When Ruth returned to Yorkshire I spent quite a lot of time at Hawkcliffe. Though I wasn't an 'official' resident until we were married. Ruth's mum and dad, Brian and Joyce, said we could live in the Granny Cottage after we were married, to save up for a house deposit. My stag weekend was in a tent in a field at Hubberholm, we had a great time. We were married at the church in Steeton, which Ruth's family attended. We were very fortunate that Brian was old fashioned and paid for the reception, while I paid for the church, flowers, photos and wedding cars. My Best Man was Geoff Stone and the Ushers were Peter Merrill and Nick Cottle. Ruth had Pam Merrill as her Maid of Honour and her sisters Janice and Sarah as Bridesmaids. The reception had about 70 guests and was at Tarn House, north of Skipton. This was followed by drinks at Hawkcliffe and being driven to Leeds station by Geoff and his wife Lynne for a train to London.

The front of Hawkcliffe House on our wedding day, 7th August 1982. My mum packed our suit cases full of confetti. This didn't see the light of day until it covered the room we had in London!

We stayed in a hotel called the Henry VIII. Then traveled by train for a week in Paris. I can't remember the name of the hotel, but it was very quaint, somewhere in the streets behind L'Opera. Ruth's french was no better than mine and we didn't have a great deal of money. We did manage a few evening restaurants, but lunches were often bread, wine and cheese somewhere in a park. I remember that we went up the Eiffel Tower, and visited the Left Bank. I also remember having my first ever MacDonald's, in fact the first I'd ever seen, sat on the Champs Élysées

We returned to live in Steeton and look for a house. Ruth travelled to Boston Spa each day and I either caught the bus or walked into school. I Got a small promotion at school, from Scale 1 to Scale 2, as 'Master in Charge of Chemistry', essentially Head of Chemistry but without the formal title! In that summer Brian had a heart attack and they found that he also had leukaemia. We got the news while we were both at SCS school camp at Bewerley Park. They fitted Brian with a pacemaker and he retired from the University, though they made him an Emeritus Professor. Brian and Joyce started to look for a house around Pickering, on the Yorkshire Moors, so it became imperative that we found a place of our own. We found a small property. A three bedroom semi; 68, Main Street, Menston, with a small garden and large garage at £23 000. We moved in sometime, I think in late 1983.

There was plenty to do in our new house, particularly decorating. At some stage I also put in a fitted kitchen, with a lot of heartache. The most interesting was plumbing in the sink. I got wet when we turned on the water! Ruth often said that it was a close run thing between selling the house and having to pay for another new kitchen. The exterior of the house was pebble-dash. I spent one very wet summer coating and then painting the entire exterior walls.....great holiday! That brings me to another car story, I had bought a Morris 1800 'Road Crab' to replace the Spitfire, Ruth called it 'Hercules' because of its size, when we were in Hawkcliffe. This had bitten the dust and we replaced it with a Mk.1 Ford Fiesta. One Saturday Ruth broke down while out shopping, it wouldn't start! The RAC repair man said that there was a lead from the solenoid to the starter motor which was in an exposed place and needed replacing, estimated cost £1. So when she got home I caught the bus to Yeadon and the car parts shop. I purchased the piece and went home.

The next day, Sunday, it was raining but we needed the car for Monday. So I got out and got under. Everything was rusty and in my effort to get the old lead off the solenoid it smashed........I didn't hit it, I just don't know my own strength sometimes. Of course the spares shop isn't open on Sunday.

We both managed to get lifts to school the next day and the guy, Martin, dropped me off in Yeadon the next evening, it was raining and dark by the time I got home with my new £25 solenoid. The next day we got lifts to work again, and I was home in good time........it was now only drizzling! I couldn't get the old solenoid off the body, the nuts were too corroded. So I wired up the new one and left it hanging in place. turned the key and......'click', nothing! Too late to go back to the shop, so I took the solenoid off and returned to the shop the next day after work. There the bloke explained that in order for it to work it had to be earthed by bolting it to the bodywork, I bought a drill and some bolts! It was dark and rainy when I got home so we organised lifts for the next day. That evening was fine so I drilled some holes and fitted the solenoid......it worked! It had taken me 5 days and cost something like 50 times the original price in labour, travel and parts. I had lost the skin of all ten knuckles and caught a chill. I vowed then that I would work hard and earn enough money to take my car to the garage when it broke down. In essence, I've kept to my promise.

Ruth had always been a keen walker and our holidays were often camping and walking in the Lakes or other mountainous regions. I was playing rugby for Airebronians and she got to know some of the wives and girlfriends and started an Airebronians Lady's Hockey Team........They had been the 'Guard of Honour at our wedding! We were always short of money but never unhappy. By 1985 Ruth was pregnant and we decided to buy a brand new and more reliable car, a red MkII Vauxhall's Astra. Ruth went into labour on the afternoon of 17th April 1986. Our friend Francis Binns (later Williams) drove her into Airedale Hospital and I met them there, walking up from school.

Christopher Richard Martin Riley was born in the late evening, our first bonny bouncing baby boy. I remember the labour, with Ruth crushing my hand and bursting blood vessels in her face and then declaring that "I've had enough, I'm going home now!"

I remember the noise, like cutting bacon with scissors, as the doctor facilitated the birth. also remember how messy it all seemed. Pam Merrell's sister was the midwife, which made it all seem a bit more like a family affair. We all went up to the ward, where I was refused entry, as it was too late! It was very surreal going home that evening to phone around and tell friends and family the good news.

My paternity leave was one day for "wife coming out of hospital". Chris had a fine pair of lungs when he got home and was never easy to get to sleep, but he very soon slept through the night, which was good.

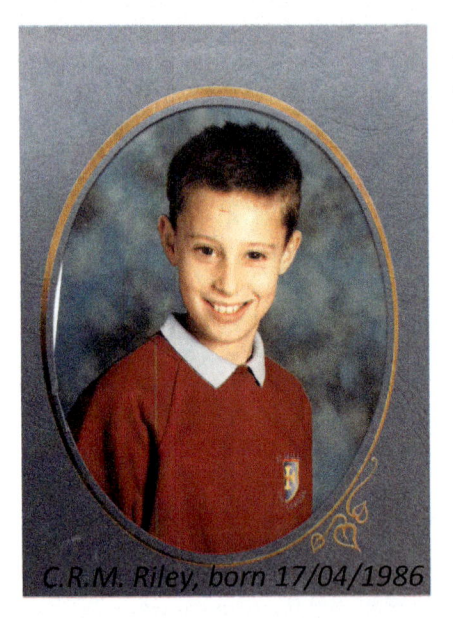

After what seemed like a very short time Ruth returned to work. We had found a girl in Menston who had just finished a Nursery Nurse course and so we employed her to look after Chris, based at our house. This really didn't seem to work. We would leave food for them both and nothing would be washed up after dinner. She was very disorganised and invited friends into the house without asking. Eventually we had to look elsewhere and found a childminder, Carol, in Guiseley. Carol was great, she looked after a number of children and each day would deliver and pick up at Guiseley Nursery School, Infants and C of E Primary School. Chris got a lot of walks out in his pram and push-chair.

C.R.M. Riley, born 17/04/1986

A couple of memorable moments with Chris come to mind. I was washing the car, my fairly new car, in the drive one day. 'Bang' I rushed round to find Chris with a hammer, he had hit the car. Helping his dad to mend it! Luckily he had done no damage. The second moment is of him tripping out of the back door, down two steps, with a head plant onto the drive. There was a lot of blood, but not from his head, his tooth had gone right through his chin, leaving a little hole just below the lip.

By early '88 Ruth was pregnant again.......we needed a bigger house. Ruth spotted a house, 77 Park Road, Guiseley. We went to have a look and immediately fell in love with it. It was much bigger than Main Street, with a large master bedroom (with a sink) & two smaller bedrooms. Down stairs was a large living room, smallish kitchen and a reasonable dining room. There was a front and back garden, shed and garage. One of the big draws was a small private road running in front of all the houses, then another small garden and large hedge before the main road. Ideal for two small boys. We paid £43 000 for this upgrade, a year later the adjoining semi sold for £75 000......we got a bargain.

Over the next ten years we spent quite a bit of money on the house. A loft conversion gave us a very nice fourth bedroom. A downstairs toilet, small as it may have been, made mornings less frantic and finally a conservatory nearly doubled the size of the lounge. The house grew as the family grew.

Alasdair Peter John joined us on January 23rd 1989. He was a bit late in arriving and I dropped Ruth off at Airedale Hospital on my way to work, to be induced. However, she didn't need it as her waters broke shortly after being admitted. I was called from school, around lunchtime I think, and Alasdair was born in the early afternoon.

A.P.J. Riley, born 23/01/89

We had been warned by the ultrasound scans that there maybe a problem with his kidneys......so we waited for him to pee. He, being stubborn, didn't. So mother and baby were taken by Ambulance for a few days to Leeds General Infirmary(LGI). I can't be sure, but I think Ruth stayed with him in hospital for 4 or 5 days. The problem righted itself and all was well. Alasdair wasn't such a good baby, we had been spoiled by Chris. I think it was something like 18 months before we got our first through night.

Early days for Chris and Al, & me with hair! Probably summer 1989

On a professional level I had a term sabbatical in the summer of '88. I completed a Certificate in Guidance and Counselling back at St John's in York. I was also interviewed soon after for a Head of Year Post and promoted to Scale 3. By this time Ruth had already moved school, to Allerton Grange High School, as Head of Home Economics, also on Scale 3. I also started, in September, of '89 a Master of Education Degree part-time, at Leeds University.

My dad died in the January of 1990, at the age of 59. He had never really recovered from his stroke of ten years earlier. He had begun to smoke again and according to my mum had stopped taking his medication for high blood pressure. We had fallen out several months earlier and I had only just seen my mum and dad a couple of times after a long absence. My dad refused my request not to smoke in front of Chris and Alasdair, either at my house or at theirs. I had said, and Ruth agreed, that this didn't work for us. My mum took my dad's side, so we didn't speak and they didn't see the grandchildren for several months. I think I was right to hold my ground, but was pleased in the end, that even though they never relented, I had made the effort to make contact, luckily, just before he died.

I received my Masters Degree(MEd) in '91, having spent most of the summer holiday writing up the final dissertation. This wasn't great for Ruth and the boys, as it took much longer than I estimated. My mum, who had been a short-hand typist in her early days typed it up for me on an old typewriter. There was no desktop/ laptop computers in people's houses at that time, and of course no Internet or mobile phones. I had done the degree at Leeds University for 2 evenings a week for 2 years.

The necessary reading was done each evening, by going to bed early and having an hour or so reading in bed. The essays were done mostly in holiday time. One essay I can remember, involved me writing under the bed, to keep out of the way of the kids! The essays were all handwritten, no word processors then, which made for an awful lot of re-writes if I changed my mind on a final read through.

In the 90's we had some great family holidays. We bought a new Espace and fitted a roof box and a trailer. We had a 'continental' family tent and the four bikes would ride on top of the trailer. Over the ten years we visited a number of different sights around Brittany, Normandy, the Vendee and down as far as Biarritz. The tent and trailer also went to Skye, the Lakes, North Wales and to several other places in the UK. Though I have to say that the unreliable UK weather was never my first choice for family camping.

We also had a French gîte holiday and a Scottish gîte with Aunty Sarah and Russell and camping and gîte holidays in Skye with Chris and Jan Ainsworth, but one of our strangest holidays was in a gîte loaned to us by some work friends of Ruth. It was in Northern Normandy, below Caan. It sat down a long farm track in the middle of high sweet corn fields, with a pool sticking up out of the garden. We arrived in the dark, as I had under estimated the time it would take to drive from Calais. We also knew they hadn't finished renovating it but didn't expect to find mud floors in the kitchen and large main room. It wasn't until I examined the floor the next day that we found there were tiles under 0.5cm of hard mud. The pool was also full of green gunk and had to be drained, cleaned and refilled. By the end of our holiday the house was spotless and the pool was in working order. The people didn't charge us for the hire, in-fact they invited us out for a meal.

Several noteworthy things happened at the house. I got a call from my mum to say that she had been taken into hospital and they had found that she had several cancers around her body. It was strange to be told by your mum on the phone that they had given her 2 years to live, she only lasted 18 months. However, she was instant that we didn't come home, because she felt there was nothing we could do that wasn't already being done.

The house itself was quite spooky and had a strange little alter in a small stone building in the garden, the lads said that they had seen an old lady sat at one of the house windows. One night there was the sound of a chain being slowly dragged up the pebbled drive........drag, stop, drag, stop etc, as if it was attached to someone's leg. Needless to say neither Ruth nor I were brave enough to look out. Back in the UK, at the meal with the owners, they asked if we had had any 'interesting' experiences in the house. We told them about the chain and the lads with the old lady. "Ah, yes" they admitted "we think it is haunted but didn't want to tell you, preferring to see what you thought". Of course I don't really believe in anything like that, but I also don't have a ready explanation.

As Chris and Al got older they both attended Guiseley Infants, then Guiseley Church of England Juniors. In this time we would drop them off and pick them up each day from Carol, our long standing child minder. They both finally were old enough to have a house key and go themselves to Guiseley Secondary, which was more or less across the road from Park Road.

In our time at Hawkcliffe I had started jogging to keep fit. This continued both in Menston and Guiseley and I completed several half-marathons. My best time was just about 100 minutes......not bad for a 'prop'. I also went to a Gym in Yeadon for a while and was in the Guiseley Leisure Centre Squash leagues. To be honest I was never very good, maxing out in the middle of league 3!

Both boys started rugby when they were 8. A school friend of mine, Nik Wood, had a son Henry & another school friend, Chris 'Bob' Monkman à son Tom, both the same age as Chris. They started at Ilkley RUFC, so we enrolled Chris there. Nik was a local 'star' having presented both BBC2's Working Lunch and Look North. He was also an inspiring coach, with some excellent players to call on, and his team did well. Chris was part of the squad which won the U8s Yorkshire Cup. Repeating the success 2 years later. Chris joined my old club Aireborough for a while. He played for the first XV at full-back before he was 17.

Alasdair wasn't quite so lucky, as I was roped into helping coach his side. The head coach was one of the boys mums, Suzanne. The squad didn't have as much talent as Chris's side. The only other good player being a long time friend of Al's, another Tom. I stopped coaching after a couple of seasons, I hate refereeing and teaching rugby was a bit like a busman's holiday. Tom & Alasdair decided they wanted to move clubs and went first to Yarnbury in Horsforth and then to Otley.

When Nik stopped coaching, after U13 I think, Chris, Tom and Henry all went to Otley RUFC. There they helped make up a rather formidable team which went on to win two more Yorkshire Cup finals. Unfortunately Al's team was never quite as good and he and Tom went on then to Baildon RUFC, but were always eager to move to Rugby League

*Chris, front right, celebrating one of his Yorkshire Cup victories.
Here with the Otley RUFC side at U15's, where he played Prop.*

Al was always something of a bruising player, being tall and very heavily built for a 'centre'. I once remember him, he must have been 15, tackling a small opponent and the lad just disappeared......'oh god' I thought, 'he must have killed him'.

Al, giving some advice while playing in the Centre for Otley RUFC.

    They both had their share of injuries, needing us to take them to hospital. Once Ruth took them both in and the nurse noticed they had been before. They were asked some questions about being mis-treated at home, but were corrected by Chris(6'1) and Al(6'3) looking down at their mum and saying "what her? it was rugby"

Al playing Rugby League, something of a bruiser but still in the Centre.

We also got both of them swimming at Guiseley Leisure Centre. Both could swim reasonably well at an early age, but it was Chris who took to it 'like a fish'. He had all his ASA medals and his 1 mile badge by the time he was 9 and, rather by accident joined Aireborough Swimming Club. After quite a few months, some initial difficulties with style and a great coach Chris started to swim for the team. He won many medals and was selected to train at the Leeds Club in the Olympic pool. This involved two nights a week travel and training in Leeds. He decided himself to give up once he started Guiseley Secondary, as it became difficult for him to do his homework. However, he did swim for the secondary school team throughout his time there. Al, never that keen to follow Chris, started diving lessons. He became quite proficient, though never at a competitive level

Two recollections of Chris's swimming. Being team house captain in his final year at Guiseley CoE, he swam last in the last relay race, one boy and one girl from each year. His team needed the points to win overall. He went into the water half a length behind the leader and beat him to the finish. Most memorable was my mum, usually very quiet and terminally ill, standing up shouting and screaming encouragement from the balcony! The other was him entering the Aireborough Club Gala at the age of 15........he hadn't been a member for 4 years, so no one really knew him. He rang me at about 18:00 to say the gala had finished and he had won some trophies and needed a lift home. I waited outside the pool as he arrived with an arm full of trophies then he headed off, "where are you going?" I asked, "for the rest, this is only half!" he had won all the Junior boy's trophies and all but one of the Men's........they never asked him back!

Al always liked mechanical things and was into mountain biking. At 15 he bought a Cannondale Jekyll, a top quality frame, from a semi-pro rider who worked with Ruth. He slowly bought bits to assemble for himself a working bike, from presents and his paper round money. I bought the bike from him when he got a car and have used it many times. It is with me here in France.

Another little technology aside. It was in about 1995 that I bought my first mobile phone. Remember that there was still no Internet and mobiles were just that......phones. There was no SMS(texts) and my first phone had no 'smart' capacity. It seems amazing now to realise that we have come so far in just 25 years, as I sit here with my iPad typing, while what I type instantly saves into a 'cloud' somewhere. It may all seem very passé to you the reader, but its high tech to a guy who used to write with a 'quill pen' and ink!

My first mobile phone, a Nokia 1011. A revolution from the old phone box. It did what it says on the box, made phone calls, and nothing else!

This was the sort of Desktop computer common in households in the late 1990s, early 2000s.

By about '96 or '97 we also had a computer in the house. It allowed access through a 'dial-up' modem on the telephone line and was often quite difficult to connect. This would have looked something like the one in the picture. Notice the 'mouse' to move the curser on the screen, it would be quite a while before the first touch screens. Of course the VDU(visual display unit) was like an old TV, no flat screens yet.

Finally the 'floppy' disc drive, no DVDs yet, and actual computer often sat on the floor next to your legs. I remember that I still had a system like this when I moved to Ilkley in 2002. It was running the Microsoft Windows '95 operating system with a Pentium processor. It mostly ran from programs on 'floppy disk' or those which made the Windows package such as 'Word', 'Excel' and 'Powerpoint'.

Much to my regret at the time, both Chris and Al left school at 16. Chris to first try College, then work as a landscape gardener and Al as an apprentice engineer/fitter for JC at Finning's in Leeds. As it turns out I have ended up being proud of both of them. But that is their story, so I will let them tell it!

In 2000 Ruth and I split and while I must shoulder some of the blame she was the one to take the decisive step towards an alternative relationship. Shortly after I rented a small house on Wilmot Road in Ilkley.

A year later buying one across the road. I spent money having it 'done up'. And made a handsome profit when I sold it in 2007. Chris & Al would come to stay on a Thursday night and some weekends. Life re-opened as a single man again. Sounds exciting, but not so much!

Wilmot Road, Ilkley. Selling this enabled Candy and I to buy the house in Aunat, France.

Trips with Chris & Alasdair

By 2001 I was living in my own house on Wilmot Road in Ilkley. The start of the summer had seen Chris and I, along with Ainsey, climb the Barre des Ecrin and now I had promised Alasdair a summer holiday too. This was to set something of a pattern for the future, though not for every year. I would go to the mountains with Chris and have other adventures with Al. This suited me well, as I always loved both sorts of trip. I have put all the mountaineering trips in Chapter 11, so here is the flavour of the others

I had got the internet and a thing called CEEFAX on the TV, and so Al scanned them for cheap holiday offers. He found one on Rhodes, 'allocation of hotel on arrival'! The price was OK so he used my card to book. "Where and when is the flight?" I asked, "It's from Newcastle at 08.00 tomorrow" he replied. Better get packing then, its already 19.00! Rhodes was fun, we stayed in the last hotel in the second bay of Falaraki! Luckily 'far from the madding crowd' Hired a Suzuki Jimmy to tour the Island and took a 2 day Paddy Scuba Course to get half the qualification. That October we finished the Open Water Divers Cert. in dry suits, in a cold and cloudy quarry near Kirby Lonsdale. We also enjoyed go-carting on Rhodes, at which Al aged 13 beat me every time, and being shot into the air in a ball on elastic bands. The one problem was in the evenings, with lots of girls in the town, Al was too young and I was too old!

Al on the hotel balcony in Falaraki, Rhodes.

101

My other international trips with Al included a week in Rome, again when he was still in his early teens, then Barcelona and Amsterdam when he was somewhat older. For the Rome trip I didn't book a hotel, as the flight was fairly early. However, with many delays and a long trip from the airport we arrived in the centre at about 22.00. Searching around we found a hotel that would take us, a room in the basement and much to Alasdair's chagrin, with only a double bed. It was this holiday we ran into a work colleague of mine in the Colosseum and Al's favourite phrase was "That was great, what are we doing next!" Argh!

Barcelona was quite a different thing. Al was quite a drinker by then and so we did sightseeing during the day and food and bars at night. We stayed in a room overlooking the Rambla and drank beer from glass boots and Tequilas in back street bars.

Now, when I go out in a town at night I never carry my wallet. It was safely in our room safe. I keep a credit card well hidden in a security pocket and carry cash spread out over a number of pockets. Going back to the Hotel, quite late down the Rambla, I was approached by two 'ladies' from a dark corner. One pulled up her shirt and stuck her bare breasts in my face. The other grabbed my testicles from behind and frisked me for my wallet. Having no success, they backed off and we walked on. "Hey dad...can we walk back and see if they will do that to me" asked Al! We did, but they had gone, lol!

Al and I went on the ferry to Amsterdam for a few days in about 2004. We had an interesting tour of the Red Light district by night, much to both our amusement and amazement, and other sight seeing attractions.

We also did some mountain biking trips, memorably to North Wales on the Red Bull and on the downhill course at Nevis Range, Witch's trails and World Cup Downhill. This latter run scared the shit out of me and I had to get off and actually climb down certain sections! Al loved it!

Ready to face the World Cup Downhill at Nevis Range.......on my 'hard tail' Scott. Whoopee.... or not!

I also did some joint trips with Chris and Al. Those I particularly remember were camping on the Isle of White, Camping at Wasdale Head and the fateful camp on the North East Coast. The Isle of White was memorable for 5 punctures on one bike ride & the lads filleting fish for those on the campsite. Wasdale head saw all three of us on the top of Scafell Pike, the highest summit in England.

Camping on the North East Coast we were being banged on the head by the tent in the wind. The only refuge we could find was a Motel on the M1 with a triple room. It was a double and a single. The lads tossed for the single and Al won, Chris insisted on sleeping on the floor?

Divorce & Beverly

One day, Ruth and I realized that sometime in our very busy lives we had drifted apart, too far apart to even try to move closer, though I at first held out some hope. Enough about that. I started to date a supply teacher from SCS, which apparently was too much for Ruth, so that is when I first moved to Ilkley. Bev was 12 years younger than me, physically very fit and good for my ego. We had just about 2 years together, but never 'officially' lived in the same house.

Bev wasn't easy to be with. On occasions she was great fun and we enjoyed walking in the mountains and going for bike rides. We had nice holidays on the Greek island of Thasos, and on Mallorca. We also stayed in the Lakes in both summer and winter & on the little lighthouse island of Devaar off the coast of Campbeltown.

It could never have lasted with Bev, for all sorts of reasons, even though there were times when I hoped I could make it work. I was either not enough or too much. By the start of 2003 we were not seeing each other on a regular basis and she admitted to me that she was seeing someone else on and off.

We still went for bike rides and the occasional walk, but the relationship was over. To her credit, or maybe to mine, Bev had made me learn how to deal with close relationships in a better way than I had with Ruth. To develop strategies and read emotions, to be attentive and see things from others' perspectives, and that was to pay dividends for the future.

Mrs Williamson, from the Art Department

At work I was responsible for the introduction, development and review of the school's Planner. This had come about as part of my job within the area of whole school Assessment, Reporting and Records of Achievement. I had also, for a number of years been a Sixth Form (Y12/13) tutor. Both these roles brought me into increasing contact with the Deputy Head of Sixth Form & Art teacher Candy Williamson. From early 2003 we had 'business meetings' in Candy's office on various topics of commonality in our roles. Somehow these didn't stop when the topics were resolved and we started to cover more personal stuff. I found that Candy was in the midst of leaving her husband, so we had things in common and a friendship developed.

By April Candy was living with a friend near Hebden and by May was looking to buy a house of her own. I took the opportunity to suggest Ilkley as a nice place and ask her if she would like to see what I had recently bought. We could then go up to my friend Chris Monkman's pub, The Fleece, in Addingham and have a meal. After some trepidation on her part she accepted my offer for 23 May. She insisted on asking me in the Sixth Form Office, if I knew how old she was. I had assumed she was my age, but no, she was 55! I can remember having to take a seat! Life was about to take a turn for the better! But before that I need to go back in time and fill some gaps: Rugby, Mountains and Mountain Rescue.

45 Wellington Road. Candy's house from late 2003, then our house from 2005 until we left for Qatar in 2008. Currently it is rented out (2020).

On 2nd April 2007 I married Candida Giaquinto at Keighley Registry Office. My best man was my climbing buddy Chris Ainsworth & the other witness was Brigid, Bea was the Maid of Honour. We ended up having a small family do on the evening before, more by accident than design. Then after the wedding we had a small reception at the Emporio Italia (£1000) in Ilkley. We wanted to give a nod to the Giaquinto ancestry! As it turns out, Candy and I seem to have managed something of an ideal partnership being, amongst other things, best friends, truly soul mates XXXX

Being married to her has been my top achievement in life, my favourite 'badge'. Twenty years on: the love, fun, camaraderie and intellectual sparing, I feel, is as strong as ever.

April 2nd 2007. Outside Keighley Registry Office

This chapter spans some 20+ years of everyday adventures, both good and bad. Mostly treasured memories for me, of Chris and Al growing from tiny babies into teenagers, that are impossible to put into words. There is lots missing I know, but it could never be anything more than a snapshot Sorry Chris & Al if I've missed some treasured memory of yours, but you have your chance to add them in your own versions.

Airebronians & Other Rugby Adventures

Before I go any further I need to talk a bit about rugby. This occupied a great deal of my life from the time I started AGS to when I played my final game in Qatar at the age of 55. It has brought me many things, not least of which are a sense of camaraderie and a group of friends that has endured for over 55 years. I have been pleased to pass my enthusiasm on to both my sons and am pleased that Chris is now doing the same with Nathan. I hope that Al will encourage Toby in the same way. My life has benefited from it in many ways and I am grateful.

I began playing for Airebronians RUFC when I was in Y12/13 at AGS. Some of the staff at AGS played and occasionally, if they were short, some of us would turn out for the 2nd Team. This usually involved playing for school in the morning, then 'Aire' in the afternoon. When I left AGS in '74 I went straight into the 'Aire' first team at prop, until I went up to York University.

I played for the University 1st team, which wasn't very good, for most of that academic year, but moved back to playing for 'Aire' before the season finished. Over the next 7 or 8 years I was a regular fixture, in the 1st XV, in the front row, moving to 1st team hooker for a few seasons. This takes me quickly through from '75 to the early 80s.

We played a lot of rugby, trained twice a week, drank gallons of beer and ate curry from a very dubious restaurant in Bradford. Zahour, the owner, was very accommodating around midnight. The toilet, outside, had a stick by the door to scare any rats before entry. The food was ordered at the counter and appeared on the top of an old TV, through a hole in the ceiling. Zahour had no knives and forks, so we ate the steaming bowls of curry with our fingers and chapatis. These were definitely my wilder years, crashing my dad's car at one point, but not too seriously. We never seemed to get into trouble, bending rather than breaking laws. Soon after getting married, in the mid '80's, I got a neck injury in a scrum and decided to move out of the front row. For my return I started to play at No. 8 for the third team, but very soon got a regular place as 2nd team No.8.

I believe I had some of my best rugby in that position. It was certainly the most enjoyable rugby I had played since school.

Airebronians 1st XV from about 1980. To illustrate my new short hair. Back: Streets, Parker, Greenwood, Boyle, Stone, Gilroy, Stead, Mackey, Smith.

I had my ups and downs with "Aire' particularly with selection and my apparent 'nemesis' Terry Lazenby, who never seemed to like me at school.

The first was in my time in the 1st team as hooker. I had played all the previous season and trained through the summer. At the end of August we had a Probables v Possibles trial match. I was surprised....shocked actually....to find I wasn't the Probables hooker. They had brought in young lad who had just left AGS, he had never even been to a training session. I gave him a rough ride during the game, making the scrums very uncomfortable, if not painful. I thought I also won more than my fair share of the ball. Nevertheless he was picked for the following Saturday. My efforts must have dissuaded him though, as he gave back word mid-week and never turned up again!

Parker, Greenwood, Lockwood, Stead, Stone, Gilroy, Whitaker, Hainsworth, Kitchen, Thompson(coach).
Fawcett, Smith, Mackey, Marlow, Denison, Wade, Riley, Hobson, Foster.

My final game for 'Aire' (almost!) was at No.8 for the second team against Workington. They beat us at 1st team level, by about 40 points. The 2nd team game was close, but we won. IMHO, and not for the first time that season, our victory was in no small part due to the back row. I had two small flankers around me, John Streets and Nick Gledhill 'Boot-head'. They were fast across the field and would delay the opposition backs, I would then arrive to take the ball. This worked so well that earlier in the season we won a match without actually winning either a scrum or line out, all the ball coming from the back row. That victory earned us three jugs of beer from the opposition Captain.

I digress, so after the Workington victory I was in the Emmett Arms the next day. Selection was on the Sunday morning and Mick Harper, Chunky, the 2nd team Captain arrived after it had finished. I had heard a rumour that a lad from University was coming home for the holidays and they had a plan to play him. Sure enough I had been dropped to the 3rds. I asked Chunky what had been said and was my performance from yesterday mentioned. "No" he replied, " they were just interested in getting this new lad into the 1st XV next week". "Ah!, thought so, I'm not available........ever again!" I replied. I only played for 'Aire' twice more.

Possibly mid-80's, towards the end of my time for Aire 1st XV:
Smith, Parker, Taylor, Cottle, Stone, Gilroy, Boyle, Drake, Peel, Hainsworth, Thompson(Coach).
Colhoune, Hanson, Pollard, Riley, Heggs, Fawcett, Wade, Tate, Waite, Hainsworth, Thornton.

"A" Team 42 Chirons "A" 13

Airebronians "A" had an easy victory over week opposition at Esholt on Saturday and cashed in to the full with eight tries and five conversions. They attacked almost throughout the game. The forwards had the advantage in the set scrums and in the loose and backed up well when the threequarters ran the ball.

Particularly impressive among the forwards were prop Mal Riley and back row forwards Tim Wadsworth and Keith Parker, who all worked tirelessly and covered every inch of the pitch. In the backs Stephen Harrison played well at fly-half and combined well with centre Roger Kitchen to create many openings in the Chirons defence. Wadsworth and Riley were rewarded for their efforts with two tries each. Further scores came from Westmoreland, Boardman, Dennison and Davey. Andrew Dale gave an excellent goal kicking display with five conversions.

Visiting the 'A' team, possibly in the early 80's, before my time as No 8

When Chris started playing for Ilkley RUFC in '95 I was persuaded to play for Ilkley 2nd & 3rd teams for a couple of seasons. It was fun for a while and I played back at Prop, but the camaraderie was never quite the same.

Playing for Aire with Chris on his 18th Birthday, at age 48

I did play half a game for 'Aire', by accident, in 2002, at the tender age of 47. Chris was 16 and playing for the 2nd XV, I went as the only supporter. At half time the Aire hooker came off with an injury. I said to the Captain that I had some kit in the car, I had played football for SCS staff the night before. So I went on, hooked, threw in at the line outs and put in some tackles that even Chris was impressed with. After the match the Aire prop, a huge bearded horse of a man came up to shake my hand. "Well played" he said, "I've never seen a supporter turn out before, it looked like it wasn't your first game though?" "No, I used to play for Aire 1st XV". "I don't recognise you.....when did you play?" "I started in 1974" I replied. Startled he said "Fucking hell, I wasn't even born then!!!!!" I played once more for Aire in 2004, with Chris on his 18th birthday.

When we moved to Qatar in 2008 I started to play staff 'touch rugby' once a week. This developed into the formation of Al Khor Amateurs RFC. We had several games, with older players rotating during the game. In 2010 we entered the Gulf Vets, over 35 tournament, 10 a side and 20 minutes each way, at Doha RFC and won in the final against Dubai Harlequins, a club supported by the UK Harlequins. That was my last game of rugby, aged 55! I did train with them when I returned for 6 months in 2012, but never played again.

Al Khor Amateurs, 2010

There is of course more to rugby than the games themselves, so I have a couple of tales of tours and off the field incidents to recount. My first tour was to London...what can I say, I was just a boy! Normally sane individuals; accountants, police, solicitors, businessmen, let loose and going wild. The coach had a large plastic barrel wedged in the back seats for toilet & sick! I had never peed in the window of a coach going down the M1 before! In the pub in London Geoff Stone fell asleep in the bar, stood up holding his glass!

Often it was surreal. I did other tours, to Wales (Cardiff) & Scotland (Edinburgh), but stopped taking my kit. This was because I really could never drink and play rugby....... touring wasn't my favourite thing and I chose not to go once I was married. 'Aire' even have a Vets tour now, with absolutely no rugby, but as my drinking days are over I have never felt compelled to join them!

Mates and the Christmas Do!

Related to the rugby, but not exactly, is our Christmas gathering. It started when a lot of us went to college, mostly rugby mates from school, but also some others who we would spend time with in our local, The Emmott Arms, in Rawdon. This is where we would be found most Friday and Saturday evenings and always on Christmas and New Years Eve throughout Y11 to 13 and onward.

We had several years where we would meet up in Leeds on Christmas Eve lunchtime. Possibly first at the Whitelock's, which is the oldest pub in Leeds, first founded in 1715 as The Turk's Head, then onto something like the Hofbrau House. Returning home to wash and change before returning to The Emmott's for the evening. It became clear that as we got older Christmas Eve became more problematic, so we changed it to the last Friday before Christmas, unless it was Christmas Eve. I became the 'convener'. Around November I would ask around where people thought we would go, usually not the Emmott's, then telephone the people in my book to arrange the date and time. We usually had about 15 lads, with the occasional guest lady or two.

By the nineties I would also arrange a Christmas meal to include wives and girlfriends. The last of these was with Candy in 2007, just before leaving for Qatar. We also changed the date of the 'lads do' to the first Friday in December, to avoid work commitments.

Kevin took over as 'convener' from 2008 and expanded the group to include ex-'Air' players. Some of whom seem to know me, but I don't really know them. There has also been a recent development in the appearance of some of the girls who were in our year at Aireborough, though numbers vary from year to year.

I'm often told that it is very rare to find 15 to 20 school mates meeting up once a year, it being 54 years since we started AGS in 1967. Its looking like I may have to miss this year though, due to the COVID-19 restrictions.......ah well!

Finally, I have been known to travel around Europe to support Newcastle Falcons. This is usually a boozy trip, though I drink a lot less these days. Over the past few years Kev has arranged trips to: Bordeaux, Montpellier, Cluj-Napoca (Romania), Grenoble and Brive-la-Gaillade.

The usual suspects are Mark Parr (who sadly passed away, Oct.2020), Alan, Jill Smith and Graham Pyle. We also, on these trips, have cultural visits/tours and make a point of finding excellent restaurants.

Bordeaux trip (early 2019): Mark (deceased 2020), Paul, Jill, Kevin, Norman, Alan and Graham

Mountains On My Mind

This couldn't be a complete story without it containing some of my adventures in the hills. Something which has become one of the focuses of our life now that we are retired to the Pyrenees. It keeps our old bones moving and has given us a small social circle of 'natives' in a foreign land. It's a long story, currently running at some 1000 days of my life, which intertwines with many others. These can only ever be very edited highlights.

Arriving at SCS and meeting Ruth got me interested in the outdoors. I started doing some weekends with the school's Outdoor Club and completed my Mountain Leader (Summer) introduction early in 1984. Also in 1984 I obtained a Local Authority, Level 1 Climbing Instructors Certificate. This pre-dated the Mountain Training Association's SPA. This allowed me to take students on Single Pitch rock climbs. I spent three or four years taking groups of kids to Earl Crag(Sutton Pinnacle) on Monday mornings, in the summer term. I also climbed at Ilkley, Earby, Brimham, Lake District and Skye with Chris Ainsworth on summer evenings and holidays. We were never 'rock jocks', but managed quite a few routes at Severe, and the odd 'VS', in the classic style. I had also been accepted by North Yorks to lead school groups in the English hills. This was done, unusually as a paper exercise, when regulations changed and schools found they were short of 'qualified' leaders. It was helped by being known to a number of staff at Bewerley Park Outdoor Centre.

In 1984 Ruth and I traveled out to Chamonix, by coach from Leeds. It took us something like 29 hours, but was very cheap. There we met Ruth's school friend Ian Cleaver, in whose flat we would spend the night.

The next day we started on our big adventure, The Tour De Mont Blanc or TMB. I wrote up the story for a friend of mine, Chris Townsend, who was the editor for an outdoor magazine called 'Footloose' and he published it! The article tells our story. (Appendix 11).

This journey gave me the thrill of travelling in the mountains, which I had never really had with the unpredictable British weather. It also gave me my first views of Mont Blanc and a determination to stand on the top before I was 35. I had six years to obtain the extra skills of working on snow and ice!

Chris was born in April '86 and in July we took him on our first visit to Skye. We went with Chris and Jan Ainsworth. On the way we camped in a big old Vango Force 10, next to Loch Lomond. Chris slept between us in his carry-cot. That year we stayed at Glenbrittle House Cottage and were grateful of being out of the damnable Scottish midges with a baby.

Camping near Lock Lomond in 1986, Chris's first camp at 3 months old

Ainsey and I were super impressed by the Cuillin, just outside the door of our cottage. Though the weather wasn't great for most of the week, Chris, Jan and I did make it onto 'the ridge' a couple of times, visiting: Mhadaidh, Ghreadaidh, Banachdich & Thormaid, then Sgumain and Alasdair(from which son Alasdair was to take his name). It was all a bit too much to haul Chris up at such a young age, so he stayed below on those days with his mum. We did camp with him again in Wales for a couple of nights that same summer.

Chris' first Munro was to come a year later. We stayed at a cottage near Kinloch Rannoch, again with Chris & Jan Ainsworth. I carried my 16 month old to the top of Shiehallion @ 1183m. It was on that trip that he learned to hold my ears for stability on rough ground...aaggg! On the way down, wearing my shortest shorts, a woman stopped me and exclaimed "I wondered how you were carrying a child down the mountain so quickly! But now I see you have thighs like 'tug boats'"........I have never heard Ainsey laugh so much. I did have another similar incident on the back gate at the UWFRA/CRO Game Show at Broughton Hall. A young woman fell through the cattle grid at the gate. I said 'Are you OK?' she said, 'That was your fault!'. "How come?" I asked......"I was looking at your legs" she replied!

Enough of that, I joined UWFA in 1989, more of that later. Between '86 and '90 I only managed to average 20 days a year in the mountains. This included the days out 'working' with the SCS Outdoor Club. Alasdair joined the family in Jan. I did however make Skye and the Cuillin again in '87 and completed the Saunders Lakeland Mountain Marathon (112/250), both with Ainsey. Ruth and I also got Chris up Shiehallion again, this time with his Aunty Sarah and Uncle Russel. '90 saw Al on his first peak, Buckden Pike, with Chris climbing it on his legs. Also in Skye again, this time to summit the famous Inaccessible Pinnacle, Collie's Ledge and the Bad Step on Sgurr Alasdair, with Ainsey and Chris Townsend. Ainsey and I also completed the 'Cleveland Classic'(56miles), the only time I've ever walked 50 miles in a day, in just over 17hrs. My feet were so blistered that the last mile took me nearly a full hour.

Despite family commitments Ruth was good enough to let me go off sometimes in the summer for some more Alpine adventures. The first was in 1991 a big year for Ainsey and I. I passed my Mountain Leadership Certificate, now ML(Sumer) over 5 days of Assessment, including a 3 day expedition in the Lakes, in April. In May Ainsey and I did a Cuillin Ridge Travers, including a bivvy on Sgurr Dubh na da Bheinn @ 915m. Over an evening and the following day we spent 13 hours on the complete traverse. At the end we free climbed Nicholson's Chimney onto the top of Sgurr nan Gillean. I was stood on the top, looking a bit sweaty when a old guy approached me. "Look at you, young lad, up here looking knackered...... and with no kit! Where have you come from today?" I pointed to Sgurr nan Eig on the other end of the ridge. "There this morning, my sack is in the bealach below!"........"Oh!" He retorted, and slid away.

Sat on top of Sgurr Nan Gillean after the travers of the Cuillin Ridge, in the background, with my mountain mate Ainsey: May 1991

The previous year I had spoken to Mike Jackson, a retired Deputy Head at SCS, at Pam & Peter Merrell's wedding. Mike had been educated at King James', Almodbury, so we had something in common. He had led many walking groups on the continent, with his wife Mary, so had lots of mountain experience. We both expressed an interest in summiting Mont Blanc and agreed to make an attempt the following year, '91. Ainsey brought Jan and his new baby, while Ruth, Chris & Alasdair stayed in the U.K. This left Mike and I to camp in Contamine. Considering I was just a year older than his son Robert, we had a great time together and became good friends. Our first trip out was to gain some acclimatisation by climbing high. We walked up to the Conscrits hut @ 2770m. In those days a tiny shack on the edge of the Tré-la-Tête glacier, accessed by climbing the glacier. At 60, Mike had found the going at altitude hard and was fairly done in as we arrived at the hut in the dark. The next day we 'played out' on the glacier using axes, crampons and ropes, up to 3000m. We fancied the Dômes de Miage the day after, but only Ainsey and I set out........a fantastic day, summiting out on the highest Dôme @ 3670m.

Domes de Miage, it has three summits all above 3500m.
For Ainsey and I our first alpine peaks: August 1991.

Then, due to Ainsey having family in the valley, all the way back to Contamine. It became clear that Mike wasn't going to make Mont Blanc. Ainsey and I had a second trip out to the Aiguilles de Tour@3542m, via the Albert 1er Refuge. I had a near death experience when I fell down a crevasse, unroped, just as we got onto the glacier. Luckily I went down just below the top of my head and got my axe in over the lip. Climbing out Ainsey said "why did you do that?" I am particularly careful to rope up on glaciers these days. We rescued a stranded Brit. on the way down from the Aiguille, he was stuck on the steep snow slope. Ainsey roped him up and I walked by his side down the hill. All acclimatised, we felt ready for the big one!

We caught the afternoon train up to the Nid d'Aigle on the 26th Aug. Staying overnight at the Tête Rousse hut @ 3167m. The dorm was full and everyone was excited, we got little sleep as there was noise from about 2 am onwards! We had a different plan, what we called a Yorkshire Alpine Club Start......6 am, ridiculous! The notorious stone shoot below the old Goûter Hut was free of snow and hence no rock fall. The ascent of the rock wall was free of ice and simple, no need for the safety chains really. We had a coffee in the busy hut and carried on up to the Dôme and on to the Vallot refuge.

The stench of vomit from inside was too much and we sat outside for a while. The Bosses Ridge was like a trench cut into a knife edge, then onto the top of Mont Blanc @ 4807m for lunch at about 13:30, in the sunshine with very few others.

Arriving on the summit of Mont Blanc, 13:30, 27th August 1991

Granted the snow was a bit sloppy on the way down, but we had great views and a memorable day so far! The Goûter passed easily and back to the Tête Rousse to save money by cooking outside. As an aside, the toilet at the hut deserves a mention. It was a wooden shack built over a 1000 ft. drop to the glacier below. When you open the door there was a sturdy wooden bar to sit on, with your bum hung into space.......then 'bombs away'. As I sat there I noticed shit up above me, sometimes there must be a tremendous updraft!

We decided to get down to the station, with the hope there might be somewhere undercover to sleep. Unfortunately we lost the path on the way down and arriving in the dark and found the station to be a locked square block. We found a niche in some rocks and bivvied as best we could without sleeping bags! It was both the longest and coldest night I've ever spent........and I have slept in a snow hole in Scotland and tent on Antarctica! The night passes something like this:
"You awake bud?"
"Yes"

"What time is it?"
"2 am"
About an hour passes, avalanches fall on the other side of the mountain, still no sleep, shivering"
"What time is it now?"
"2:15!"

Bivvy at the Nid d'Aigle, the morning after. All our clothes on. Feet in our ruck sacks. Then a bivvy bag and a third size Karrimat.....luxury.....not!

We got the first train down and Mike cooked me some breakfast.

'92 saw us in Skye again with the Ainsworths. Our challenge that year was an exciting ascent of Pinnacle Ridge on Sgurr nan Gillian and our first ascent of the Bhastier Tooth. Then quite a few outings in the Lake District over the next 18 months.

Ainsey and I, along with Mike Jackson and and a friend of Chris' called Paul Mason, went to Grindelwald in '93 and camped under the Eiger North Face. It was a rather wet couple of weeks and Switzerland was very expensive for beers and eating out. By the end of the trip we had two hut stays, both with Mike: Gaspaltenhorn hütte @ 2458m and Mutthorn hütte @ 2898m. We also managed to climb the Tschingelhorn @ 3576m and Faulhorn @ 2680m, but without Mike. '93 was also the year Ainsey and I started to help out with the Duke of Edinburgh's Award, on their expeditions. I was to continue with this for nearly 20 years. Also at this time Vanessa Derwent, 'Ness', arrived at SCS and we teamed up on many occasions to lead expeditions.

Ness, third from the left, checking in with a couple of groups out on their DofE expedition (mid '90s)

'94 began with me attending the Glenmore Lodge Winter Mountain Rescue skills course. I remember the head of the lodge sitting all course members down in the lounge. He talked about all the courses on that week, then about the awful weather forecast. "Some changes will have to be made as sometimes it will not be possible to get on the hill", he said. Adding, "Oh, you might see some people going onto the hill. They are on the Winter Mountain Rescue course and will be going out every day, irrespective of conditions!" We were to experience 'working' in the Scottish mountains in all their winter ferocity, while other courses at 'the Lodge' were holed up, practicing inside. One morning we were building ice belays but had to return to the Lodge as the wind and driving snow were so strong that we could no longer hear the instructor shouting at us from 1m away!
I spent the week learning Northern Irish with a team from the now defunct Royal Ulster Constabulary(RUC). It was also the year that I took son Chris Out backpacking and wild camping around Kettlewell and Grassington; he was 8, we had a great time.

While '95 saw me mostly using my outdoor time for UWFRA and DofE in the Yorkshire Dales, '96 saw us moving further afield with Gold DofE groups. We wild camped in Green Hole near Bow Fell with Martin Woodhead & Ness, in a snowy March. Then took the same group to Arran in July. Ness and I also did 10 days at Humphrey Head Outdoor Centre, with the Y9 outdoor pursuits group. Later in July Ainsey and I met up with Chris Townsend on Skye, to help him complete his round of all the Munros and Tops.......continuously under his own steam. We even got a mention in his book of the same name! There is a copy on my shelf.

In '97 Chris and I did the Cumbrian Way, with his scout group, 15th Airedale. It was on this trip that Chris famously brought me a 'Pot Noodle' and asked me how to cook it! Poor boy, deprived childhood or what! In '98 we took the family to Norway, mainly car touring. It rained quite a bit, but we did manage three days walking in the Jotunheimen, from Gjendesheim out to Memurubu. More DofE the following year, '99, with Ness and Julie Greatorix, a fellow chemist who joining the DofE team. I did my Winter ML training in preparation for the European Mountain Leader(EML) Assessment, that I intended to do at some stage. This included a night in a snow hole with Chris, a guy from the lakes MRT and a girl called Robyn who chose the two of us as her 'room mate'. In the mini-bus the previous day she had approached us, "I've been watching everyone, and I'm with you guys for the snow hole" a compliment indeed! We had two days of high wind and whiteouts, or 'in the white room' as the staff call it, navigating, assessing Avalanche risk and ice belay making, on Cairn Gorm. An interesting 5 days.

That summer Ainsey and I did a French outdoor adventure for the kids at school. This involved an excellent 2 day and 1 night bivouac, descent of the Ardèche River, by canoe. It was also time for another Alpine adventure, this time to Gressoney in the north of Italy. I met The Ainsworths out there and we added some big peaks to our tally. Starting with the Quintino Sella refuge @ 3587m we climbed Castor @ 4221m. On the arete up to the hut there was a humming noise. I asked Ainsey what it was and he replied "its your ice axe!". "Hey" I replied, "yours is doing it too!". It was the warning buzzer for the electrical storm arriving. We dropped our sacks ran down the hill some distance, then sat low, on the rope for insulation. The lightening storm arrived and circled the cirque, then moved on. At the hut there was 25cm on fresh snow.

Then, later in the week, from the Gnifetti hut @3647m, we climbed up to the Margherita hut on the top of the Signalkuppe. At 4554m it is the highest accommodation in Western Europe, it has oxygen available for anyone in need. I remember running up stairs to get my camera for a photo of the sun setting behind the Matterhorn. By the time I reached the top step I was on my knees, breathless.

On top of the Signalkuppe, outside the Margarita Refuge, with Ainsey, August 1999

The next day we had a peakfest: Parrotspitz @ 4432m, Ludwigshohe @ 4341m, Corno Nero @ 4321m, Balmenhorn @4167m and finishing on Pyramid Vincent @ 4215m......so standing on 6 x 4000+ m summits in a day! Without a doubt our biggest summit day ever.

2000 saw us on a family holiday to Scotland at Easter. Chris and Alasdair climbing Meal nan Tarmachan@1044m, Benin Glass@1103 & Ben Lawers@1214m. Then in the summer we had a family holiday to the Pyrenees. Making it into the Cirque de Gavanie, the Refuge below the Bréche de Roland, into the Cirque de Troumousse and finally walking up the Pic de Midi de Bigorre@2872m from the col de Tourmalet. The end of 2000 also saw the end of my marriage to Ruth and, in many respects, the start of a different life.....but more about that later.

The following Easter '01, I took my new girlfriend, Beverly Bolton, to Mallorca and we did some walking in the north of the island. This included an ascent of the Puig des Jou. Sitting for lunch in a sunny little valley I became spooked. I have no idea why, but something just wasn't right. I was eager to move on to the summit. On the summit, at 1051m her highest peak, Bev said "didn't that lunch stop have a scary feeling, I was glad to move on?" It has ever happened to me in the hills before, or since! Apart from that it was a sparse mountain year.

The following year, 2002, was better and I did a number of 'Wainwright's', summits from Wainwright's seven books of Lakeland Peaks, with Bev. The culmination was another Alpine trip. This time with the Ainsworths and son Chris. He was now 16, and I thought it was time to introduce him to the Alps. He was in the Ardèche with his school. So I drove down to Briançon to drop Bev and her friend off, they were doing part of the GR5 to Nice, then on to the Ardèche. I picked up Chris and we returned to Les Deux Alp to camp.

Our first outing was to the Sella Hut and from there we climbed the Replas@3428m and the next day the Rateau@3809m.

Chris looking cool on the Replas(3428m), his first real Alpine peak: 2002

I have to say that the last bit to the top of the Rateau was very tiring. Coming down Ainsey was above me and unroped, he slipped and started to slide. I can remember his crampons coming towards me in a hail of snow....."I'm coming, I'm coming" he shouted as he tried to get his axe in! We passed lots of French climbers, taking it very steadily, and asked if we could push ahead of a large group abseiling onto the glacier. Chris did well, despite a large gunky septic hole in his foot, from the beach! This was followed by a Via Ferrata, for Chris and I, on the Torrent du Verizon, very vertical in a deep river canyon and our first together, then on to the Barre Des Ecrin.

The Barre Des Ecrin is a biggie and Chris's first 4000m peak at only 16yrs. On the way we stayed at the Refuge Du Glacier and then visited the Pic Neige Cordier @3614m, and finally the Ecrin Hut.

Chris and I on the summit of the Pic de Neige Cordier(3614m), 2002

The ascent to the Neige Cordier has a steep and 'chossy' gully near the end, with rocks and mud sliding all around. The next morning was another start in the dark, in a long line of alpinists. Then steeply past some tottering towers in the icefall and a long rising traverse. A steep and awkward icy arete to the top of the Dome de Neige de Barre des Ecrin saw us at a cold and draughty summit @ 4012m. The true top was far too windy for an ascent on the day we were there. From there we did another night at the Écran hut, where it snowed several centimetres, then down into the valley.

On top of the Dome de Neige de Barre des Ecrin, 4012m 5th August 2002

I left Chris on the campsite with Ainsey to pick up Bev. Not to my great surprise she had fallen out with her companion and refused to fly home with her, so now needed a lift! We met in Avignon after I had driven from the Ecrin to Marseille, to find the train didn't stop. It didn't stop at Avignon either, instead going direct to Lyon.......a lot closer to where I started. I didn't know this, as Bev's mobile battery died. So I got a room in Avignon and waited. At about 10pm I got a call to say she would be in Avignon by midnight, so I waited at the station. When she arrived........remember I had breakfast in the Ecrin Hut and ate late lunch In Marseille.......she said "you don't look very pleased to see me!' Then didn't speak until we got back to the hotel. We returned to the campsite the next day and three days later the three of us travelled back to the U.K. together.

In 2003 I did the Howarth Hobble with Bev, 31 miles in just over 10 hours. Then in April I did the Aonach Eagach, Ben Nevis and Buachaille Etive Mor in three consecutive days with Chris. We had interesting 'company at the 'lodge' we stayed at in Kinlock Leven, Chris will tell you the story. Suffice to say we locked the room securely that night! We also had a bit of an adventure in May on the way to find a DofE group on a wet, dark and misty night over Mardale Ill Bell and Harter Crag. The bad weather freaked Chris out a bit. Being his first time on the hill in such bad conditions I couldn't really blame him. We were pleased to find the group cosy in their tents in Wrengill Quarry. At the end of May I was proud of both Chris and Al. We camped at Wasdale Head and had two full days on the hill which included: their first ascent of Scafell Pike @978m and a spirited climb of Scafell@964m via Lord's Rake and the West Wall Travers.......proud dad that day! We also did the Gable Travers and the scree run down Hell's Gate the next day.

Chris and Al on the top of Scafell Pike, May 2003

My first 'proper' mountain with Candy was on 18th Jan. 2004, an ascent of Penyghent@694m. With not much experience of walking in the mountains I was highly impresses. Little did I know that mountain walking would become a regular feature of our retirement together. Candy did her first Munro, a Cuillin peak no less, in June of that year. It was Brauch Na Frithe@958m. In her excitement she did take something of a tumble on the scree on the way down. True to form she bounced back up with no more than a brief tear! Signs of the grit and durability to come. I also did both the Blaven/Clash Glas travers and the Dubh Ridge with Chris and Ainsey on the same trip. Memorably on Clash Glass, I dislodged a huge boulder as I climbed a rocky corner. I tried to 'push it back.....lol, but it chased me down the hill, and I only avoided death or serious injury by ducking round a corner. How the two Chris' laughed! Summer saw us in a mobile home in Chamonix, with Chris and Brigid, then later swapping Chris for Al. Ainsey had his own family apartment and we intended on looking at some high alpine routes. To be fair the weather was never that kind, with lots of rain, even at higher altitudes. We managed to literally wade up the Argentier glacier to get to the Col du Tour Noir@3553m. Then wade across the same glacier to climb steeply up to the Grand Montet cable station @3293m. Ainsey unhooked a crampon up a particularly steep piece of ice and Chris and I had to hit the deck while he re-fastened it! His first stop back in Cham' was to buy new crampons, with better fixings!

Further outings saw us at the Albert 1er refuge. This was Candy and Brigid's first Mountain Refuge visit. On the way up Chris and I found a woman with a badly broken wrist on the steep snow going up to the hut. I could not persuade her to move, and she was very cold and 'shocked'. I carved out a seat in the snow and sat her on my knee. I sent Chris up to the hut to get the guardian to call for a helicopter. This arrived in due course and did a one runner touchdown on the steep snow! When we got to the hut Chris and I were greeted by all, who had been watching from the balcony, as heroes........free drinks all round! On the next trip out I wasn't going too well. I made it to the Trient hut and several cols on the Trient glacier: Col Doit@3200m, Fenêtre de Saleina@3200m and the Col Supérieur du Tour @3289m. Chris and Ainsey reached some peaks, culminating in the Aiguille du Tour @3542m, a peak I had done with Ainsey 13 years earlier.

By mid 2004, early 2005 Candy and I were settled together in her house, 45 Wellington Road, Ilkley. We decided to go to the South of France in the summer for a camping holiday, without realising that this would soon become our home. We camped with the bikes in a village called Palau del Vidre, inland from Argeles. We only had one mountain day on foot, to the Roc de l'Grivel@902m & Pic d'Aureilla@1030m, from where we could see a 5km queue on the A9 into Spain.

The interesting thing was the return to the campsite. We were setting up for tea when the owner came around. "You were supposed to be off today, I have someone waiting to pitch their tent!" Bugger, we had the dates wrong, we packed up and moved on as fast as we could. We found a nice hotel for the night, in the middle of a 'zone industrielle', surrounded by a high wall, but with a pool and restaurant. It gets worse! The next night we had a hotel in Valence. In the morning we looked at where we might stay that night as the boat was midnight of the day after. I thought I would just check the ferry time, it was just after midnight of that day, 850km away...oops! We made it, a bit sweaty, but in good time.

After a slow start in '06 Chris and I did a semi-winter ascent of Snowden via Crib Goch. Followed by Helvellyn and Catstye Cam via Striding and Swirral edges. In May/June Ainsey and I went up to Glenmore Lodge for 5 days of training, the EML was now the International Mountain Leader(IML). Though this was 'training' we had a day which included a navigation test and the final day was 'Speed Navigation Assessment'.

For this we were taken out into the Cairngorms and had to complete a large mountain orienteering course in a set time. I found all my checkpoints fairly easily and with a bit of running was half an hour inside the time, having done a rather cold and wet river crossing to get back to the lodge.

Chris on Striding Edge, Helvellyn, winter 2006

Candy and I returned to the area of France we had visited the year before, this time camping in the Black Mountains north of Carcassonne. Against my advice we camped on a little hillock and lost the new gazebo in a spectacular storm on the first night! We also climbed the Roc du Nouret@1073m and the highest point Pic de Nore@1211m. The only time we have walked in those mountains. The same holiday, camping near Maury, we visited several Cathar castles: Perypetuse, Queribus and Montsegure, familiar now to many of our guests. We also made it to the top of the Pic du Canigou@2784m, from Los Masos, staying in the Cortalets Refuge@2150m. This was on the second attempt. The first time we had used the track to climb most of the way and had a problem with the radiator on the Freelander. We descended to Perpignan after a night at the Cortalets, for a replacement at their Landrover garage!

I also managed a couple of Scottish peaks that summer, staying with Chris at the famous Clachaig Hotel in Glen Coe. A place I'd always wanted to stay. We managed Bidean Nam Bian@1150m and Stob Coire nan Lochan@1100m on the first day. Then Buaichaille Etive Beag and Stob Dubh@958m on our way home, having done Buaichaille Etive Mor, Stob Dearg@1022m in the same way in 2003.

Since doing the Mont Blanc trip with Mike Jackson and Ainsey in '91, we had taken to doing an overnighter just before Christmas. Though we didn't know it at the time 2006 was to be our last one, at the Wasdale Head Hotel. Another 'famous' climbing hotel I had hankered to stay in. For more about this hotel, the history of rock climbing and its climbing connections read *'The First Tigers'* by Alan Hankinson........like the other books I've recommended its somewhere in my little library! Mike was close to 77 in '06. We got him up Rough Crag@317m and Stords Hill@384m. Quite rightly he was happy to wait for the photos of Scafell@964m via Lords rake and the West Wall Travers in the snow, the next day. Happy to wander around Wasdale and breath in the air and atmosphere of the hotel. Unfortunately for the next few years I wouldn't be around, busy with my own adventures. Sadly, Mike died in 2020 in a 'home' in Skipton, he had suffered from dementia and no longer recognises even his son. I last went to see him in about '17, it took him a while to remember me. I had taken some photos of us and we talked about our old adventures. Despite our age difference we have had some good times!

2007 saw the end of my final year at SCS. I also had a number of other memorable experiences in the outdoors. Candy and I did Scafell Pike @986m in late April, and I followed this with a National 3 Peaks round in May. This was with step-daughter Bea and her strange friend Terry. They were doing it for charity and asked me to go along and give them some help on the mountains. Candy agreed, and with Terry's wife Sue, drove us between Ben Nevis@1343m (Scotland), Scafell Pike@986m (England) and Snowden@1085m (Wales) within 24hrs. I had a feeling that it might be hard going, when Terry arrived without a waterproof and insisted on buying the cheapest he could find in Fort 'Bill'. He then laughed at the walking sticks on my pack. Finally he had the great idea of wind up head torches for Bea and himself, but didn't give them a trial first…..surprisingly, all three of these things he would come to regret!

It was our intention to do the Ben in daylight, then drive to Scafell Pike and do it overnight. Starting at 16:00, all went well on the Ben and we were up and down in 4.5hrs, a good time…..funnily enough nobody laughed at my sticks as they fell over coming down the loose scree. Then onto England! The forecast was poor and we set off in rain at 02:30. It soon turned into a hooly, with strong wind, heavy rain and next to zero visibility….broken only by the winding of head torches every few minutes! Short of desperate, even I found it interesting! We got back to the car at 06:30, guess who was very wet indeed! There were branches and trees on the road as we left Wasdale, we were lucky to get out of the valley. Snowden from Llanberis Pass isn't that difficult, so I was fairly confident we would get down in under the 24 hrs, it was 11:30 when we set off. Bea was doing well but Terry was moving slower, it took us 2.5hrs to reach the summit. Going down was even slower, so as the weather was clear, the path was good and there were lots of folk about I decided to head down by myself. I arrived in the cafe after a total of 22hrs and 56minutes, the others were some 0.5hr later. As a footnote, Terry did an article, for their sponsors, I didn't get a mention………arse!!

August saw us in Zinal, Switzerland for a family holiday and my IML assessment. First we had Bea, Ewa and Roo then later Brigid(Lob) and John. We took B,E&R for a night in the Petite Montet Refuge@2145m and L&J to the Cabane de Moiry@2885m. R,L&J all had sleepless, fairly turbulent and noisy nights due to altitude. They were lucky to survive unharmed!

My IML assessment 19-24th Aug. went really well and after the day one de-briefing on the expedition I was asked to keep my contribution to the group to a minimum. I was asked by the assessor to spend part of the evening in the first hut teaching some simple French phrases to two of my group. I spent most of the next day telling jokes, to keep myself amused. My navigation leg was on a ridge, looking at the map I could see the end point from the start........I just followed the path. Two of the guys in my group of four eventually failed the assessment. Their navigation wan't great, also they hadn't bothered to look up the local culture, geology, language, flora and fauna. To add to their distress they hadn't arrived early to acclimatise. You can never over prepare for an assessment. On 24th August I became an International Mountain Leader: Accompagnateur en Moyenne Montagne brevet d'Etat d'Alpinism in French.

Accompagnateur en Montagne 2007

In October I had a big adventure with Chris Monkman, Graham Ogden and Geoff Stone. We went to Nepal for 3 weeks to attempt the Annapurna Circuit.

Annapurna Trek, 2007, Yak Kharka @ 4000m: Geoff Stone, Graham Ogden, Me and Chris Monkman & porters.

Chris and Geoff had been on the Everest Base Camp trek several years earlier, but Graham and I were 'newbies' to Nepal. I loved Nepal and trekking in the high mountains with Katie Melua on my iPod, even though the following account may not sound like it was such fun, personally I had a ball. The trek started well, in the tropical region of Besisahar, and we climbed slowly to get acclimatised. Chris was recovering from a hernia operation and his marriage had, that very week, gone down the pan...so he wasn't in a good place! By the time we got to Manang@3500m on Day 7 for a rest day Graham had 'Delhi belly' and Chris was suffering from the effects of altitude. It was snowing lightly. Graham and I got an en-suit to share. This was a Concrete room with two beds and a table and badly fitting windows. The bathroom was an adjoining concrete room with a hole in the floor (toilet) and a tap! By this time our porters were providing double sleeping bags plus "washy water and bed tea" each morning..... luxury. We were also being garlic soaked at mealtimes, with garlic soup and Momo's. This was also my first experience of Tibetan Bread and deep fried Mars Bars.

We got Chris to see a French doctor in the village and he prescribed some Diamox (acetazolamide), but said it may take a couple of days to work. By the time we climbed to Yak Kharka@4000m, the next day, Chris was if anything worse. While Graham, now fully recovered, and I climbed a ridge close to the hostel @4150m Chris and Geoff took to their beds. The following day we reached a small village Leder@4140m Chris could go no further. We had agreed on two things at the start; no alcohol on the trek and we would stick together, we headed back down to Manang and another rest day.

There were a couple of other things on the trip worth mentioning. The first was how I lost a job in Qatar and gained another, without being involved! This I will cover more fully in Chapter 13. The second was my complete loss of respect for Geoff. We had been friends and played rugby together since our schooldays. Playing side by side on many occasions, in the front row for both School and 'Air' 1 XVs as well as much social time. However in Nepal I saw a different side to him, his favourite phrase being "Johnny Foreigners"when referring to the locals. He also thought that they were all on the take, which was sometimes true but for such small amounts it was not worth mentioning. As an instance we were sat in a small open restaurant one night when the village had an electrical outage. We waited, not unexpectedly in my view, for quite some time to be served. We could see the staff in the kitchen cooking on wood burning stoves in candlelight. At the end of the meal Geoff refused to tip the staff as we had such a long wait. FFS! I put in the tip for us all, a few measly dollars. He was also bothered by the fact that I was much fitter and unconcerned by rocky and narrow paths. Finally I had to explain that this is what I've been doing for the past 20 years since I gave up rugby! We have spoken only briefly a handful of times since returning. In my defence I'm not the only one who friendship with him has cooled in recent years.

In January 2008 we moved to Qatar. I had no experience of the desert, which in Qatar is often more like a builders yard full of rubble than lovely sand dunes. Candy and I helped to start the International Award(IA/DofE) there, led by Lucy & Kevin Davies. Our first expedition was from school to Al Khor island to camp, with the first group of Bronze candidates. We were to plan many more outings and have weekly training for things like camp skills, cooking, map work & navigation. To be honest most of our supervision, unlike my DofE in the UK, was by car. We did always need to camp with the group though, as we had many Muslim girls. This first year also included beach camping with Ewa, Roo & Bea, down at the Inland Sea.

Our first summer based in Aunat saw us climb a few local peaks. The most obvious being the Pic d'Ourtiset@1933m and its neighbour the Picou Negre@1856m. Both massive peaks by UK standards, but with only 500m of ascent from the end of the track. The Ourtiset, which I can see from the settee in the new veranda, is also my most climbed peak, currently with 25 ascents(2020)....Candy isn't far behind! We also managed the Madres@2469m and Pic de St.Barthelemy@2349m, both visible from our village.

Candy and I also did Candy's first backpacking trip. From the house to camp at Nebias in the valley, visit Puivert and back to the house. The highlight of the trip was running out of cash and no cash machine or point for using the card in either village...yes this was 2008! Our evening meal was a giant tin of ravioli and a giant tin of runner beans, it was all we could afford in cash!

In December I got permission to leave school early to do a British Association of International Mountain Leaders(BAIML) continuing professional development(CPD) in les Contamines-Montjoie, near Chamonix. On Day 1 I had my first experience on snowshoes. This was interesting as my IML qualification already allowed me to take groups out in winter on snowshoes. To be honest the change in temperature from Qatar to sub-zero France was not good and I found myself at La Balme@1706m with all my clothes on and still freezing to death.

The second day we were supposed to do some mountain biking, instead we did a morning of bike repair then built a full size Igloo in the afternoon. Catching up with Candy and spending Christmas in Aunat we were pleased to find it snowed. So we bought snowshoes and did some practice! The best day out was above Camurac ski station. We did the ridge of Penedis@1876m, Quercourt@1820m, Taillade@1808m and Assaladou@1721m on a fabulous sunny day, returning by the woods to the north, traversing steep slopes. This is still one of our favourite places both in winter and summer, not too testing but with brilliant views over the Eastern Pyrenean chain. We have done it lots of times and hope for many more.

Raquettes around the Quercourt with the Tourism & Loisirs (T&L) from Carcassonne

In 2009 we were still working in Qatar. We had set up a Silver IA expedition for last year's Bronze group, in the deserts and waddies of Oman. This was a great experience for Candy and I as well as the kids. We loved the people of the villages and waddies as they always seemed friendly and wanted to communicate. We were in Aunat again for part of the summer, managing the Canigou@2784m again, this time with Bea after a night in the Cortalets@2154m. As a change we ascended by the Crêt du barbet and the intimidating chimney on the south face to the summit. To their credit, both girls coped admirably.

Our time in Qatar never gave us much opportunity for mountains, the highest point on the peninsula Qurain Abu al-Bawl, which we visited, is only 103m above sea level. We did get many nights under canvas and a few good trips. In 2010 we took the now Gold group, still with 22 students from something like 19 nationalities, to Nepal for their residential and final expedition. We had a local 'guide team' and some backup porters, but I had worked hard to get the kids to do route cards and maps from Google Earth. It ended up being something of a guided tour, as the route was very obvious, but all the kids.....and us staff.....got a lot out of living a different lifestyle to that of luxury Qatar. We managed to do a circuit from Nayapul, which included: Ghorepani@2874m, Tadapani@2590m, Ban Thanti@3180m and Ghandruk@1940m. It snowed overnight in Tadapani and many of the students, all 17-18yrs old, had never been on snow. I never realised that standing and walking on snow was a skill you had to learn. They were falling about all over....laugh out loud(lol).

Ainsey and his wife Jan came out to see us in April. We took them camping to Oman on the side of Jabel Shams@2500m, then on to its South Summit at 2997m. Unfortunately the highest point at just over 3000m is a military installation and restricted. The Ainsworths had a bit of a meltdown in the heat on our return to camp. Insisting on packing up and literally running down to the car, instead of waiting in the shade of the tent until the sun got lower in the sky! We felt obliged to follow, but they didn't feel obliged to wait! We had some nights in good hotels, but also a night camping high in Wadi Dam, swimming in the pools. When Ainsey and Jan took their tent down there was a small Scorpion sleeping under the groundsheet..

We finished in Qatar in the July of 2010 and I had plans to go to Antarctica with Ainsey and Graham Ogden. Nothing much in the way of mountaineering, though we did climb some way up the Martel Glacier @900m, just outside Ushuaia, on Tierra del Fuego. We also camped for one night on Pléneau Island just off the cost of the Antarctic continent and made a continental landing in Neko harbour.

Camping on Antarctica. Our ship was the MS Expedition. This is a photo taken at about 1:30am and is as dark as it got.

By New Year of 2011 I had managed to find yet another international post. This time in Wuxi, Jiangsu Province, 100 miles west of Shanghai.

Though we got out for many ascents of our local hill, Huishan Forest Park, with its 'interesting' cafe and ridge walk, we didn't meet many mountains. We had one weekend trip to climb Mount Huangshan, Lotus Flower Peak@1864m. Where we stayed in a 'hotel' just below the top. This was more of a tourist honeypot/sacred mountain, with paths and steps to the summit. However it was impressive on top, very Chinese.

Returning home in the summer we met Ainsey and Jan at the Refuge de Ruhl@2185m, to pick them up from a section of the GR10. Candy kindly walked with Jan, who found the big rocky ground hard going. On the Col de la Lhesse@2439m it began to rain. Saying they only had light waterproofs they ran off down to a hut in the valley, leaving us behind. You think I would expect it by now! Later that year Ainsey and I, Candy, Jan and my Chris ran a Gold IA expedition for AKIS north of Bonne, towards Lake Geneva. We included two preparation days and a final rock climbing/tourist day in Chamonix to finish. I'm pleased to say, all went well and Chris performed brilliantly with the students.

'Expedition Awards International': Paul, Candy, Jan & Chris in the Chamonix valley with AKIS BS IA, 2011.

I was invited back to Qatar to work for 5 months at the start of 2012, so got nothing done in the mountains until I returned home to France at the end of May. I helped my school friend Peter 'taff' Williams climb Snowden, with Alan Wade and Phil Wright. Keith Parker turned back on the Pyg Track as he felt it was too steep.......what? It was a long haul with what can only be described as a 'fat lad', but we finally made it. I persuaded everyone that the train down was the best thing, and we rode down in the guards van.

Taff (Peter Williams, front), Phil Wright and Myself on the wet bit up the Pyg Track on Snowden, 2012

2013 was a full year off work, but I had started my OU degree in PPE and this was taking up a lot of my time......I had set my sights on seeing how well I could do, fr once, if I gave it 100% effort. Candy and I did quite a bit of local snowshoeing in January and February, including two ascents of the Ourtiset@1933m. In the summer I arranged an Alpine trip with Ainsey, it had been a while. We invited Mark Bonner who taught Physics at SCS and had joined, then taken over, the school's DofE. Mark is quite a bit younger than us and his main love is sailing. Though he had quite a bit of U.K. experience he was new to the Alps. We decided to base ourselves at Ainsey's French house near Grenoble and start by repeating our Ecrin trip of 2002. I wasn't really fit, so just joined in where I could without pushing myself. We went to the Sella Hut@2671m for some altitude training and on to the Replas the next day. I waited at the col@3286m while the other two scrambled to the south summit.

The Sella Hut (2671m) in 2013, behind is the Replas, with its higher South Summit. Access is by the glacier to the col.

Then on the Ecrin I waited at the Ecrin hut@3175m while they went and climbed the Dome de Neige. We then moved on to Contaminés Montjoie and climbed up to the Conscrits Refuge@2602m via the lovely Tre-la-Tête hotel. I was surprised to find that the old glacier route up to the top hut had been abandoned and a suspension bridge built to facilitate a rocky ascent. Also much of the lower glacier had vanished over the past 20 years. Then on arrival at the Conscrits, what a magnificent spaceship of a building to replaced the old ram shackled hut, see earlier picture. Once again I had a hut day while the other two went off to do the Domes de Miages.......my first real Alpine peak, 22 years earlier!

Sat on the balcony of the Ecrin hut. Barre des Ecrin is on the left, with the Dome de Neige, 4012m, just on its right flank.

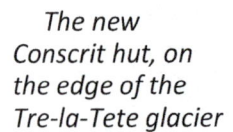

The new Conscrit hut, on the edge of the Tre-la-Tete glacier

I got a six month contract in Singapore starting in Jan. 2014. So we took the opportunity to go out in mid December and then fly on to see our friend Graham Ogden, who had married a Kiwi girl Maree and was now living in Wellington. We first booked a camper van to look at the South Island, and took the opportunity to get into the outdoors. On Arthur's pass we climbed to the Devil's Punchbowl and to 1500m on Mount Aicken, missing the summit by some 300m as the weather was on the turn. We also walked the coastal route from Bark Bay to Anchorage in the Able Tasman National Park in the north of South Island. Returning to Graham & Maree in Wellington they drove us up to do the Tongariro Alpine Crossing. This is a 20km hike passing close to Mt Ngauruhoe AKA Mt Doom from Lord of the Rings, with active volcanoes in the Red Crater and Emerald Lake.

One of the laughable things on the walk was a sign which recommended that if the volcano started to erupt you should "turn and run in the opposite direction! That said, some 3km from the active sight there was a 'recently' ejected 5 tonne Boulder………eeek! We also went on to see the geysers and geothermal mud pools in Rotorua.

'Mount Doom' at the start of the Tongariro Alpine Crossing, with active volcanic sites at Red Crater and Emerald Lake

After Christmas we returned to Singapore to start work. In Singapore we climbed to the highest point, Bukit Timah@164m a couple of times. It's interesting because it is surrounded by original primary rain forest. Which is strange as there is nowhere in it that you can't hear traffic! We also walked the Kent Ridge from Harbourfront right through to the Science Park, via Faber Peak and the Kent Ridge Canopy Walk a number of times. I joined the Hash Harriets to run once a week for an hour and a half around the lesser known green areas of Singapore.

Part of the Kent Ridge, our favourite walk in Singapore. Some of which is a canopy walk through the jungle.

Paul & Vic came to visit us in Singapore and we flew off to Kuching in Sarawak on the island of Borneo. Paul wasn't very well so Candy and I decided to have an adventure in the jungle. Rather than book a trip we caught a local bus to a small quay. From there a local motor boat took us to Telok Beach and the Bako National Park. There was a set of trails marked on a crude map/sign, so we chose one, the Lintang Loop, 3.5hrs, took a photo on my phone and set off. We had a great day, seeing only two other groups and moving through seven types of climate/vegetation zones. The highest view point was Bukit Tambi@140m. There is a cafe back at the beach and we took the opportunity to have a drink and food before returning to Kuching by boat and bus.......a great day.

*The Lintang Trail in Bako National Park, Sarawak, Borneo.
A self-guided tour of some real jungle.*

We left Singapore in June, I became officially retired and my days per year in the hills started to grow. Returning to France Candy and I joined two walking clubs. I had never walked with a club before, or been led on a group walk. At first it was strange but we thought it might bring us into contact with more French speakers.......improve my French and getting to know more of the area in which we were to live.

On 19th Feb. '05 we did our first walk with the Tourism & Loisirs(T&L) of Carcassonne. It was a snowshoe from Montsegure up the Taulat ridge. This group was usually 10-15, good walkers, enjoying 800-1000+m of ascent or 'dénivelé'. Then in July we also went out with a more relaxed club, the Haute Vallée Randonnées (HVR), based in Quillan. Their groups were of a very varied standard, from 20-30 walkers enjoying 400-800m of ascent, in lower mountains and on the local plains. The T&L was a group of French speakers, until I introduced my Irish friend Brian some years later. The HVR had a smattering of British, Dutch, Australian, New Zealand and from time to time a Yank. The two groups have certainly become a big part of our lives and many of our friends here in France are connected to one or both.

Leading a group from the HVR on Pic Fourcat, 1928m, and Rocher de Scaramus, 1868m, in 2016. Our fellow Aunat resident and friend Mari-Jo Dagneaux is front and centre.

We had quite a few snowshoe adventures with the T&L in the first four months of the year, particularly helpful in getting to know the Ariege mountains. Having being critical of the standard of the HVR I note that the Roc d'Aude@2325m, Roc Blanc@2542m and Petit Peric@2690m were some of the earlier summits I did with them!

August saw me journeying to Saas Fe in Switzerland, with Ainsey and Bonner. We went up to the Britannia Hutte@3030m to acclimatise and got stuck there for a full day due to snow and bad weather. We next went up to the col Freejoc @3826m, made easier by the uplift of the Alpine Express!

Mark and I on the glacier, heading towards the Freejoc(3826m)

Repeating the ascent the next day all the way to the top of the Allalinhorn@4027m. Our 'time off' turned out to be an exciting ascent of the Mittaghorn@3143m via a superb Via Ferrata.

148

Mark and I on the Mittaghorn Via Ferrata

Two days later we went up to the Hohasaas Hutte@3200m to set out for the Weishorn. Unfortunately I wasn't going well and we called it a day at 3800m. Regrettably it was too cold for them to leave me behind to completed the last 250m of ascent! I went immediately to bed on return to the hut and had a good solid 4hrs sleep? 2015 gave me 33days in the hills, something I had only managed twice....... 'since records began' in 1983.

I had 10 outings with T&L in 2016 and 6 with HVR. Candy broke her ankle descending from around the Bassies refuge on 24th March. Luckily she was just above the access road to the electrical station. I was able to run down to get the car while Jean(aged 72 at the time) heroically carried her down the path on his back! With two screws in her ankle she was out of action for some time, but up and walking without a pot or sticks after only 5 weeks.........incredible! In late June she climbed the Ourtiset@1933m with Ewa........fantastic.

We went to Australia for Alasdair and Sara's wedding in September, doing the Four sisters and Tropical Forest walk in the Blue Mountains. This was fairly trivial walking but interesting. We also had a camper van and searched out a Grade 4 coastal walk from Horseshoe Bay near Bowen. We were 'gob smacked' to find that the final rocks had a yellow line painted to the top, showing the way!....lol.

Can't find the way, follow the balisage.

Notable at the end of the year was a scramble up the North ridge of Tryfan, a favourite route, with Chris. He hopped over the summit twin boulders to claim 'the freedom of Tryfan', it looked slippy that year so I didn't bother. Near the top we got a fantastic view of a Brocken Spectre, my first. Wikki says, "A Brocken spectre also called Brocken bow or mountain spectre, is the magnified (and enormous) shadow of an observer cast upon clouds opposite the Sun's direction. The figure's head is often surrounded by the halo-like rings of coloured light forming a glory, which appears opposite the Sun's direction when uniformly-sized water droplets in clouds refract and backscatter sunlight".

Quite a few walks with the clubs in early in 2017, more being curtailed by the final project for my degree and step-son-in-law John's sudden death in early May. Chris, Charlotte, Jess and Nathan came over to France in July and we managed to get them up the Ourtiset@1933m, being my 14th time!

*Camping with Jess and Nathan near Le Bousquet de Sault.
Outside cooking and girls and boys mini-tents.*

In August Ainsey and Bonner came to Aunat for a 'Pyrenean adventure'. We started with some acclimatisation: The Cortelets hut@2150m from Los Masos, then the next day the Canigou@2712m via the chimney. We had a day at home. Then followed up with my first visit to the Carlit@2932m, staying at the CAF hut next to the Lac de Bouillouses. Moving on to Spain and the Renclus hut@2140m we visited the Pic dAneto@3404 via the Pas de Mahomet.

*The awesome finishing ridge, the Pas de Mahomet,
to the Pic d'Aneto, Spain*

*The tiny Maupas hut, full to the brim, 45 people in three bunks on
three layers in the same room.......now that is full!*

The Aneto is the highest peak of the the Pyrenean chain and has the largest glacier to cross. Returning to France we went up to the Maupas Hut@2430m, a tiny hut with 45 people in 3 bunks of a tiny dorm. This was to climb the Maupas@3109m via its easy 'mauvais pas'.

Candy went caving for the first time in October. A free day's training was offered by the Maison de Montagne in Esperzel. This was to facilitate the assessment of some young underground leaders. We visited the Aven Jean-Bernard on the big Pays de Sault plateau. I thought it would be a simple cave trip, but it turned out to involve 3 Single Rope Technique(SRT) pitches in both ascent and descent to the main Avon. With the added attraction of lunch in the Avon itself. Candy did really well, enjoying the abseils, but finding the SRT ascents quite challenging. 2017 saw 43 days in the mountains, the most so far, but it was to get better.

We went to the UK for Christmas, first visiting Kev and Val Boyle in Newcastle. Out on a walk on Hadrian's Wall, near the famous tree close to Vindolanda I slipped on a wet rock and fell on my bum. Candy ran to help and slipped on the same rock. Getting up she was holding her wrist, when she finally let me look at it, it was a classic 'dinner fork' fracture! It was set by the doctor in Hexham Hospital, after much heaving, pulling and sweat. A real 'Victorian' job.

He was not happy after the x-ray and wrote us a note of referral for the fracture clinic in Nottingham, our next days stop. The Consultant in Nottingham agreed that they could do a better job and after numbing Candy's arm suspended it from five 'Chinese finger traps' for 20 minutes, it was done. This painless and effortless system seemed to relocate the bones and she was plastered up. On return to France the doctor their said they would have operated and pinned it, but it was a reasonable fix. Once again, with lots of exercise, Candy was able to get more or less full movement back into the joint.

By the end of January 2018, only a month after the accident she was back walking with the T&L. In early February we snowshoed for three consecutive days. First around the Bois de Linas@1200m, then La Racounade@1120m followed by the Pic du Midi@1179m(Esperzel), near home. My healthy heroine xx.

In May we went over to the UK and stayed with Chris, Charlotte, Jess and Nathan in a cottage on Skye. We had arranged to meet Ainsey there, and Mark Bonner was up with some of his other mountain buddies. It was an absolutely glorious week, the best Skye had seen for some time. Though it was also a family holidays we managed a coupe of good days on the Cuillin Ridge. Chris and I both soloed the East Ridge of the Inaccessible Pinnacle (the In Pin) on Sgurr Dearg@986m and summited Sgurr na Banachdich@965m and Sgurr nan Gobhar@613m.

Dad and lad, bored with waiting for the climbers with ropes, 'but in' and 'free climb' the East Ridge of the In Pin on Sgurr Dearg, Skye

Two days later we mounted Sgurr nan Gillean@965m using the 'Tourist Route'.....a misnomer if ever there was one. Then I showed everyone the 'easy gully' way up onto the Bastier Tooth@917m ....Chris dashed off and did Am Bastier@935m too. In mid August Chris, Nathan and I did Snowden@1085m via the Pyg Track and down by the Miners Track........an impressive effort for an 8 year old.

Chris and Nathan (age 8) on the way up ....or maybe down, Snowden, August 2018

On our return to France I helped Ainsey achieve a long standing ambition, climbing the Obiou@2789m via the long and often very exposed Arrêt du Rattier. A long and exhausting 8hrs, but very rewarding, with magnificent views and exposure and a little technical difficulty here and there.

Candy finished off the year with her first big mountain. We climbed to the Refuge de l'Etang du Pinet@2246m with Mari-Jo and a woman from the T&L, Nicole. The next day we climbed the Pic du Montcalm@3077m, the highest peak in either Aude or Ariege. A 3000m peak at 71yrs. a magnificent effort!

A lot of continuous exposure on the Rattier ridge on the way to the Obiou, but little real technical difficulty. It was a long day, though!

With 67days in the hills and 116 peaks/tops, 2018 is going to be a hard year to beat. Though this total doesn't include two cycle tours, which I will describe later. A truly outdoor year.

2019 was to start with a few snowshoe trips, then a visit to Australia involving several nights for us under canvas with Al, Sara and Hemsley. My best experience was to wake up one morning with a large Kangaroo sleeping peacefully just next to me outside the tent. We were both shocked when I opened the fly sheet! At home I had become more involved with the HVR and led a number of walks for them in 2018/19. The most stressful part of this is deciding if we should go when the forecast is a bit uncertain. Candy did her duty by going out on the 'recos' with me and duly being my 'serre file'. I had also managed to get my new Irish friend Brian O'Raghallaigh, who lives part-time in Quillan, to share some walk leading with me and we made a good team. Bea and Andy came in the summer and we three did the Ourtiset@1934m and the Bentaillole@1965m.

In July Candy and I went to the Lakes with Chris and family to do some small 'Wainwright's'. We stayed in a beautiful house with its own wood at Troutbeck. The first day out the whole family: Candy, Chris, Charlotte, Jess(10), Nathan(9) and Emily(7 weeks) did Wansfell@488m.

This was my first Wainwright with Jess and Nathan and my first mountain, of course, with Emily on dad's front.

All out on Gowbarrow summit, hiding from the wind. Emily (7 weeks) is tucked away on her dad's chest. Photo by Candy

The next day Chris, Nathan and I did Great Mell Fell@537m in the morning, then we all did Gowbarrow@481m in the early afternoon followed by the three 'boys' doing a late afternoon rush up Little Mell Fell@505m.

Chris, Nathan and Emily on a windy Wansfell. Emily's first 'Wainwright" at only 7weeks!

In August I met Bonner and Ainsey in Cauteret, central Pyrenees for another 'Alpine' adventure. The first trip out was via the Breche de Roland@2805m to the Goriz hut in Spain. This hut was packed, with 100 in the hut and a further 100 camping outside. What was nice to see was that there were not only 'grizzly old men' like us, but many mixed groups of all ages and groups of young women exploring on their own. We sat at a table with a young couple, where the girl had brought her boyfriend trekking for his first time.......great stuff. From there we made an easy ascent of Mont Perdu@3348m in just 3hours, including one 15 minute stop.

Mont Perdu @3348 with Mark, 2019

Next day, back over the Breche from a quiet arid valley into the metropolis of a verdant France. Our second trip took us to the Bayssellance refuge@2651m and on to the Vignemale@3299m, the highest of the French Pyrenees. This involved an easy glacier crossing and then a steep friable rock finish.

The team:- Mark, Myself and Ainsey on the summit of the Vignemale, @3299m the highest summit in the French Pyrenees

It was after this that Ainsey got an emergency call from Jan to say that their French house had caught fire......needles to say he had to rush home. Luckily there wasn't too much damage and the insurance came good. Bonner and I were left to have a nice night at the Espuguettes Refuge@2027m in the Gavarnie valley. Followed by an early morning ascent of the Pimene@2669m in 1.5 hrs and a descent to the valley in time for lunch.

160

Back home for only a couple of days I set out to join Brian and a small group from Dublin: Gerry, Donal, Mario and Onya on a section of the GR10. We did about 22/25km a day with suitable 'dénivelé' (1000m) for each of 2 days from Ustou (St.Lizier) to the Maison du Valier. Followed by a trip to the Estagnous refuge@2222m and Mont Valier@2238m the next day.

Brian, Onya and Myself on Mont Valier @2238m

This included a knee knackering descent of 1950m back to the Maison du Valier. 2019 finished with an astonishing 62 days on the hills and 94 tops and peaks.

By 2019 I had become a regular leader for HVR, with of course, my beautiful assistant Candy. I hoped for a bigger year than last year in terms of both days and peaks and and had arranged for a tour of the Grand Paradiso with some of the T&L group and a bike tour in Scotland; Arran to Inverness.

It started well with 14 days and 38 peaks/tops by mid March...........then we had the COVID 19 lockdown. All plans were cancelled. From 15th March to 11th May we were not allowed to walk out of our house for more than 1 hour a day and no more than 1km distant. We visited Le Crausse@1027m.......or telephone tower as we call it........ by various routes 43 times in that time. The HVR started up again, for groups of 10, on 18th May.

I lead some local tours of Aunat/Fontanes and then later the Ourtiset, my 25th visit to the summit. That day we had two groups and Candy led her first group, after a trial run the day before. Unfortunately the T&L closed down and intended to restart on 1st October, but didn't! I managed only 58 days in 2020 but with a record 114 peaks and 8 snowshoeing days.

Leading some of the more intrepid of the HVR up the Pic Carlit @ 2921m, in early winter conditions, 7 Sept. 2020.

A Bit of Cycling to Add to the Mix

Like most kids I had a bike. However, having been knocked off it at 11, without injury, cycling alone between Horsforth and Guiseley, I never had it repaired. Ruth and I bought Mountain Bikes when Chris and Al were old enough to go for little rides and we would also take them away with us on holiday. It wasn't until I started to live in Ilkley that I started to ride mountain bike routes with Ainsey and sometimes with Al. I also bought a custom made road bike from Geoff Stone, who didn't like it because it went too fast! I bought a mountain bike for Candy soon after we started to go out and she took to it with some delight. Since getting to Frances we have used the bikes often to get around the countryside and along the coast for days out.

Our favourite local tours have been up behind the church, through the woods and onto the road to Bessede. From there up to the Col de Pradel towards Aunat for 1km before dropping down through the woods to meet the same road. At first Candy and I took nearly 1.5 hrs, with Candy having to stop at least 3 times for drinks. We now do it in under 1 hr, without stopping. Our other favourite is to go to Rivesault. From there, there is a tarmacked bike route along the Agly river to Le Barcarés, 15km. It can be extended along the coast to Port Leucate or even the fabulous sea food 'cafes' at the Grau de Leucate. With a stop for lunch, 5 hrs on our bikes..on the flat! As I sit here writing this Candy is nursing a broken finger. She fell off on the Agly route a couple of weeks ago (Feb '21).

At Christmas of 2017 I met an old school friend, Bryn Griffiths, and we talked about biking. He was going to ride the WW1 Western Front in the summer and I asked if I could go along. This was to be my first extended bike tour. A few years earlier I had helped Chris out by buying an almost new Trek road bike from him. With touring tyres and rear panniers this converted into an ideal touring bike for me. So on 20th July I was dropped off by Candy in Caterham, just south of London. My plan was to get some practice in before meeting Bryn and John in Dover. I cycled from Caterham first west(??) to Dorking. Then east to Pembury, near Tumbridge Wells and Canterbury before picking up the coast near Sandwich to head to Dover. By the time I reached Dover my bum was both sore and had got better! I did try a couple of Sustrans routes but found that in general they were not suited to my ladened touring bike. A VTT would have been better, but then much more effort on the French roads to come. We crossed on a morning ferry, interesting on a bike with all the cars and lorries, and landed in Dunkirk. We headed into Belgium, roughly following the line of the Western Front.

We stopped off at Talbot House or 'Toc H' as it was called by the soldiers, in Poperinge, for a refreshing cup of tea before our first night in Ypres. A note for the future, Talbot House does accommodation! In Ypres we took a trip into town in the evening to watch the Menin Gate ceremony.

The Vimy Ridge Canadian monument near Arras, France ....and my bike!

The next day we cycled to Arras via a museum with preserved WW1 trenches and visited the Vimy Ridge memorial. From there we again roughly followed the Western Front towards Albert, stopping off at the Thiepval Somme Memorial and museum. This was an especially hot day, getting up to 36 Celsius in the afternoon. That evening we stayed in Peronne. From there we headed still further south to St Jean aux Bois, just south of Compiegne, where we finished our Western Front trip.

The next day we headed into central Paris, an interesting if not attractive ride, with time on some very busy roads. A central Paris hotel was quite different to what we had become accustomed to

The following day was the arrival of the Tour de France in Paris. I left early to cycle through empty, traffic free, streets to the Gare du Nord, leaving Bryn and John to watch the finish of the Tour. I managed to make it by train to Dover by the end of the day. Then on to Aberystwyth via London, cycling through London to change stations, to Birmingham and Shrewsbury. The hardest part of the journey was making sure that I could get my bike on each train!

In September of the same year Candy and I decided to attempt the Canal du Midi, from Toulouse to the Med. coast. We adapted our bikes with panniers, I chose to take my old Scott VTT (Vélo Tout Terrain). It was just as well that I did as several sections were not suitable for a touring bike. We stayed in accommodation each night at: Montguillard, Lauragain, Arzens, La Redorte(staying in the Chateau de la Redorte), Le Somail, Bezier and ending in Port des Onglous. Lunches were either a picnic or a meal in a cafe/restaurant. With no rain an excellent 275km journey. One vivid memory was riding behind Candy, along the towpath, some way after leaving La Redorte. "Did you forget a pannier" I asked. "No" she replied. "Well you only have one now!" "Oh shit........!" We returned along the towpath, about 2km, to find it stood up in the middle, as if someone had found it and placed it there......unopened! Lucky girl.

Somewhere on the Canal du Midi, 2017

In 2019 Candy and I cycled the other half of the Med. to Atlantic connection, the Canal de Garonne from Toulouse to Langon.....just short of Bordeaux. We stayed in Grisolles, Pommevic, Port Saint Marie (two nights due to heavy rain), Marmande (glamping in a wig-wam)and a wonderful cordon bleu evening in Langon. We did 210km in all, along well made (tarmac) paths by the canal and small roads, which would have suited my Trek road bike but was OK on the Scott........once again we loved it!

The end of the Canal du Garonne, 2018

Having broken her ankle in March 2016 walking in the Ariege, then her wrist in December 2017 on Hadrians Wall, she fell of her bike in 2021. This was on the paved way between Rivesault and Le Barcares and resulted in a broken finger on her right hand and some damage to her right fore arm. Later in '21 she again fell, getting off her bike and fractured her coccyx.......very painful. This became her longest lasting injury, full recovery taking in excess of 6 weeks!

I must take better care of her!

Back to the high hills

The pull of a high mountain adventure always stirs the blood. Sometime in '21 I came across an advert on the Internet for Jbel Toubkal (4167m), the highest peak in the Atlas Mountains & North Africa. It's three main attractions being: I had never done a high 'desert' peak, I hadn't climbed a 4000m peak since the Allalinhorn in 2015 and thought that may have been my last, and Africa was my missing Continent, having visited Asia, S.America, N.America, Antarctic, Europe and Oceania.

I was soon in contact with my long time mountain buddy Chris Ainsworth, and he jumped at the chance. At our age we don't mind a bit of suffering, but not too much. We booked with 360 Expeditions, so it was a package tour! The group met in Marrakesh and consisted of our leader, Ben & his girlfriend Holly. Plus three seasoned 'expeditioners', Susan & Heide in their late 50s and David at 75! The other two were on their first expedition, Sarah Jane about 40 & Helena at about 30.

The actual trek was only 3 days, and we we're accompanied by 3 donkeys to carry our main luggage and food, plus two cooks to supply us with three hot meals a day. Local guide Omar & his apprentice Mohammad would guide us on the trek.

Day 1 was from Imlil to the refuge at Azib Tamsoult(2200m), summiting Tizi n'Mzik(peak) at 2610m. A 5hr day with 1200m of ascent and 13km.
Day 2 was more of a challenge, rising to 3600m near Aguelzim mountain pass and onto the Refuge des Mouflons(3200m)
Day 3, started at 3:30 for a 4:30 depart. Summit of Toubkal 9:00 and back to the refuge for 12:30. 1000m of steep ascent and 9km. I actually recorded less than 5 hrs of walking for myself, we had several waits for David. This wasn't the end of the day. After 1.5hrs for lunch we descended back to Imlil, arriving at 19:30. A day of 15hrs, 20.5km and with a 2580m descent overall. We were all a bit jaded!

Of all the mountains I have climbed, certainly in the UK, the most continuously difficult expedition was to traverse the Cuillin Ridge of Skye. This I did, with my long time mountain mate, Chris Ainsworth, in May 1991. It gets a mention earlier, but I thought it was worth expanding.

Recollections of a Cuillin Ridge Traverse, 1991

This short account is as accurate as the intervening 31 years will allow, correct in overview if not in every detail.

This wasn't our first time in the Cuillin. It had been a long term plan to investigate the ridges more interesting portions before our attempt. This began in 1986, 3 months after Chris was born. We stayed for a week in a cottage which was part of the famous…..though we didn't know it….Glen Brittle house.

On this first trip we managed via An Dorus, Sgurr a' Mhadaidh, Sgurr a'Ghreadaidh, Sgurr n'a Banachdich & Sgurr Thormade. On our second outing Sgurr Alasdair via Sgurr Sgumain and off by the Great Stone Chute & Coir Lagan. The second visit was in 1988, which was very wet. We managed Sgurr Nan Gillian via the 'tourist route'. Then later: Am Basteir, Sgurr a Fhionn Choire, Bruach na Frithe and off via Sgurr a Bhastier. In 1990 we were back again for two big days, first: Sgurr Dearg Beag, The In Pin(Sgurr Dearg), Sgurr Mhic Choinnich and Collie's ledge, Sgurr Thearlaich, Sgurr Alasdair and down Via the ' bad step', Sgurr Sgumain & it's Stone Chute. The second day took in Coir a' Ghrunnda, Sgurr Nan Eag, Sgurr Dubh na da Bheinn, Sgurr Dubh Mor and down again via Sgurr Sgumain & it's Stone Chute. We were missing a small section N. of Sgurr a' Mhadaidh but felt we had at least seen most of the obstacles.

So, we set off in good weather on the afternoon of 28th May, from Glen Brittle, well prepared and confident, so long as the weather held. We would assess each obstacle as it arrived and decide to attack it or circumvent it.. as it turned out, in most cases, we elected to make best progress by avoiding them. Perhaps not a purist travers, but a travers non the less! Walking S. along the coast round to the entrance to Coir a' Ghrunnda. We had reasonably large packs, containing not only cold & wet weather gear but also minimal cooking equipment, food for a full 24hrs, gear of sleeping: bag, bivvy bag and mat as well as helmet, harness, rope, slings, crabs, belay device and a few pieces of climbing 'protection'. We hoped to fill up with water in the Coir above and take it onto the ridge.

Looking South along the ridge from near our bivvy

The path into the Coir involves a few scrambles and then steep scree onto the ridge to the N. of An Casteal a G-c. We ditched our packs at that point, as we intended to get the southern peaks done, and return, before our bivvy for the night. The first problem, An Casteal a G-c looked formidable and we sneaked round it to gain it easily from the S. Then onward and upward over our first Monro, Sgurr Nan Eig and onto Sgurr a Choire Bhig and Gars-Bheinn. This, only to turn around and start our ridge travers for real, taking all four tops again before regaining our packs and taking them up to bivvy among the summit rocks of Sgurr Duhb na Da Bheinn as the light dimmed.

We found a spot sheltered from the wind, in a ring of stones built by others. Here we cooked and made ourselves as comfortable as possible. The weather was kind and the night clear and not too cold. We chatted and watched as sunset dissolved into the darkness of the Black Cuillin all around. This first bit of the travers took us only about 2hrs.

Sunset from the bivvy, looking North, Sgurr Alasdair far left.

Morning dawned early, bright and set fair, we were in for a warm travers. After a brew and breakfast we loaded up and by 06:00 we're heading off towards the famous T-D gap. Here someone has taken a chunk out of the ridge and an abseil is required, followed by a climb out at V. Diff. on the other side. Neither of us was keen on the climb and it looked steeper and more polished from below…..what to do? I reckoned we could head down the S. side of the gap and skirt round the head of the Coir and climb up towards the 'bad step' between Sgumain and Alasdair. We had climbed between these two the year before, so would be on familiar ground. We avoided the 'bad step' via a loose corner on the right and were soon over it and up onto Alasdair.

From there it was down, delicately into the top of the Great Stone Chute and steeply up onto Sgurr Thearlaich. From there the ridge falls to the col between Thearlaich and Sgurr Mhic Choinnich. This gives a direct ascent via a quite long and verticale Kings Chimney or round via Collie's ledge, which we knew from an earlier visit. Neither of us fancied it, so it was round the corner onto the ledge followed by a there and back to the summit of Mhic Choinnich.

The ridge descends from there along the crags of Coireachan Ruadha until it begins to climb again towards An Stac, Sgurr Dearg and it's 'In Pin'. We were sat at the lowest point when a small group passed, including a girl who had been in my form at school, some 20 yrs ago. " Hello Anne, what are you doing here?" "Woh! Hi, a travers attempt, and you? I didn't know you did this sort of thing!" "Same thing, a travers attempt. I didn't know you mountaineered either."….. we chatted for a while and she was on her way, I never saw her again. A few years later I was to hear that she died as a result of a climbing fall, somewhere in Scotland.

Next came the In Pin - here viewed from near Sgurr Mhic Choinnich – with few people on it, it went quickly and we were into the up and down of the middle part of the ridge. Much of which was to some extent familiar. Sgurr na Banachdich, Sgurr Thormaid, Sgurr a Ghreadaidh and then via An Dorus to the four tops of Sgurr a Mhadaidh. On leaving Mhadaidh the route takes a right angle to the E. with a descent and no way on except a steep wall. This was new to us and I led the wall, not knowing if we would need to down climb. However there were some signs of a route above. We stopped in some shade to look at Bidein Druim nan Ramh…..it was hot and our water was low.

We decided to skirt the top on the W. flank, staying as high as we could, to rejoin the ridge beyond and climb up to Sgurr na Bhairnich and the familiar top of Bruach na Frithe. We looked at Naismith's route onto the Tooth, but it seemed too late in the trip to attempt something of that sort. So we headed onto Sgurr a Fiona Choire then ducked below the crags of Am Basteir to arrive at the Coll between it and Gillean.

There was no question of missing Am Basteir summit, so dumping our loads we returned west along its ridge to the top and back. Once again we left our sacks, free climbing Nicholson's Chimney to arrive on the summit of Sgurr Nan Gillean at around 16:00. Ten hours from our bivvy.

This next bit I wrote earlier, as part of my mountaineering chapter.

I was stood on the top, looking a bit sweaty when an old guy approached me. "Look at you, young lad, up here looking knackered...... and with no kit! Where have you come from today?" I pointed to Gars Bheinn on the other end of the ridge. "There, 6 this morning, my sack is in the bealach below!"........"Oh!" He retorted rather embarrassed, and slid away.

The descent to Sligachan went well, back via the col to collect our sacks, in just 2hrs. A celebratory beer in the bar of the hotel, followed by several Dalwinnie's in the bar near where we were staying in Dunvegan.

Looking back along the ridge to Am Basteir and Sgurr a Fiona Choire, from Sgurr nan Gillean

We started from Glen Brittle at 16:30, arriving in Sligachan at 18:00 the next day. The ridge is 12km from end to end and has approximately 3000m of up and down between those ends. There is a further 900m of ascent to get onto it and 8km from Glen Brittle. At the end Sligachan and the car are about 5km and 900m below the summit of Gillean. This adds up to a massive 4000m of ascent and descent over 25km. The ridge, end to end, took us 12 hours (2+10, to be honest a good time, the average for a travers being 16-20 hrs), the walk in and onto Gars-Bheinn was about 4 hrs and coming down 2 hrs......to be fair not a ' classic travers', but one that suited us..........that is a lot and looking at the figures I'm amazed we made it.

**Upper Wharfedale Fell Rescue Association
Mountain and Cave Rescue.**

I joined UWFRA in 1989 after a conversation with Tony Dean at the Allerton Grange H.S. leavers ball in Roundhay Park. In those days, if you were accepted by the committee you went straight onto the bottom of the 'surface' callout list as a probationary member, attended practices and hoped you may get called out. As there was no interview, pre-probation and no personal skills test, it really meant that you needed to know someone on the committee. I was accepted on 20th Sept. UWFRA is one of only three rescue teams in the UK which is both an MRT (Mountain Rescue Team) and CRT(Cave Rescue Team).

The Fell Rescue 'Hut' in Grassington.

To my credit my personal skills were improving all the time. I had recorded over 100 outdoor days and 350 peaks and high places in various mountainous areas of the U.K. The rock climbing I had been doing made me confident on steep ground, abseiling and with ropes and belays. All they had to do was to teach me the skills and techniques for the specialised kit of mountain rescue.

On my first practice, a month after joining, I got a ride in a RAF Sea King rescue helicopter...... sometimes called a 'Paraffin Budgie' due to its bright yellow colour and smell.

A view over the winch man's shoulder, from my seat in the Sea King. This was over Great Whernside.

There were other practices and I got to know some of the other lads in the team, but no call outs for me! Early in '90 I decided to do the Welsh St.Johns mountain first aid, run by Bewerley Park. This was a 'hands on', anything can happen, lots of scenarios affair. I did very well in the examination and the experience held me in good stead for the future. I also met 'Cokie' Van Der Veld, an outdoor pursuits instructor, from whom I would learn some local caving.

My Very Own Rescue

Some of the lads from the rescue team helped out at the farm owned by the Daggetts in Burnsal. Jeremy Daggett was the President of UWFRA and his son Michael was the team mechanic. They asked me if I fancied a night of haymaking, which sounded fun and was to become a regular summer exercise. Their old hay-baler made large oblong bales which had to be loaded by hand and pitch-forked onto a trailer and moved into the barns, then unloaded and stacked. This started around four and we would work until it was too dark to see. Then back to the farm for haymaking supper made by Margaret. I had come straight from SCS that first summer and set off alone, back home. Along the road to Bolton abbey I was flagged down by some teenagers in a couple of cars. Their mate, who was drunk, had jumped over a wall for a pee. The trouble was that it was a bridge and he fell about 10 metres into a small stream. They were just looking over the wall and no one had dared to go down!

A second car arrived in the other direction and I asked the guy to go ring an ambulance. Car phones were very uncommon. I expected Pete Miller and Pete Dransfield, two senior UWFRA members, to be along soon, going home in the same direction. I also recognised that we would need some kit to get the casualty out of the ravine. So grabbing my call out rucksack and leaving the 'kids' on the road I went down to investigate. The lad was semiconscious with a beer can in a hand with an obviously broken wrist, and partly in the stream. I didn't want to move him, in case of back or neck injuries, so started my examination. I was amazed at how all the stuff I had learned, along with not a little adrenaline, kicked in. I was part way through when Pete & Pete arrived. I asked one to go back to the farm and start a callout and the other to descend. Pete Miller went back and 'Dranny' came down. I finished my examination and we decided to lift the casualty onto the bank and wrap him in some sleeping bags, which came floating down from the kids above.

While Pete dealt with his wrist I went up to brief the Paramedics who had arrived in the Ambulance. We agreed that more people and some specialist kit was needed and they were very pleased when I told them that UWFRA was already on the way. I helped one Paramedic to the casualty and the Rescue landrover arrived. We got the casualty onto a stretcher and used ropes to haul him up the ravine side and into the ambulance.

Driving the Landrover on a bit of an incline. I have the distinction of being one of the few people to crash on a 'blue light' call. I hit some ice as the car in front braked and glanced a car coming in the other direction, taking off its front wheel! Fortunately nobody was injured, but it was a while until I got to drive again.

From then on I often got callouts, both to surface events and assisting on the surface with underground rescues. These included many searches and the occasional 'snatch and grab', getting in and out to pick up a casualty for the air ambulance or paramedics.

By mid '90 I had started caving, a few times with Cokie and some trips with Pete Dransfield who had a Cave Instructors Certificate. I also joined Cottingley Caving Club(CCC), which was largely UWFRA members and was run by team member Mick Balmer. I taught myself Single Rope Technique(SRT) from a book, using the beams in my garage. My first trip using SRT was in Lost John's Cave, which has 'Centipede', a 100 foot pitch. Unfortunately my trips with Cokie caused problems with Ruth, unfound I might add, so these had to stop!

Going underground

I was also going underground with UWFRA on practices. After a few Ian Watson or 'Watto' asked me why I wasn't on the underground call out list. I told him I wasn't really a caver, but he put me on the list anyhow! I had been to a few underground callouts, working on the surface using the 'mole phone' to communicate underground. However, my first full callout, of quite a few, came on 10th. March '92, an evening that a few of us were having a hut night. It was for two cavers, well overdue. Their car had been found near two caves, one of which was Sleets Gill.
Four of us went up in a team landrover to examine the two caves.

Hauling on a rescue practice, possibly in New Goyden Pot.

I went with Julian Griffith to Sleets Gill. This is a large cave like entrance which descends via a steepish slope to a more horizontal crawl and then a good length of walking passage. When we got to the bottom of the slope, we met water blocking the crawl. On the way back out I found a small tackle bag containing some Mars bars and car keys..........we knew where the cavers were!

This was going to be a big callout! Cave divers from all across the north of England would be needed and lots of manpower for a recovery which may be very slow. I was sent back up to the cave to monitor the water level, while things were organised. I don't know how long I was down there, maybe three hours or so, but I did find that I could use my radio to communicate with the landrover down on the road. The water went down about a meter in that time. By the time I re-surfaced the cave entrance was ablaze with lights and activity.

Roy and Les entering Sleets Gill Cave for the reconstruction of their rescue. Also found on You Tube as 'Hard Decisions at Sleets Gill, by Sid Perou.......can you spot me in the video?

I was taken back to the hut to get warm and have some food, then returned to join in the underground effort. On descending I found that the crawl was now out of the water and the drop into the mainstream passage had two divers heading into it. They found the two cavers sat towards the end of the passage, fit and well. However, the weather forecast was for more heavy rain later that day, which may flood the cave to the roof. Food was sent to the 'casualties' as was diving equipment. The team were going to teach them to dive and then dive them out. In the meantime we were ferrying diving bottles of oxygen to the water entrance.

By daybreak the first 'casualty' was out, closely followed by the second. There were television cameras and reporters at the entrance when we finally all got out. One of the 'casualties' was a Producer for Tyne-Tees TV and the team helped him reconstruct the rescue for a documentary, 'No Pick-nick at Sleets Gill' I had a small part, in the wrong place!

In the early '90's there were quite a few underground callouts. Mostly getting me out of bed on a Saturday night. I became an active member, often going in the backup team with drinks, food or to set up and use the Molephone.

*Recognise those legs? It is my turn to go get a sheep from down a hole!
The tripod, built with scaffolding poles and joints allows a straight hang in a hole with 'dubious' sidewalls.
Then you chase the sheep round the hole with a net, attach it to your waist and get hauled out!*

Many of the callouts were for what is called the Dowbergill Passage. This is a 1km piece of passage linking Dow Cave to Providence Pot, beneath Great Whernside. It is a classic of northern caving trips, and was in those days the most called out cave in the country. Occasionally I would be pushed up to the 'sharp end'. In Dowbergill we usually didn't know where the casualties would be, it is a 20m high vertical maze. So teams would go in from both ends. On one such trip I was going in from the Dow Cave end, as part of the first group. We found the group who were still some way into the cave, but with no light. I think there were five, with one girl who seemed quite hypothermic. The problem in Dowbergill is that manoeuvring a stretcher is difficult and very time consuming. The route goes up and down, with only width for someone back and front. If a casualty can walk assisted, that is by far the best way to get them out. We put the girl into a harness/jacket with lots of handles. I held her from the front, walking backwards, while someone else held her from the back. At one point we had to crawl through a tunnel half filled with water.......for this she went on my back! Up and down ladders, through waist deep water, we eventually got her to the main Dow Cave tunnel and put her on the waiting stretcher. I learned a couple of days later that she had arrived at hospital with a core temperature of not much more than 30 Celsius, but made a full recovery.

From about 1992 I was elected to assistant secretary of the UWFRA committee and in 1998 I became an assistant surface leader. There I became responsible for aspects of surface rescues and very occasionally running one at the 'sharp end'. One such was in Buckden Gill. An oldish chap had fallen some distance and it looked as if he may have ruptured his spleen, as he was showing signs of medical shock. He was in an awkward position on a steep slope. We roped up a stretcher while the Paramedic pumped him full of liquids. It became obvious that the situation was critical, so I called for an RAF Rescue helicopter. This was in the days before there was an Air Ambulance. Unfortunately, despite our best efforts the casualty stopped breathing just as the helicopter arrived. We all had a go at cardiac massage, but eventually we handed him over to the helicopter team. He was dead on arrival at Airedale hospital.

Thinking of helicopters. We had a fallen climber on Embay Moor and the Paramedics needed him lifted to the hospital. Unfortunately the RAF were busy, but we got the Police Helicopter instead. To get our stretcher in, along with the doctor they had brought, both the Observer and his seat needed to come out. The Observer was wearing unsuitable 'Doc Martins', totally useless on wet steep grass and mud. So I ended up carrying a helicopter seat off the Moor!

A couple more short stories. I was called out to Kettlewell from school for a "long stretcher carry". I arrived by the bridge to find an empty landrover and one of the Paramedics from Grassington in his Ambulance. He told me it was a school secretary on a primary school walk who had died of a heart attack by the river. Steve, the other Paramedic was there as were 6 team members and a stretcher. I said I would walk along and see if I could help with the carry back to the Ambulance. I met the group heading back and asked if I anyone needed to swap. Someone on the front said yes and we changed over. The body was in a body bag, but the head was wrapped in a towel! Strange, but not wishing to look foolish I said nothing. It was a bit surreal having this nodding head rock about next to me, but hey it's UWFRA! Arriving back we put the stretcher down next to the Ambulance........the towel/head rolled off the end with a thud. Steve rushed to pick it up and shoved it quickly under the Ambulance seat. "WTF" I exclaimed, what is that? "Shhhh!" Steve exclaimed, "It's a walling stone I've pinched for my garden!"

In 2002 I received the Queens Golden Jubilee Medal, for those with more than 5 years serving in the forces, police, and rescue services.

My Medal, presented by the Lord Lieutenant of North Yorkshire

Last one, or two, honest! We picked up a body somewhere on the moor above Patley Bridge. It was dark and raining, and several of us would need to walk back for the stretcher to fit in the Landrover. So rather than walk, we put the stretcher and corps on the roof and climbed inside the cab. Fortunately the guys at the Ambulance saw our lights coming down the hillside and someone must have guessed what we had done. A call came in, "Just to let you know the press and some family are here". As we drove just out of sight, we put the stretcher in the back and some of us paraded slowly behind the 'hearse'.

My saddest times were always fatalities. Early in my time with UWFRA we were searching for a suicidal man in his early 20 who had an impending jail sentence coming up. My small group found him hanging from a high tree above the Kilnsey road. Beautiful view, beautiful hangman's knot. It is very surreal eating your lunch with a body swinging in the light breeze in your peripheral vision. Once out of the tree, We put the stretcher on the wall by the road, waiting for the hearse, but we found it was disturbing the traffic! On another occasion we were asked by the police to look for a family camping, after retrieving the body of a dead mountain biker near Kinsey Crag. He had broken his neck going over the handlebars. I went with Ken Robinson, one of the team's Controllers, and the soundest of MR colleagues. We found his family: wife, two small children and grandparents, in a static caravan.

We had been told by the Paramedics just to say that he had been taken to Airedale hospital after a serious accident, and that they should travel there at once. This we did, but I think they had an idea that the news was not going to get better! The third which is clear in my mind is the recovery of two soldiers from Howstein Gorge. They had been floating down the river, 'gorge running' after a flood, and been caught and held underwater, by a fallen tree which was trapped across the river. I belayed another team member while he went to cut the tree branches so we could haul them out.

Have I ever been scared on a rescue, no is the simple answer. However, I have been sort of stuck in a cave, on a trip with the CCC, which did scare me. We went to look at Aven Entrance to Meregill Pot on the Ribblehead side of Ingleborough. The wet entrance was flooded and the dry entrance is a crawl of about 2m, followed by a right angled bend, then flat out to a pitch head after a further 3m. I was last in, got around the corner, then couldn't get through the tight section to the pitch head. I shouted to the others to go on, I would meet them back at the car in 5hrs or so. Trouble was, I struggled to reverse around the tight corner, as I was fairly flat out and couldn't see where my feet were going. After a minute or two of panic, worrying that the others couldn't get out past me, I calmed down. If you panic in a situation like that you could be there the rest of your days! Eventually I ran the process of crawling into the tunnel through my mind, how did I get round the corner? I replayed it in reverse, and much to my relief I was out.........did I mention I am a bit claustrophobic even now when I think about it and I have woken up sweating about it on more than one occasion.......mild PTSD?

In wellies and wet socks, sandwiches in my pocket and no map, I then went on to pass the time by climbing Ingleborough in the mist. This went OK until the descent towards Ribblehead. I finally came out of the mist towards a familiar sight, Alum Pot, on the wrong side of the hill......oops. My feet were in a right state when I finally got back to the car, narrowly avoiding two ignominious ends in one day.

I have had one other near miss caving. I can't remember the pot, but the passage to one pitch was a tight vertical squeeze through, followed by a very small stance and a reach into space over a 20m drop. I needed to take off my descender and put it on a gear loop at the side to squeeze through. Through the squeeze I put in a bolt and attached a 'cows tails'; a short rope with a karabiner ('crab'). I then swung out and screwed in two more bolts and attached the static descent rope, attaching my second cows tail to the Y-hanging rope. I attached my descender to the main rope and swung out fully over the pitch. I untied my cows tails and slowly lowered my weight onto the descender and.........'pop'! It had still been attached to the gear loop....rookie mistake. I was dangling 20m up on my arms. I managed to get one foot on the stance to the side and attach a cows tail. Then put my descender on the main 'maillon' and made an elegant descent. They say you learn from your mistakes......if you live through them! It works, I haven't made another 'rigging' error since.

I also did some TV work with UWFRA, usually behind the scenes. My first was when 'Watto' the Underground Leader asked me if I was free to carry some kit into Dow Cave. This ended up helping the Cameraman for a Children's TV show, film an interview with Watto about Caving. I got to carry the camera down to the far end of Dow Cave. We also did two sessions for Emmerdale Farm in 1997. One was helping actors get to an awkward place to do a sort of river rescue, but the second was to provide men and an ambulance for a Search and Rescue scene. I got on screen for this one, just sneaking into shot!

We also supported a period drama, being shot at night on Ilkley Moor. My job was to take care of the leading lady. We were introduced and she was a little frosty. After her first scene on the moor she came back to warm up in my Landrover, Fell 2. I had coffee, snacks and the heaters on. She opened the door and looked up, "I can't get in there, I'm wearing a full corset. I will need help!" I dutifully went round to help her, being a bit shy as to what I was going to do. "Just grab my arse and haul me in........
I'm fucking dying from the cold!" she instructed me. The ice was broken.

As I said earlier I also got on screen in the documentary 'No Picnic at Sleets Gill'. Sat by the side of our Underground Controller, Harry Long. In the real rescue I was actually in the cave at the time we got both casualties out.

With Harry Long in the UWFRA control room during the filming for the documentary 'No Picnic at Sleets Gill'. Re-edited and available on You Tube as 'Hard Decisions at Sleets Gill'

However, by 2000 my personal life and the rescue team had been entwined, as Ruth had joined the team with the help of Tony Dean. Our split up made callouts more difficult and my involvement in the team became less frequent. I had few callouts up to 2008, when Candy and I left for Qatar. I finally resigned from UWFRA in 2014, after 25 years as a member. It had brought some real excitement into my life, and sometimes an excuse to leave school in the middle of a lesson. It gave me patience and endurance, sitting for hours on end soaked to the skin and in a cold draft on 'gypsum travers', waiting for something to happen. I enjoyed the camaraderie, such as four of us sharing one pair of glasses to map read on a night search. Many days and nights practicing with the team, organising practices and other times in the Hut just maintaining the equipment. Sometimes a sense of a job, which could end up helping the injured and saving lives, well done. It also brought close up the sad experience of death a number of times, sometimes by accident, sometimes by suicide.

Fund Raising

Two other times of year also come to mind, in later years, when Chris and Al were a bit older they became family days. The yearly fund raising efforts:

The Game Show at Broughton Hall was an annual event organised between UWFRA and CRO. We used the main grounds, in front of Broughton Hall, near Skipton. There was a hunting, shooting, fishing, farming and crafts theme, with several hundred stalls. Clay Pigeon shooting and a 'Main Ring' with events running all through the day. It was an enormous undertaking and took several evenings and weekends to set up.......then the same to clear up afterwards. I spent many years working on the 'back gate', with Pete Dransfield. This was the entry point for the Stall Holders and parking for disabled traffic and those from the teams working at the show. We also took people who walked from local villages/parking. The mornings were very hectic, directing stall holders to their allocated plots, but things were more relaxed as the afternoon went on. As Chris and Al got older they would help out, running errands and working on the gates.

I remember Alasdair, aged about 10, in one of the Landrovers. It was driven by a new member, a bit of a know it all........now a Controller! It was struggling to get up a grassy bank pulling a heavy trailer. Al leaned across and said it would be easier if you put it into the 'Low box' with 'Diff. Lock'. The guy was much embarrassed as the Landrover then easily glided up the slope.

Dickensian Christmas weekends in Grassington Village was also a family affair. The Fell Rescue Hut would be opened to visitors for three weekends prior to Christmas. Tea and cake was served in the hut, tours were given. I was usually to be found in the kitchen caravan used on long call outs, serving bacon/egg butties and hot soup outside the gate. Playing my annoying Christmas pop CDs. Once again the whole family became involved. It was no surprise that when Chris became 18 he signed on as part of the surface rescue team, which he continued for something like 10 years. He qualified as a Swift-water Rescue Technician and became an Assistant Surface Leader, responsible for River Rescues.

Al was never so keen, though after his apprenticeship with Caterpillar he did work on the Dagget's farm for a number of years. It was also through UWFRA that all four of us got into the yearly 'Hay Making' at the Dagget's farm outlined above. At first it was just me, a night of moving bales onto a trailer and then off, into a barn. Followed by a supper. Then as the lads got more useful Ruth and Chris could carry bales while Al, at no more than 6, would drive the enormous modern tractor around the field. Showing a passion for vehicles which he still has.

Caves and Caving

As I have said, I have never considered myself to be a caver, but I have done a bit of caving over the years, in fact some 90 caves. In the early days I caved with a few of the lads from UWFRA and some evenings with Pete Dransfield. I didn't keep the same sort of log for caves as I did for mountains and it sort of drifts off around the mid-90s. However a list of caves, all in the North of England is possible.......if not very interesting (Appendix 11)

Moving East: Qatar, China and Singapore

It was late in 2006 or early in 2007 that Candy had an epiphany. She came home from school saying that she was going to be 60 in August and that she had had enough of teaching at SCS. She could retire on her pension and looked at doing a Masters Degree in pottery. That was fine for her, but I was only 51, and I wasn't going to get up each morning and keep going to school! Tesco was an option, but I could earn more from 2 1/2 days teaching than a full week at Tesco's.

By mid 2007 our mind moved towards some adventures, towards the end of our lives as we both had the urge to see the world. Candy's 'children' were all settled and in their 30s, Alasdair was 18 and Chris 21 and both were working. We felt for us it was now or never! We first looked at Voluntary Work Overseas(VSO), but they seemed only to want electricians, plumbers, builders and joiners. This made me think of looking at the International School section of the Times Educational Supplement(TES). I also went with Candy to an International School recruitment in London, with no success. Later I found what looked like a couple of interesting jobs in a place called Qatar, in the Persian/Arabian Gulf.

The first interview was for Doha Academy, which I didn't get. The Head gave me a excellent de-brief, but he had managed to secure a teaching couple and said it would not be long before I got a job. My next was for The Newton School, a new school as Head of Science. This must have been just before the May Bank Holiday, as I got the job confirmation at a cyber-cafe (a place to access the Internet, before Smartphones) on the Isle of Skye. It was for January 2008, as I had booked to go to Nepal in that November.

We left SCS in July of 2007, Candy had done 26 years there and I had done 28. I remember no sadness at leaving, just an overwhelming sense of relief that I had made it through in one piece. I felt that I owed them nothing, in fact it was more the other way round. The biggest insult was to be charged for a ticket for our own 'retirement' do. Evidently as there were too many long term staff leaving at the same time? Between us, our retirement gift was enough money to buy a decent Laptop computer for our travels.

In preparation for leaving the UK I had sold my house in Wilmot Road. I made quite a nice profit from the sale so we started to look for a 'home' in France. I will give more details about this in Chapter 14, enough to say we had found something suitable by the end of 2007. We decided to rent out Wellington Road and move all our possessions to the new French house, for our duration in Qatar.

I wrote about the Nepal trip in Chapter 11, it was not exactly a turning point in our lives, but it did change our plans.....for the better! We had been on the trail for several days when I found a cyber-cafe to look at my e-mails. The first I opened was from the Principle at the Newton School: "Don't come here! I have been suspended! It's a complete mess...........by the way, I hope you don't mind but I have passed your details to another Head I know and he is very interested!"

The second e-mail was from Bill Turner, Secondary Head of Al Khor International School, also in Qatar. He said he had spoken to Candy on the phone and would like to offer us BOTH jobs! ......who? what? where? why? how? .... The last mail was from Candy who had taken a mystery phone call from Bill, having no idea about the first e-mail. She, after a short chat, had accepted Bill's offer. In under 20 minutes: I had a job in Qatar, I didn't have a job in Qatar, I had another job in Qatar, Candy had a job too......... and I hadn't done anything!

Later we would have a short interview with the Head of Science, Kevin Davis. This took place in the living room of a friends of his in Morley, a strange venue. He was a nice guy and we got along very well. We started in January 2008!

Furniture was put into storage at the end 2007 and we spent the last few days in Wellington Road sleeping on the floor on an old mattress. We drove to Bea's in Candy's little Peugeot, having already left the Freelander in France. From there it was on to Heathrow and finally, at about 06:00 we landed in Doha, after an 8hr flight. Getting off the plane was amazing. It felt like the engines had overheated as we stepped out in 30 degrees of heat.

We were met at the airport by the Secondary Deputy Head, Bradley Roberts, a white South African. He drove us out of the city up the desert road we would come to know well. There were camels on the desert, which wasn't sand, more like builders yard rubble. Al Khor town

(Al Khawr) looked more like a scene from an Indian movie, with hundreds of scruffy men moving around the Main Street. We were to find that these were the unskilled labour, mostly Nepali and Indian who lived in camps and worked around the oil fields.

Location and extent of Qatar (dark green) on the Arabian Peninsula.

Al Khor (Al Khawr) is on the coast north of the capital, Doha

Through the town took us past a large new hospital and into the modern walled Al Khor Community, sat surrounded by desert, housing about 4 000 people. It had security on the gate and we had to be checked in. We were taken to our flat, it was half of the second floor of a block of four, C87, and we thought it was huge: master bedroom with en-suite, two other bedrooms, main bathroom, laundry room, large kitchen, living room with adjoining dining area.

Al Khor Community, a walled community north of Al Kohr, surrounded by desert of the 'builders yard' type.

I can remember Kevin arriving with some cans of beer at about 10:00 and taking us down for a look at the school. We met a number of members of staff, including Kevin's wife, Lucy.

Al Kohr International School, British Stream(AKIS BS) was a 4-18yrs fee paying co-educational school, with some 800 students in the secondary school. It was mainly staffed by white Brits, Australians, New Zealanders and South Africans and its first language was English. Its buildings were nowhere more than 8 years old and it had a huge 'capitation' grant. The school was owed and run jointly by RasGas and Qatargas for its employee's children, 95% of whom were Asian and Muslim.

The Community had small D apartments, larger C apartments, B villas, and A villas for gas company top brass! These were allocated on status, size of family and to some extent how long you had been there. Senior staff and those who had been there from the start had large B Villas with maids quarters, we like most teaching couples had a large C Apartment.

Everyone, including the students were very friendly and helpful. We were give 'buddies', Brett & Julie Young to help us get accustomed to life and bureaucracy in Qatar. They were a teaching couple from the Bristol area, about our age, who had been there for a year. Brett was a Geography teacher and Head of Sixth Form, Julie was Head of Special needs and would be Candy's boss. We have stayed friends and they have visited us here in France.

AKIS BS, Secondary School entrance.

The school started at 7:00 and originally finished at 13:00 (later 13:30), with only breaks and no lunch. The difference between teaching here and in the UK was, for me, the students! Discipline was, usually, not an issue and the vast majority of students saw it as their duty to learn as best they could. As an example one sixth form student, from Pakistan said to me, when I asked if he was going home for the summer, "No, it's horrible there! I'm going to stay here and study, so I can go to University in the US or UK and never have to go back". The students were also friendly and would come and talk to you as you moved around the community.

With subsidised food from the three restaurants/take-aways life was not expensive in Qatar, if you stayed on the community. We insisted on the waiters calling us Paul & Candy, but the best we could get was 'Sir Paul' and 'Ma'm Candy'. We were paid quite well, not as well as the UK but we paid no tax on what we earned. As the flat was free, including electricity for cooking/air conditioning and our medical was free our outgoings were minimal. On average we saved one full salary per month. We would treat ourselves to rides down into Doha most weekends to visit the shopping malls. Our favourites were City Centre, Landmark and the one and only Villaggio. Il had famous outlets, restaurants, cafes and cinemas, but Villaggio had a canal with electric gondola rides running through its centre! The money enabled us to have several good holidays and also pay for our family members to visit. At some time over the, nearly, three years we entertained Chris, Al and his girlfriend Kelly, Bea, Ewa, Roo, Brigid and John and Paul and Vic.......some were lucky and came twice! It was unfortunate that Charlotte was never able to make it, but she was pregnant or had very small babies the whole time we were there!

Qatar was both old, with traditional culture and also exceedingly modern and hot(35-45 degrees). We had many trips to deserted habitation, but most Qataris live in modern luxury. There was a never ending supply of 'dodgy pirate videos' to entertain, as well as cinemas in Doha so cold with the 'air-con' that a blanket was needed. Some of our time was spent by the pool in the Waha Club in the community. It had its own cafe/restaurant. Then there was the indoor Cafe de Paris which had the most wonderful looking, but quite inedible cakes! The Batile bakers in town was the place for the best chocolate cake I've ever tasted. The Ex-pats on the community were always friendly and we were often invited to parties.

Graham Ogden, my ex lab technician from SCS had come for a weeks visit and asked me to look out for a job for him. The IT was in quite a mess, being run mostly by a teacher. So I dropped the idea with several staff, including Lyal the Principal, of appointing a Systems Manager. In a follow up conversation he asked me if I had anyone in mind..........of course I did. We fitted Graham up with a job and later a wife, leading to a life in New Zealand! We had a similar incident with Paul and Vic. They came on a visit and liked what they saw. We introduced them to Jarlath Madine, the Primary Head, and he spoke to them about working at the school. He offered them jobs for the following year, which they accepted, staying for 9yrs.

There were sports as well. I played Squash with Graham on many Friday mornings at the Nakeel Club, very close to our apartment. The weekends in Qatar are Friday and Saturday! Candy played sometimes and we also played some tennis, but in the end we found that we preferred badminton. There was also staff 5-a-side football on Thursday afternoon, when school finished for the week. The Nakeel also had a gym, but I preferred the large gym in the Waha, down the road. There was also touch rugby each week, organised by the PE staff from school. This was a co-ed event with some of the female staff taking part. With the arrival of Lyal French-Wright, a Kiwi, as Principal and Coach the idea of a club was floated and Al Khor Amateurs R.F.C. was born........I was always the oldest player!

You will have seen my 'founders' shirt in Chapter 10. I had learned to dive on Rhodes a few years before, and Al Khor had a 'Dive Club'. Candy did her PADI Open Water and I did a refresher. We had a few trips, usually a weekend camping on the coast, but Qatar is much the same under water as on the surface. To make it more interesting they have sunk old toilets, slides, and even an Ambassador's car to attract fish. They do have some dinner plate sized Blackfin Butterflyfish. These fish would come and eat bananas from your hand. They also liked to try and eat my mask, as it had a yellow frame. Unfortunately the cheap and easily available food outweighs the exercise and putting on the 'Qatar Stone' is more under statement than illusion!

Our other favourite recreation was to take the Pathfinder out of the compound and drive across the desert to Al Khor or Purple Island .

Al Khor Island, we camped on the far side of the Jebel (the naughty Jebel!) a number of times with International Award kids.

This was connected to the mainland by a roadway which had been destroyed in a couple of places so that vehicles were not allowed. We could park and walk.....sometimes wade.....onto this island, which in those days was inevitably deserted. We would sit on tiny seats and listen to Podcasts.......particularly The New's Quiz with Sandi Toxvig, which was our way of catching up on news from home!

Finally a couple more tales of bureaucracy. There are about 300 000 Qataris, with 1.5 million ex-pats. Qatar is very rich due to the natural gas. Even young Qataris are encouraged to work. Often there will be a Qatari in charge in government and quasi government businesses, but some skilled Indians actually running things. It was my ill luck at Q-Tel, the telecommunications firm, to be served by a Qatari. I had a problem with the Internet connection at home and was explaining when he got up, said "excuse me" and left. After a few minutes I asked another attendant what had happened......"Its 12 o'clock, he has gone for his lunch!" At several shops in Qatar the locals would drive up and sound the horn. A shop worker would come out and take their order......the original drive through.

Though the large hotels in Doha sold alcohol, there was only one shop to buy alcohol in the whole country, we called this the 'Booze Souk'. For this you needed to provide them with a statement from your employer, including your earnings. You were then issued with a 'licence' at a refundable cost of about £150. This limited your monthly spending according to your earnings, I believe it was 10%. Only those with a certain level of income were allowed a licence........or for that matter to bring their wives and families into the country.

The International Award

We both really enjoyed the teaching and the kids. Lucy and Kevin were wanting to start a Duke of Edinburgh's Award, called The International Award, and Candy and I were keen to get involved. The great thing was that we managed to get 23 kids from 18 countries from Bronze to Gold in three years! I was asked to buy some kit for the kids to borrow/hire, as sourcing outdoor kit is not easy in Qatar. I asked how much I could spend and Lucy just said "Order what you think we might need and let's see how it goes!" No joke, I ordered £10 000 worth of the best kit I could find: tents, rucksacks, stoves, sleeping bags, compasses, GPSs, First Aid kits.......for 30 people plus staff!......the order went through, with a grant from the gas companies, no questions asked!

The other great thing was maps. There are no walking maps for Qatar, so Kevin and I we went to the Qatar equivalent of the Ordinance Survey, in Doha. We met an Indian chap who asked us what we wanted: area, scale, contours(colour and spacing), roads, buildings, electric pylons etc. All of which he put up on screen for us. We asked for 10 copies on water resistant paper. He sent us away for a coffee and had them ready for us in less than an hour. Brilliant! We repeated this every time we used another area in Qatar.

For each expedition Kevin and I would spend a day driving the area, searching out routes and campsites and working out logistics for water drops and checkpoints. Sometimes we would make it a family trip and camp out......our first experiences in desert camping......often finding a place close to the sea, the Persian Gulf. Barbecue was usually the order of the day, with a big driftwood fire, eased down with G&T or beers. A couple of the guys also had motorboats we were invited to play on. We had some great trips in the confines of this little spit of a country. Al Khor Island, mentioned earlier, was used for our first overnight expedition with the IA, and every following first expedition. Very few people visited the Island and the kids could see 'home' from a nearby Jebel. Another aside: we had an incident between two of our first cohort, resulting in them having a food fight. I sent them each to sit on a Jebel top in the dark to think about their behaviour. This became known as 'being sent to sit on the naughty Jebel'.

Camping on the Zecreet Peninsula (Internet photo). We used this for Silver Award IA.

Because many of the girls were Muslim we had to always camp close to the groups, between the boys and girls! This was good because each time a group went out we got to camp out too.......these were very social affairs. Apart from IA we would also go and camp as a group of teachers. This might involve a trip south to the Inland Sea, which had real sand dunes to drive in. Getting stuck was always on the cards! Candy and I bought a brand new 4.0lt. 4x4 Nissan Pathfinder, top of the range, leather seats, for an incredibly low £20 000. With petrol subsidised at 15p a litre..yes 15 pence, it cost virtually nothing to run. It had massive 18 inch BF Goodrich All-Terrain tyres and running them at ultra-low pressure it was virtually unstoppable in the desert.

Visits from Qatar

One of the advantages of being in Qatar was its location. It was some 8 hrs further east, by air, than the U.K. This made holidays interesting, without being too costly. We had a lovely bespoke trip to Sri Lanka, organised by a Sri Lankan travel agent in Al Khor. We toured the Island from Sigiriya, climbing its Lion Rock, a 200m high volcanic plug with an old fort on top, to Kandy and its tea plantations. We spent our final night in the Galle Face hotel in Columbo, the only hotel in town with its own beach. After some re-negotiation over rooms they gave us the late owners apartment. The living room was so huge it took 2x8 seater dining tables and 2x4 seater settees and still looked empty. The attached bedroom was bigger than any luxury hotel room we have ever stayed in. The plaque on the wall in the room showed such worthies as U.K. Prime Minister 'Ted' Heath and First Man to stand on the Moon, Neil Armstrong had stayed in it. On another occasion we went to Jordan, staying in a 5 star hotel in Amman. We visited the old Roman town of Jerash as well as a day at Petra, the city carved from rock. There was also time to 'swim' in the Dead Sea, a very weird experience. It is so salty that you can sit up in it to read a book and it is incredibly difficult to turn over while laying flat! We visited Mount Nebo, allegedly Moses first saw the Promised Land from there. On other trips we also visited Istanbul, which we enjoyed immensely. One of the most memorable things for me was catching a boat from Europe to Asia Minor for 50p. Actually it was just the ferry across the Bosporus!

We had adventures more locally, driving and camping around the desert coast of Qatar. Further afield, the drive from Qatar, through Saudi Arabia to the UAE or Oman was done on a couple of occasions. The transit involved a number of visas and several boarder posts. Candy would wear an Abaya and Hijab and just dip her sun glasses to be seen. Once, we arrived at a non English speaking boarder and our Passport was not recognised until we had some help from a passing Qatari and I mentioned Manchester United! We stayed on Desert Island, off the coast of the UAE, and the Jebel Haffeet Hotel, near Al Ain in the south with its bar 'in' the swimming pool. We also visited Muscat in Oman and the mountains and Waddies of the North on a couple of occasions, once with the Ainsworths (see Ch.11). I also remember a trip to Dubai with some teachers from school. This was titled a Stag Night & Football Tour. However the 'stag's' fiancé flew over from Wales and wouldn't let him go on the trip and we played no football.........we did, however, have a great trip!

China Adventure

We left Qatar in June of 2010, having had a great time. I took my schoolteacher Pension from the U.K. in November and Candy already had hers, so we didn't need to work full time. However, we decided that we liked the itinerant ex-pat life, so I joined 'Teacher's on the Move'. This was an internet based organisation which provided short length teaching posts all over the world......what we in the U.K. would call 'supply teachers'. They sent me an advert for a job in China to start in January 2012.

We were in Whitby, having breakfast in a hotel on the cliff when I got a call from the company which ran the school, Dupont in Shanghai. From January to June in a place called Wuxi (pronounces Wooshee) in Jiangsu Province, about 150km to the north west of Shanghai. The school was Wuxi No.1 School and had a fairly new building to hold 4500 Chinese students, 11-18 and co-educational. The school had its own International unit of some 250 students. They were doing GCSE and A-Level courses, in English, from the Cambridge Board in the UK. Evidently, after a short chat, I was found to be ideal to teach just A-level Chemistry. This turned out to be Y13, and only 2 groups........10.5 hours of a 30hr teaching a week, teaching the same thing twice! Wednesday was a particular blast, in school teaching at 7.30 and finish by 9.10, then home for breakfast and off on a local adventure.

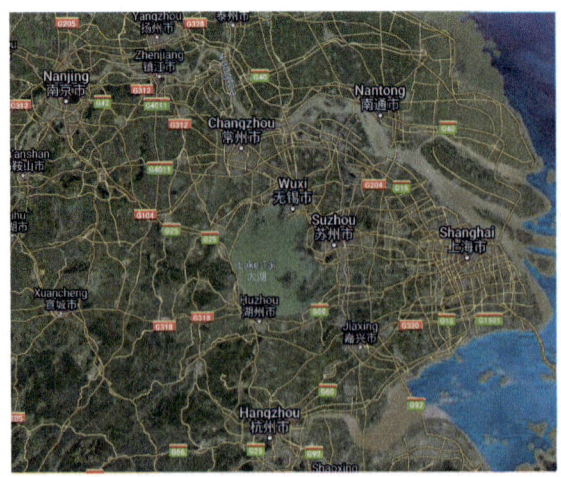

Wuxi, a small Chinese city of 5 million, 150 Km North West of Shanghai, on Lake Tai. The pollution was so bad at best we only ever got a view of the lake shore.

Still, I'm getting in front of myself.

We needed to travel to the Chinese Consulate in Marseille for an initial entry visa, which took 24hrs to process. While still in England we had already obtained Medical Certificates and had Chest X-rays. We organised flights from Toulouse via Munich to Shanghai, having caught the bus from Quillan and the train to Toulouse. We were met at the airport by Vanessa who had interviewed me. She took us to a bus station attached to the airport, bought us a ticket and had to leave, saying "someone will be waiting for you in Wuxi!" Luckily in China buses and trains all have Arabic Numbers, so we eventually found our bus and loaded the luggage. It wasn't exactly luxury travel and when it stopped we didn't know if it was a 'pee break' or getting off time. Eventually we arrived in Wuxi, a huge modern city of 5 million, with very, very few Westerners. We were met, as the only westerners on the bus, by what can only be described, at first view, as a 40 year old 'tart' in a tutu and leopard skin tights, carrying a cheap plastic brolly. This turned out to be the marvellous Polly, the schools secretary and general facilitator.......a tiny power house, lovely but with a forceful personality and wonderful lack of appropriate dress sense. In the taxi to the hotel she explained that she had a couple of flats for us to look at, but we would be in the hotel Grand Park for a week. The hotel was very grand, but a bit 'down at heal' in a Communist regime sort of way. We had three meals a day from the buffet, but the ample buffet never changed from one meal to the next. Candy got a liking for pork & chive dumplings, something which has stayed with her. Only chopsticks were available and nobody spoke English! We were the only westerners in the hotel.

Over the next couple of days we saw a suitable flat, not as big as Qatar, but with two bedrooms and windows which nearly fit. On the 18th floor our main window looked out over the famous Grand Canal which runs from Beijing to Hangzhou, nearly 2000km, it is more like the Thames in London than any UK canal. Our apartment was Flat 1807, Unit 35, Golden Horse International Gardens, which you needed to know in Chinese to get home by taxi!

金马国际花园
Jīnmǎ guójì huāyuán

We also needed a bank account with the Bank of China and a cheap mobile phone and local SIM card. The flat had furniture but we had to buy utensils. In our case: a wok, 2 bowls, a kitchen knife, a ladle, a large pan, 2 mugs and chopsticks........we were going native! We also needed bedding including pillows and a duvet. Drinking water came from a store in the entrance
to the flats complex in 5 gallon bottles. We did have wifi installed, but it never worked and only China News was in English on the TV. However, we made contact with a girl who sold pirate DVDs from first a shop and then a garage, these were very cheap, up to date and in English.

Wuxi No.1 School, with the famous 1776km Grand Canal in front.

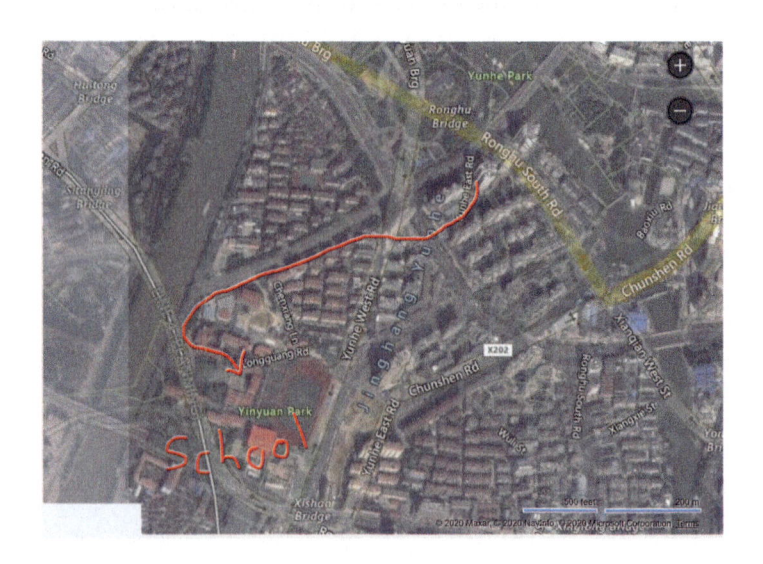

Route to school

Candy didn't have a job in China, but the first week kept her busy trying to clean the flat and explore the local shops. We found a Starbucks a short walk from the flat, in the centre of town, which did wifi(Smartphones were still not common). This meant that we could speak to those 'at home' cheaply using the Skype we had used in Qatar. This was before Skype video, Zoom, Facetime or Messenger video. However, the timings were difficult as Wuxi is GMT +8 hrs, making weekends our best contact time We found our way to 'Carrefory', as Polly called it, and also a place we called the Japanese Supermarket. We also joined a gym at a 5* hotel. This was partly for the gym and partly for the sauna just to get occasionally warm. The weather was cold, below zero most of the time and though we did have a decent heater our flat was hardly hermetically sealed. There was also noise 24hrs a day, which we eventually got used to. Wuxi was also very polluted. We never had a blue sky day in all the time we were there, the visibility from 'our hill' was never more than 5km. Periodically they would put fish into the Grand Canal, which the locals would eagerly fish for, to eat! These would turn up, floating dead, after 3 or 4 days.

School was strange, my lab. technician spoke no English, so each week I would order apparatus with a lot of laughing and pointing. Every day except Monday I could have at least a 2hr lunch break, as I didn't teach either just before or after lunch.

So Candy and I would meet to have lunch out. We found an interesting bakery with rice bread, which had a cafe upstairs. Staff would come and sleep at the tables in their break. I did try school lunches, but my first was a piece of inedible pigs trotter.......so I never went back. As it got warmer Candy would walk to school and we would go find a cafe in the park opposite. Two interesting thing about the school: first, because we were south of the Yangtze river.....just, there was no heating in the classrooms or any public buildings. Remember its below zero outside, so I taught in a wooly hat, fingerless gloves and a duvet jacket for 3.5 months; second, the internet was restricted by the government, no Google etc. however the students always had access to a VPN (Virtual Private Network) which allowed you past the filters. Each would last a week or so before it would get closed down, then some student would let you have a new one!

I had 2 classes with about 15 students in each, all Chinese. The idea was that I should teach them A-level Chemistry in a Western style. They had learned English since their junior years, but I would be one of the first native speakers they would hear. Chinese students in the past had found it difficult moving from the Chinese system, which is very didactic, to the student being expected to think or ask and answer questions. Interestingly the students had all chosen sometimes quaint and sometimes just odd western names for themselves; Agnes and Black stick out in my mind.

The kids, also in coats and hats, would fall asleep at their desks during breaks between lessons........they had interesting night lives on their computers. There was also a Chinese 'shadow staff' with their own staff room. These teachers were the Form Tutors and taught just one or two lessons a week. Many had other night time jobs and their staff room was more like a dormitory. I had one help me with exam invigilation and had to wake him twice during the session. Each morning all the 4500 students would do eye exercise for 10 minutes, to some very Chinese music. I thought this was hysterical and only went once, as I couldn't keep a straight face.

Life and Travels in China

So what did we do with our time in Wuxi? Our main interest was the local hill, Huishan Forest Park(329m, so 300m of ascent) which we could see from our bedroom window. In previous times there had been some sort of communication post on top, but now people used the hill for recreation. Stretching, pull ups, slow walking with a purpose(very strange) or just banging against a tree with your body. We tried to get quickly to the top.

On the top there was a source of refreshment, it could hardly be called a cafe. It served green tea in large flasks and a wonderful noodle soup with a fried egg on top. We took other westerners from school up there but the somewhat unsanitary nature resulted in them just buying bottles of Coke. There was a long ridge behind the cafe which led towards a more salubrious looking establishment.........which was never open. We often did this walk 2 or 3 times a week!

Our hill top cafe on the top of Huishan Forest Park, Wuxi

Nearby Citangqun, next to Xihui Park, was a 'reproduction' of old Wuxi canal town, as the original old town was knocked down during the cultural revolution/destruction. This sold mainly tourist 'tat', but the skills with which it had been reproduced were substantial. On Wednesdays and weekends we would often travel by taxi or train to local 'sites', old gardens or housed. Suzhou was not far by train and more historic as was Nanjing, a former Chinese capitol city. Nanjing was also the home of the famous 15th Century trading fleet of incredibly huge ships, built by Admiral Zheng He.

One evening a week we would go to the Blue Bar in town, with Nick & Linda and a few others from school. This was an American style bar which did burger and chips and attracted both locals and ex-pats. Sometimes there could be as many as 10 westerners at a time, the most we ever saw in Wuxi. Around the city we never saw a western face, but locals were very friendly. They would often want us in their 'selfie' or push their children towards us to speak english. If they did have limited english they were often disappointed to find we were English not Yanks. A final observation; toddlers in China don't wear nappies. There is just a slit under their trousers, where their usually cold red bum can poke out.

As far as longer trips go, we started early. I taught for three weeks and it was Chinese New Year, a three week holiday! We were told not to travel in the first week as some 800 million Chinese head west, home from big cities of the east coast. I had imagined that this would make the continent tip! We found that the sister of our other school secretary was a travel agent, so she came to our flat to help us organise a trip.

Beijing for the Chinese New Year holiday, 2012

We had a problem with Candy's visa, which was only single entry, so we couldn't leave the country....Tibet, Taiwan and Hong Kong were out. Still China has quite a bit to offer.

My mum had been planning to visit the Terracotta Army when she found that she was terminally ill with cancer........I felt obliged to fulfil that ambition for her, so Xian was a must. If we were heading north then Beijing and the Great Wall were two other musts.....so the plan was set. It was arranged that we would first fly to Xian and be collected by a driver and guide for the tours. We then had an overnight sleeper to Beijing and again met a guide and driver. We did get some free time in both places, to both eat and explore. Our Xian guide was quite young, he had been born in the time of 1 child per family. Our Beijing/ Great Wall guide was about my age and had lived through the famine of Mao, where they peeled the bark from trees to make soup! We had a memorable time, as it was still very festive after Chinese New Year. It snowed on our visit to Tiananmen Square and the Forbidden City, leaving a blue sky and bright sunshine. The first in Beijing for about a year; the air had the strange metallic taste of seeded clouds.

We visited Guilin in early April, getting more adventurous our 'travel agent' booked flights and hotels only. The hotel organised trips so we went to a barbecue on a riverboat trip and bamboo rafting on the LI River to see fishermen using Cormorants to fish for them. Then at the end of April we went to the beautiful old Lijiang in Yunnan Province, staying at the equally old Zen Garden Hotel. This is very much in the southwest of China, next to the Tibetan boarder. We visited the 'First Bend on the Yangtze' and 'Leaping Tiger Gorge'. For this we hired a young girl in her car for the day. We also hired cycles to visit some local villages for lunch, near the Jade Dragon Snow Mountain.

Passing through Kunming on the way home we had a 4hr delay, 1.5hrs of which was spent standing on the runway in the heat of the day.

Lijiang , internet photo.

On our last day we took the train from Wuxi to Shanghai, traveling at 300kmh. There we stayed in a huge corner suit at the Crown Plaza in Century Park with access to the Executive Floor. I was quite ill the next day, by the time we got to switch aircraft in Germany.......could it have been the free food?

Qatar Again!

Like Qatar, we had a great time in China and once again we were sorry to leave. In late 2012 I was snowshoeing in the woods above Aunat when I got a call from Kevin Davies, my old boss in Qatar. "Was I busy? Could I come to Qatar for a couple of terms asap?" They had a teacher who had left for half-term and not returned, they were a bit desperate! It suited us, the paperwork was done and in early January of 2013 we were off to Qatar again. Actually we flew to Rome, watched some International Rugby with Kev, Val, Alan, Marg and Mark, beat some Romans in a snowball fight in the city centre, lost all Candy's credit cards, well not lost, left them in Rome, and flew straight to Qatar. This had presented somewhat of a packing challenge, zero degrees in Rome......thirty five in Qatar! They gave us a tiny 1 bed flat just opposite the school, which met our needs as we didn't have a car. Step son Paul and his wife Vic were also there at the same time, so we had the availability to lone our old Pathfinder if we needed it. To be honest I don't remember too much about this trip. We visited Istanbul again, this time with Graham Ogden and his fiancee Maree Carlton. Candy came back to France a couple of weeks before I finished to spend some time with Brigid (Lob). This was brave, as she had to get the car started after it had been left in a covered car park in Toulouse Airport for 5 months! All it needed was a jump-start, good old Freelander.

Further East, Singapore

Some time towards the end of 2013 I was contacted by an ex-colleague Bradley Roberts. He had become the Principal at St. Joseph's International School in Singapore. He was looking for a chemistry teacher to cove a maternity leave from January 2014 for 6 months, and wondered if I was free. Why not, another very different place to live, lets get the paperwork done......there is always paperwork! We decide to fly out to Singapore, to leave our things there, going via a quick visit to Doha in late November of 2013. We stayed with Paul & Vic in their new 4 bed detached house on the Al Khor community. They now had 6 indoor rescue cats and a further 5 or 6 outside! We had barbecues in the desert with the Davies', Roses and the Akers' and tea at the Ritz, on 5th of December we flew to Singapore via Columbo. We arrived in Singapore to find that we had a lovely 2 bedroomed flat, with private lift and balcony - Flat 09.02, 23 Akyab Road,
f

flat 2 on the ninth floor. The cost to the school was going to be £1750 (UK) a month.......gulp! The previous teacher in the flat had 'done a runner' and we took over the lease. The plus side was that the flat was fully furnished.......though this system was to cause us some problems when we left. The flat complex had a swimming pool, sauna and gym. Singapore is very humid and cloudy and a constant 30-35 degrees Celsius all year round, being just 1 degree (100miles) north of the equator.

View from the flat in Singapore across to Tan Tock Seng hospital and Novena MRT(Mass Rapid Transport) Station.

We had a couple of days in Singapore then flew to Wellington NZ via Sydney. My idea of this part of the world was a bit vague, I thought it would be a short trip, in fact it is 5 time zones! We stayed a couple of days in Wellington and then sailed to the South Island to pick up a camper van. This was our first, and brilliant. We slept on the coast next to seals in Kaikoura, meeting a Kiwi lady who recognised my Yorkshire accent and gave me the latest copy of the Dalesman. Then shared an evening meal with her and a fisherman, who supplied us with fresh Abalone and Crayfish. The main road, A1, south was no bigger than a small A road in the UK and we met hardly any traffic. In Christchurch we stayed one night with Tracy and Garth Jones. He was a Kiwi and they had met while teaching at SCS.

Then onto Akaroa, which was fabulous. This was followed by meeting the Kia birds at Arthur's Pass. They will pinch your coffee or sandwich from the table or your windscreen wipers or the rubber which keeps your windscreen in place......they are also big! We then crossed to the west coast to Hokitika, Punakaiki & Picton. We ended up in Motueka near the Abel Tasman National Park, taking a boat ride North, then walking South down the coast......again fabulous. We spent our last night at 'Tez' Hardwick's house in Nelson. Tez is an old rugby from school that I hadn't seen for 40 years. He was no less strange than when we last met!

Back on the North Island with G & M we did the Tongariro Alpine Crossing and I got to see my first live volcano close up. We also went to Rotorua to see the geysers and mud pools. The visit finished with Christmas dinner, sat in the sun on Maree's sister's balcony, looking out over the bay. Surreal!
I did consider emigrating with the family to NZ in the mid-90s, but eventually Ruth thought it would be too far from her family. NZ felt so safe and quiet, like a different age.

The volcanic Tongariro crossing, with 'Mount Doom' from the Lord of the Rings films.

We were back in Singapore for New Year and work. I needed to walk to school, or catch a bus. Walking took about 35 minutes, so I would leave 'home' at 06:45, which was in the semi-dark in equatorial Singapore. I always carried an umbrella, as torrential rain was possible during the early morning and late afternoon. The school was 4-18, co-ed, fee paying and one of the top school in Singapore. It was run by a catholic order of Lasallian monks or 'brothers'. The Primary and Secondary schools were quite separate, but on the same site. The school had about 36 nationalities of all faiths. It also took about 40 students a year in each of Y10/Y13 as residents, from poor areas all around the Eastern Pacific. Bright students were chosen to cope with the learning in English, but those were not the only criteria. Those who might benefit most from the opportunity were top of the list.

I was allocated a laboratory in the older area of the school. All access was from outside, as with all laboratories, and the essential air-con was very noisy. The language of the school was English and I was to teach Cambridge O-Level Chemistry.....yes O-Level! plus International Baccalaureate Chemistry at Advanced Level. I had been warned in China that this was a "pain in the arse" due to its individual practical assessments. Regretfully, I found this to be more than true and one of the banes of my time there. There were five of us in the Chemistry department and I had more than double the number of teaching years of the other four combined, including my new boss. I was to find that this was a very dynamic department, which is probably why the staff were all so young.

The other bane of my life was to be a form tutor to a Y9. A surprisingly unruly bunch of 25 mostly Malaysians, Singaporeans and Indonesians..........to say the least they were un-co-operative and on the whole we didn't get on! So from the outset I can't say I enjoyed the work experience, but life in and around Singapore was novel and interesting and Candy and I had a fun. Candy was employed on a part-time basis to teach some Art and do some supply. She also did sports trips, accompanying students to after school sports events around Singapore, mainly Tennis and Netball. She also spent a week camping and doing outdoor things on Bintan, an Indonesian Island just south of Singapore.

Enough about the school! Candy and I thoroughly enjoyed living in Singapore, mainly because it was like nowhere else we had lived. One plus was that the language was English, so we could communicate easily with the locals. Singapore has some very strict laws, such as no spitting & no chewing gum in the country! These sorts of laws make it a very safe place to live, except for the mosquitoes, which can give you all sorts of nasty things.

A Street food centre, Balestier Market, near our flat

We would regularly visit the Cinema at Shaw Plaza, a few minutes from the flat. We never seemed to be charged the same entry fee and needed to wear a coat! We also ate out at the 'Street Food' markets. Street food was made illegal, but the vendors had been allowed to create food markets.

The food varied from Chinese to Tai, from Indian to Indonesian and Malayan.......along with Tiger Raddler's, we loved it. We also ate 'posh' at places like the Polo Club and restaurants in town, but the street food was our favourite. The two key dishes for Singapore were Chicken Rice and Chilli Crab, both were great. There was also Raffle's Hotel, with its famous Singapore Sling at £15 a glass, peanut shells to throw on the floor and my first experience of cold red wine! We would also visit the local shopping mall at Novena, which was the local station for the underground or MRT(Massive Rapid Transport).

At weekends, as shopping is not our thing, we would often get the MRT to the south coast and walk along the Kent Ridge. Here they had linked some small ridges with walkways and canopy walks. We also enjoyed wandering around the Bukit Timah Forest. This is an area of primary jungle and also the highest point in Singapore at 163m. We also visited Pulau Ubin island, where we hired bikes and got caught in a tropical down pour.

The Hash

One of the other supply teachers and a long time inhabitant of Singapore invited us to go jogging with the 'Hash Harriets'. Their motto being "a drinking club with a running problem". It was a female version of the Hash Harriers clubs found all over the ex-pat East. However the Harriets had a twist: men were allowed, but could never run in front of the front woman. The club had ex-pat men and women, but also local Peranakan, Indonesian and Malayan members. Each week a starting location was found and a run planned: streets, rugged land, jungle, all were permissible. Some walked, some joggled, others jogged. The course was usually 1:15 to 1:30 hrs, in 30 Celsius 100% humidity.......a sweaty job. After many years of not jogging, I found it surprisingly comfortable fairly quickly. Candy joined 'les femmes de certain age' towards the rear. For me it was something to look forward to midweek, and I loved it, getting to visit bits of Singapore only known to the locals. I had a Hash name, as everyone does, 'Tight Arse' or TA; partly from the strapping on my thigh and partly from my Yorkshire roots.

After run drinks with the Hash Harriets. Wearing the cap for 'Dick of the Week', for tripping up twice while jogging and talking

At the end of the run the club had a van, driven by a local, which provided cold washing water and drinks: water, beer, wine etc.. We washed in the car park, donned our club tee-shirts, and formed a drinking circle. Here drinking penalties would be handed out for club rule misdemeanours by a 'girl' in a mini-skirt and high heels! Chants of "He's alright, he's alright, he has a teeny weeny willy but he's alright" or "She's alright, she's alright, she's a little flat chested but she's alright" would echo round the parking lot. It was like a rugby club but without the preceding pain! Afterwards a nearby restaurant would have been booked to eat out.

Visits from Singapore

Once again we were in a good location to visit outside Singapore. We caught the executive coach up the coast to Malacca, in Malaysia, a couple of times. Once by ourselves and once with Graham and Maree, who came to visit. Paul and Vic also came to visit and we took them to the Island of Borneo, Kuching in Malaysian Sarawak. Paul was ill for most of the visit, but Candy and I had a chance to wander alone in the jungle.
We also visited an Orang-utan sanctuary.

The jungle trail in Sarawak, Borneo

Visiting the Mekong Delta, by boat. Vietnam 2014

Chris Horsfield and his wife Cheryl also visited for a few days. Chris & Cheryl had come to Qatar after us and we had been their 'buddies'. We also managed to get a trip to their place in Ho Che Min City (Saigon) Vietnam. This was a fabulous place, Candy especially loved it. We took a boat ride on the famous Mekong Delta, as well as visiting the city sights. From there we flew to Cambodia, Siem Reap. Not far from Siem Reap is the famous Angkor temple complex, containing Angkor Wat, something which had been an ambition to see for Candy for many years.

A friend of ours from Qatar and Singapore, Julie Thompson had unknowingly booked the same time as us in Siem Reap. We found a Tuk-Tuk driver that we could hire and he took us to Angkor Wat. The next morning he picked us up for the day, first to see the sunrise (it was cloudy!), then he gave us a thorough tour of all the main temples. We also bumped into some other friends from Qatar, Martin Jones and his wife. They had brought a school trip from their latest job in Kuala Lumpur.

The magnificent Angkor Wat at Siem Reap in Cambodia.

(KL).......a refuge of many ex-al khorians! A small world indeed.

Our last visit was for a weekend on Bintan Island. We booked a wooden hut built out over the sea, with a restaurant, spa facilities and canoes. It was on arrival in Bintan, an Indonesian Province, that Candy found she had no space in her Passport for the immigration sticker. We were threatened with the boat back, but after a great performance from Candy, including copious tears, we were let in.

In our last weeks in Singapore we had a visit from Alasdair. He had decided to do a year visit/work in Australia, meeting up with the brother of his best mate, Tom. We had a few days of fun around Singapore before he had to leave for what was to become his permanent new home.

Al stopping off in Singapore for a 'steamboat'. Setting off for an adventure of a lifetime which became a lifetime adventure, 2014

We had some problems leaving the flat. Evidently we were responsible for a full cleaning, including curtains and air-conditioner servicing. Every scratch to the skirting board, every mark on the wall. We hadn't realised this on arrival, and had taken over a flat which was a bit grubby. We also were nearly left with the problem of the furniture we had 'inherited', but passed this responsibility onto the school. Cleaning by Candy and plenty of tip-ex did the rest. Our last day/night was spent on the Executive Floor and a suit at the Fullerton, the old Singapore Post Office on the river. We do like to leave in style!

I was rather put off by the work in Singapore, so wasn't keen to take up other offers. I had also been studying for a BA from the Open University and this hadn't been easy while working........I think I will retire! So at the tender age of 59, having taught for 35 years......granted not all of every year since 2010......I could stop banging my head against the brick wall. I was a full time student again!

Family and France: The Aunat Years

Before moving on to actual retirement and living in France I need an opportunity to catch up on my increasing number of family members. This is just a brief 'catch up' to 2021 as a comprehensive tale would occupy many volumes. This is really just a set of 'thumb nails', as each person has their own story and their own memories, best told from their perspective. I've already introduced some of the main characters, but perhaps I need to update these. I will start by taking a step back as far as 2003...and Candyand her surprises!

On my first date with Candy, 23th May 2003, at The Fleece Hotel, Addingham owned by my friend Chris Monkman, we talked about many things, including the fact that I was an orphan.......though I failed to add it happened when I was 40 yrs old! Her first 'news' was that she had three children by her first husband......three children!!! her first husband!!! Yes she was currently organising her second divorce. Children was something of an overstatement: Bea, Brigid also known as Lob and Paul were 35, 34 and 33 respectively. At the time Bea was married to Marek with two small children: Ewa(10) and Reuben or Roo(7) and both Brigid and Paul were single..........I have, for them, over the years gone under the self styled 'nom de plume' of WSF or WSG......Wicked Step Father/Grandfather!

Candy was born in Addis Ababa in 1947 and after a brief sojourn in Iran, was brought up in Geneva. Her father was an Italian medical Doctor working for the World Health Organisation. He often worked abroad. Candy went to a French speaking primary school & then to the prestigious International School(French section) of Geneva. She is thus, as are her two brothers, truly bilingual. We had been going out for a while before she mentioned this fact! Candy had her three children in quick succession, starting at the age of 20, so didn't start her degree (BA Hons. French and Ceramics) until she was 28. Coincidentally she went to Ripon & York St. John, where I was also a student concurrently. Another coincidence was that in 1978 Candy was living at Grantley Hall near Patley Bridge, where her first husband, was working. At that time it was a North Yorkshire Adult Education Centre, where I had to spend time at as a newly qualified teacher. She started at South Craven School in January 1981, exactly one years after me and 22 years before our first date.

My beautiful Candida, slumming it in a seafood bar at the Grau de Leucate, half way through one of our coastal bike rides. 2018

Chris and Charlotte, mad as ever, 2019

    Chris tried the 6th Form at school and then Outdoor Ed. at Skipton College, but neither suited him. He worked at landscape gardening and working in pubs, where he met Charlotte in 2008, while Candy and I were living in Qatar. Jessica was born on 17th Jan. 2009 closely followed by Nathan on 4th Jan. 2010. They have, so far, lived in Ilkley; Chris first living in my house on Wilmot Road, then with Charlotte and the kids in Weston Road followed by several years in our house at 45 Wellington Road.
So not only does Charlotte have the same birthday as Candy, 31st August, and my dad, but she was brought up in 45 Wellington Road as a child.
After a short time again in Weston Road they now live again in Wellington Road, this time at no.7.

After a 10 year gap, Jess and Nathan were joined by Emily, born on 29th May 2019. Chris moved to being a tree surgeon & finally settled to an outdoor life as a roofer.

Sadly, he died on 10th March 2022.

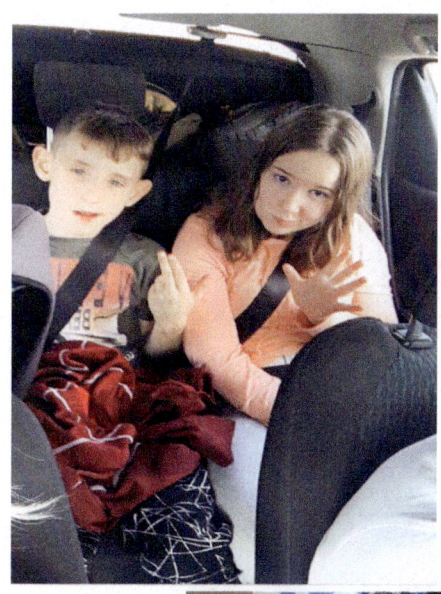

Jess and Nathan, always perfect travellers, 2020

Emily, 2020

Hemsley, first day at nursery and very keen. I hope it lasts!
November 2020

Al and Sarah on holiday with us in Barcelona, 2017

After Alasdair finished his apprenticeship as a 'fitter' for Finning's Caterpillar he worked for a number of years at Hartlington Fencing. In 2014 he headed off to Australia for a year of work and travel. He moved up to Queensland to stay with a friend from Finning's and ended getting a job in the warehouse of an open cast coal mine.......and a wife and family. Sara and Alasdair were married in 2016 and have made their home in Dysart, a mining town in the middle of Queensland. Hemsley was born on 19th December 2017. She was followed by Toby, our latest addition so far, on 22nd April 2020

Toby, a big boy, 2020

'21/'22, Al, Sara, Hemi and Toby had a big adventure. Al has taken a year off his job to work on Mornington Island with his friend Dave. Dave owns a butchers/store on this largely Aboriginal Island with 500 inhabitants. They had 10 month contract and seem have relished the experience.

Al at work as a butcher on Mornington Island
Al and Sara had their third child, Candy and I's 8th. grandchild in January of '23. A girl, Remmi.

In the course of our relationship Bea has divorced Marek and now has a new husband, Andy who she lives with in Nottingham.
They were married on 1st April 2022.

Ewa is living with her boyfriend Charlee. *(Above, Christmas 2020)* As I write, January '21, Charlee is working with disadvantaged youngsters and

Ewa is recovering from a debilitating auto-immune disease. She has just begun a new job with a graphics firm.

Roo, with his new girlfriend Natasha, with Lob, Bea & Ewa

Roo had recently moved to Bristol, once again to work with young people/ disaffected youths.

Brigid met John Corton the year after Candy and I met, 2004. John ran his own internet business, doing on-line biology courses. They moved in together onto John's canal barge, permanently moored in Todmoreden.

John was accepted onto a PhD at Aberystwyth University and they bought a house near to his department in Wales. They were married in 2011.

Brigid or 'Lob' as the family calls her. Out with the HVR in 2018.

Unfortunately, in 2017, just after achieving his PhD John died suddenly. Brigid found him in their house on her return from a week spent in France with us. The coroner was unable to find a cause.

Brigid still has her house in Wales. She spends a lot of time traveling to 'pet sit' while people go on holiday. Lob spent 3 months in France at the start of '23. She has booked to spend another 3 months around Quillan and the Mediterranean coast at the end of this year.

Paul married Victoria(Vic) and they worked as junior school teachers in Newcastle and London for some time. After visiting us in Qatar in 2008 we set them up to talk to Jarleth, the Primary Head and he was able to offer them teaching jobs. They moved there in 2009, staying until 2019. Currently they live in the 'granny cottage' next to Vic's mum and dad's house near Hexham. They have 16 rescue cats from Qatar!

Paul & Vic in Sarawak, Borneo, 2014. They came on a visit to us in Singapore, while they were working in Qatar.
It's difficult to get a photo of Paul, as he is not keen to pose.

Paul & Vic have recently bought themselves a house near Hexham, potentially as their 'forever home' with their cats. They are still teaching locally, though Paul is on a half timetable.

In total, so far, for Candy and I this amounts to 5(4 as of 2022) children with 4 partners and 8 grandchildren with 2 partners. A grand family total of 18, from 1 Boomer with no obvious older living relations..........that is certainly another BOOM!

Life in France

Having decided that France would be a nice place to own a house and having some funds to buy one from the sale of Wilmot Road, we decided upon somewhere near Carcassonne. We had visited the area for camping holidays on two occasions: first to a campsite in St Palau-del-Vidre near Argeles-sur-Mer, then a tour including the Black Mountains north of Carcassonne and Maury in the valley of the same name. It seemed the ideal spot, mountains and the Med. and not a British honeypot. Also a wine waiter in Monkman's restaurant in Ilkely had recommended that we look at Limoux, Esperaza & Quillan. We booked a week in a hotel in Carcassonne and wrote a list of requirements, we had about €100 000 or so to spend and wanted: something in a small town/village, possibly with a shop and bar; at least two bedrooms, a small garden and garage for storage, near an airport that did cheap flights, fit to live in straight away with no major renovation. We organised an 'agent immobilier' for each day and gave them our requirements. We saw the house in Aunat, 1 Rue De l'Eglise and it ticked all the 'required' boxes. It was 1.5hrs from the airports at Carcassonne and Perpignan and had no shop or bar, but these were flexible requirements. We put an offer in for it at lunchtime on the Wednesday, by mobile from nearby Esperzel and it was accepted. It cost us €105 000, at the time, about £74 000. We now owned a house in France!

1 Rue De L'Eglise in 2015, before our friend Rene built us the conservatory, but after we had the garage and house re-roofed.

We traveled down with Chris to sign for the house in December, but the contract would not go through until early 2008. This was an interesting trip. First, as we got to the check-in at Dover I realised that my passport was not in its cover. For some reason nobody asked for it and we drove straight onto the ferry. At Calais we drove straight off the ferry and out. I had arrived in France 'sans passport'. My problem was that we were leaving the car in France and flying back to the UK. There was no way I could do this without a passport. The nearest UK Consulate was in Toulouse and we had a day there to get me a one time entry visa to the UK at about €80. I gave it to Candy and she put it in her handbag with her's and Chris's passports. We then went to do some shopping and have a celebratory coffee and cake. About 20 minutes after leaving the cafe Candy declared "Where is my handbag?". Rushing back to the cafe the waitress said, "I was wondering when you would be back" and returned the bag. Candy took out the passports and my papers to check they were their and Chris grabbed them and put them in his pocket, "I think I'll keep hold of them!" he said confidently.

As we had decided to let out 'Welly Road' the furniture was to arrive from the UK and we paid for Brigid and John to travel over and move us in. So we didn't actually get to live in the house until the summer of '08. When we arrived Brigid and John had done a good job of getting the furniture and boxes into the right rooms. We were pleased to find that the previous owners had left the cooker, dishwasher and washing machine and all the light fittings. But not so pleased to find the garage full of old furniture and other stuff, that they hadn't been able to sell. There were bits we salvaged: dining chairs, a TV, a yoke, a strimmer, big garden table, chairs & brolly, a dog grate for the fire and a barbecue outside. The rest we managed to have collected by "Parchemin", they took it all for what they could get for some of it......garage cleared!

From 2008 to the summer of 2010 the French house was effectively a holiday home, mostly used in the summer. The Freelander was kept in the garage and always started first time when we arrived....what joy. I remember Chris, Charlotte and baby Jessica visiting us in 2009. When we left Qatar in 2010 Aunat became our permanent home. About this time Chris, Charlotte, Jessica and their new baby, Nathan, moved into 'Welly Road'. So when we visited the UK we were a bit itinerant. Staying with whoever we were visiting and for longer stays in a flat near Skipton, Cawder Hall Cottages, which we hired a number of times. This suited us, as on a long stay we needed our own living space sometimes.

Even our friends from Aunat, Rene an Mari-Jo, came for a week to stay with us at the cottages. I can't remember the year, possibly 2012 or '13, but I do remember that Rene said "Isn't everybody very white!" I think their favourite memory was Fish and Chips in Whitby. Welly Road has now been rented out since November 2016, via an Estate Agent in Ilkley.

Making the house our home

The garden in France was really just a couple of small trees and some scrubby grass. While we were in Qatar we had two locals put some more bushes and plants in and make a small rockery and flower beds. This was a birthday present for Candy.

We had the house re-roofed, and later the garage which had been ceramic/asbestos! Also we had our friend Rene, who has building as one of his many useful skills, put a door through from the lounge/kitchen into the garage.

Then he built a platform and stairs in the garage to accommodate a fridge, freezer and dryer. This gave us garage access without having to walk around through the garden. It also gave us a 'wet room' entrance into the house in winter.

Other jobs that Rene has done for us, often but not always, when we were working or travelling are: pointing the outside garage wall, re-wiring the garage, putting in a loft access hatch/ladder, and building the small 'veranda' or conservatory as we might call it in English. The veranda has been as, if not more useful than the other things.

It has made the house feel bigger and also given us the ability to sit 'in the garden in the lovely, but very cold, winters we have here. His final effort was to help me at no cost, or rather I helped him, to build a room in the garage……. which we have named the 'Oubliette' or Shed, as it is down stairs.

This project was finished in 2020 and it has given us a gym we can now use in the winter, a studio area for Candy's art and an overflow/3rd bedroom. We connected it to the house in 2022, giving us a second small kitchen area, the Link'. Sept.2021 a plumber also fitted a toilet in the back bed room.....for our old age!

Rue de l'Eglise in 2021, with the new veranda

France "Full-Time"

Singapore was our last contract, that finished in June of 2014, so we headed home to France full-time. My main aim for the end of 2014 was to finish my Level 2 Politics course from the Open University, including an exam held at Bradford University, just before Christmas. Working and studying had taken something of a toll, but I managed a 2:1 (Grade 2) in both the assignment work and the exam. In 2015-16 I did the Level 3 course in International Relations, for which I was to receive a 1st (Distinction), followed by Level 3 Economics in 2016-17, for which I also received a 1st (Distinction).

These courses took a lot of my time and I am forever grateful to Candy, not only for keeping me fed and watered, but also for giving me the time and being a sounding board for my ideas as they developed. It has to be said that the intellectual journey, if not the assignments, over the 6 years of the course, became a joint one. I put in the legwork, but through my explanations and our joint discussions Candy shared in the outcomes....except Econometrics, which was mine alone!

My final dissertation in 2017 was on Econometrics: a critical study of the use of Linear Regression Analysis to put a value on air pollution, using house prices and other housing data. Not only did I receive a Distinction(87%) for this, but also a Commendation from the world's largest academic awards programme, The Global Undergraduate Awards, which brings together the world's top undergraduate students.

As well as study, in 2015 Candy and I also joined two walking clubs: Murray, an English man who had arrived in Aunat in our absence introduced us to the Haute Vallée Randonnée(HVR) of Quillan and Marie- Jo, also from Aunat, to the more formidable Tourism & Loisire of Carcassonne. Through these we were to meet and make friends with a number of 'locals' and One or two English speakers. The two groups have provided us with many enjoyable exploits........some of which get a mention in Chapter 11. So studying, walking and making a small effort to improve my French became the focuses of 2014-17.

In 2016 we also spent a few months back in the UK. We had recovered Wellington Road from Chris and Charlotte after the 5 years we had promised them and needed to rent it out to improve our pension income. Though Candy had been able to take both her Teachers Pension and State Pension in 2007, at age 60. I had only been able to take my Teachers Pension, with 25% deductions, at age 55 in 2010. I got my State Pension this year, 2021, at age 66.

The HVR, through its Chair Claudine, provided us with the opportunity to watch 'Opera Live from the Met' in the cinema 'Cap Rouge' near Carcassonne. It took us no time at all to become monthly devotees. We also gathered a few closer friends, for meals. At first this was Rene and Marie-Jo, which extended to their friends Bertrand and Isobelle. Bertrand and Isobelle didn't live in the village, but were regular visitors from Perpignan/ Montpellier to Isabelle's cottage. Later they also bought a modern bungalow on the edge of the village, which they tore down to build a large barn like house.

More recently we have had meals with members of the HVR, in particular Annie, now Chair, and her partner Narcis, Patrick and Christine who taught on La Reunion for many years and Brian and Rose Mary who are from Southern Ireland. We also see Murray from time to time to have meals. Occasionally we also meet with Jean-Luc and Collette, who have a holiday cottage over the road from us. They live on the West coast, but Collette's mum was born here.

The village has three main 'get togethers' each year and we attend when we can. At New Year there is usually a meal and dance, preceded recently by Bingo(Lotto) and a lottery. Two years ago Candy won a dried leg of pork and last year I won a whole assortment of things: wine, cheese, meat. The meal is served at large tables and will often last from 10pm until 3 or 4am......with wine and Limoux Champers throughout, it is not for the faint hearted. There is usually a similar get together in the summer, but without the Lotto. Also there is usually a barbecue and music night. The village will have karaoke........my absolute favourite thing in the world......NOT! This will be followed by live music lasting well into the early hours. Most of these events have 100-150 attendees, which is remarkable as the residents of the village average about 50. This year Candy and I have joined the Committee des fêtes, with Candy on the actual Committee.

Travels from France

Many of our travels since arriving full time in France have been our itinerant tours of the the U.K. On most of these tours we have been pleased to be invited for a couple of nights to stay with Kevin & Val Boyle. Along with their friends Alan & Marg we have always had convivial evenings. I've known Kev for many years, he was a mate of mine when we lived in the New Inn in Guiseley, back in 1969.........so over 50 years. We played rugby together both at school and for Airebronians and of course his sister Julie was one of my first girlfriends.

Val, Kev, Alan, myself, Marg & Candy: Bologna, Italy, 2014/15

Newcastle, or at least Catton, also allowed us visits to see Paul & Vic, since their return from Qatar in 2019. The remainder of our U.K. trips were visits to Ilkley to see Chris, Charlotte, Jessica and Nathan, and now Emily as well. Then Nottingham to visit Bea, Ewa, Roo and Andy and finally to Aberystwyth to see Lob.

We have had a few holidays with Chris and his family, memorably on Skye and in Northumberland. We had another planned when the dreaded COVID-19 retreated, but events with Chris overtook us.

We have also been lucky enough to get a couple of trips to Italy. First with our bikes around Luca and Piza. Then with Maree and Graham Ogden in Rome. Followed by Kev, Val, Marg & Alan to Bologna. Finally we had a 10 day tour of Luca, Florence and Piza with Paul & Vic. They flew to Piza from Qatar to meet us. We also did a journey down Spain, through Valencia as far as Córdoba with Paul & Vic. Again meeting them, this time in Barcelona, from Qatar.

With Vic and Candy in Córdoba, 2015

By far our biggest adventures have been to visit Al in Australia. First for his marriage to Sara in 2016 and then for a visit in 2019. On the first visit we started with a short tour, 'locally, of Dysart with Al and Sara. This involved driving for 7 hours, in what seemed like a straight line, over no hills, via Emerald to Longreach. There we visited the famous Quantas Museum and the Stockman's Hall of Fame. A veritable Outback adventure. From there we headed north, in a straight line and over no hills, to Hughenden. There we met some original 'Outback Men', stockmen and road train drivers, with whom we had a fun evening around the pool table. From there we went to the coast at Cunguella, near Townsville, where Sara's parents, Christine and Bryan have a beach house. Leaving Al & Sara to finalise their wedding we were able to hire a camper van in Airlie Beach and drive up the east coast. Unfortunately I was ill for a couple of days, so we didn't make it to Cairns, but loved Bowen, Ingram and Cardwell.

The Groom and Bride with the Groom's family and friends Alasdair & Sara's outdoor wedding, Airlie Beach, Queensland, Australia, 2016

235

*Paul's third graduation, BA, with 1st Class Honours in
Politics, Philosophy & Economics, The Barbican, 2017*

Candy's 70th: Roo, Vic, Candy, Toby (Jess), Charlotte, Bea, Brother Andy, Chris........missing from this photo was: Paul, Lob, Brother Micky, Bea's Andy, Eva and Charlee ; 2017.

This was followed by time at the Airlie Beach Hotel and the wedding, including snorkelling on the Great Barrier Reef and Candy and I's first Jet-ski experience. Plus I ate Aussie 'Surf & Turf'.......Crocodile and Kangaroo.....lovely!

In mid September we left the wedding party and headed for Sydney, staying at the Travelodge on Wentworth Avenue. We did the normal stuff. A Midsummer Night's Dream at the Sydney Opera House, Bondi Beach and coastal walking and a visit to the Blue Mountains. Finally we flew to Brisbane, our favourite Aussie city, to meet up with Graham and Maree Ogden, for a few days and visit our favourite breakfast spot, River-bar + Kitchen.

One of the highlights of 2017 was renting a house in Derbyshire for Candy's 70th birthday, see picture above. A chance for our two families to get together.

Aireborough Grammar School, 50yrs since we started. Includes some wives/husbands, 1967-2017

       This time in the U.K. coincided with my school reunion. It was 50 years, September 1967, since my year group started Aireborough Grammar School. There were quite a few old faces, including my very old friend Stephen (back row, 5th from left), who lived next door to me in Horsforth.
    I hadn't seen him since 1975!
Our second Oz trip was in March '19, and was to visit the latest addition to the family Hemsley (Hemmi).......now one. Al had taken time off work so that we could travel. We started with a camping trip, Al had bought 2x2 man 'swags'. I woke up the first morning with a Kangaroo sleeping just by my head.

We had a couple more nights around Gladstone, including snorkelling and an island lunch using Al's powerboat. Then bailed out into a luxury apartment, it was too hot for the Aussies! On a second trip to an inland lake we camped again, with Al's friends Dave and Chucky.

Again playing on Al's boat and barbecuing at night. As the light fades Cain Toads make their way onto the beach, some of our party........I'm pleased to say not Al.......took to hitting them back into the water with golf clubs! Though to be honest like rabbits, the Cain Toad was introduced by Westerners, has no natural predator in Oz and is something of a growing pest. After a fun time with our Aussie family we had a few days in Brizzy, followed by a week with Graham & Maree in and around Wellington, NZ.

The COVID Year(s)

I started these Chronicles in April of 2000, after an idea from an old school friend, Bryn Griffiths. It seemed like an interesting project and would fill some of our 'lockdown' time in France. The lockdown had been caused by a pandemic virus SARS-CoV 2, which causes the disease COVID-19. To date, March 2001, it has been caught by 116M people and 2.58M have died worldwide. (UK 4.2M & 124000: France, 3.9M & 89000). These figures, from March '20 to March '21 show the COVID-19 mortality rate to be somewhat higher than that for Influenza. Particularly worrying for us oldies, I'm 65 and Candy is 73, is that mortality for oldies is much much higher than for the the younger generation. On the up side the mortality rate is hugely increased by pre-existing conditions, such as diabetes, heart disease and respiratory disease, non of which we have.

By March '20, here in France, we had begun to be locked down. We needed an 'attestation' to leave the house, signed by us with a date and time. Our journeys out could be only for food shopping or a walk of no more than 1hr and no more than 1km from home. In this first instance we shopped once a week, with face masks and social distancing, at the Superette in Belcair. We could not visit others or they us. We walked to the top of Le Crausse (1027m)......or Telegraph hill as we call it.....on 43 occasions between 17 March and 11 May, a day short of 8 weeks. After that there was a respite and we went out with the HVR using groups of 10 and strict social distancing. These groups grew through the summer and a full program was resumed. Candy and I were reluctant to join other social activities, visiting Rene and Marie-Jo in their garden on one occasion and having Isabelle and Murray round to sit in our garden on separate occasions.

Apart from 1 meal at Bertrand and Isobelle's house and 1 night in the Grand Duc Hotel at Gincla for Candy's birthday our social activities were just between the two of us.......its a good job we never tire of each other's company.

We were locked down again on 30 October 2020 until 27th November, just a month.....in the first instance. More or less the same rules as before. Then from 28th Nov until 15th Dec things opened up a little. We could move up to 20km from home for exercise, but with only 3 hours out of the house and an 'attestation'. We moved to walking around the Bois de Linas with a sandwich and coffee, about 2.5 hrs. Also thankfully the 'Shed' is fully finished as a gym and art studio, so we have kept ourselves in a reasonable state of fitness and entertainment. After 15th Dec. the 'Attestations' and time limits were dropped and we could travel further afield.

We had a couple of walks with the HVR and two trips to the Med. cycling from Rivesaltes to Le Barcares and back, along the Agly cycleway, 38km. January '21 saw France having a curfew between 18:00 & 06:00 for non essential movements. However this allowed both the HVR and T&L to recommence their weekly walks. By April 2021 we had both been double vaccinated against COVID and although this is not a total prevention it tends to alleviate major symptoms and death. The HVR was in full flow, with me leading many walks, while the T&L had virtually ceased due to the accompagnateur Jean-Claude having bad knees.

Technology 2020

Since last I spoke of technology, in my youth and early teaching there have been quite a few changes. To those of you reading this in years to come they will seem 'old hat', but here are just a few:

Let's start with my lovely new car. The Dacia Duster in its basic form is a cheap car, built by an offshoot of Renault, in Romania. We bought the top of the range model with 4x4 and a Diesel engine. The idea of 'hybrid cars', which are part battery and part petrol has been put into practice over the last 5 years or so and all electric cars have started to appear on the roads. Unfortunately 4x4 hybrid or electric are still very expensive. Also the idea of self-driving cars has also developed over the last few years, though these exist they are not yet legal to run on the open road.

Things like electric windows have been around for some time, my 1986 Vauxhall Astra was the first car I had with those, but my Duster has some new gadgets which I have never had before. It has a fitted GPS, which replaces the portable one I have had since Qatar(2010). It has a media centre which attaches to my iPhone by Bluetooth for making hands free telephone calls and playing music from my mobile. The headlights come on by themselves when it's dark, but it's windscreen wipers still need operating by hand. In some cars the headlights also dip automatically and the wipers start when it rains. The Duster also has cameras for parking, front, rear and sides, while the 2 to 4 wheel drive works at the flick of a switch....this was also a feature of the Nissan Pathfinder we bought new in Qatar in 2008! The Duster has anti-lock brakes (ABS) and anti-skid technology as well as descent control and the engine will switch off when you come to a halt, re-starting when you touch any pedal. The ABS and descent control had also been features of the 2002 Freelander. Finally the Duster has rear, though not front, parking sensors.

Mobile phones have become Smartphones, replacing iPods and iPads and similar technology by other firms, these have become part of everyday life for most of us. The internet is available across the world, wherever there is a 3G, 4G or in some cities 5G signal, all in the last 10 years or so. In Qatar (2008-10) and even in China(2012) we used Skype internet calling, voice only, to communicate with family at home. Text messaging was also popular, but sending an image was expensive.

iPod Classic, notice there is no touch screen. I bought mine from the Apple Shop in New York, while on a school Art trip.

I bought my first Smart(-ish) phone in about 2006, before that Wi-Fi, but not internet, was generally available at home or in pubs and cafes. I also bought a state of the art iPod 'Classic', 6th Edition, 80Go, in New York at about the same time. This is neither internet, touch-screen nor Bluetooth connected and has no sound of its own except ear plugs, it will also wire into a speaker/amplifier. This iPod still holds all my music collection.

iPhone 4S from 2012

I bought my first iPhone in 2012, a 4S, after we returned from China. I am happy to say that I replaced it with an iPhone 12 mini in 2021, as many of the Apps no longer work as the operating system and it no longer updated from iOS 7(we are now on iOS 16.3 and iPhone 13, as of Sept.'23).

The camera on the 4S also left something to be desired. Candy now has a iPhone SE. I bought Candy an original iPad when I left Qatar for the second time in 2013 and I bought myself a first generation iPad Air in Singapore in 2014. This last pad is the one I am using now, with a Bluetooth keyboard and an App called 'Pages', to write these memoirs. It will connect to the 4G network in Aunat via my smartphone or the house Wi-Fi, but doesn't have its own SIM card. Candy's has bitten the dust!

The 'Pad' and Smartphone along with internet connectivity by mobile network or Wi-fi have changed the way we live in as few as 10 years. Prior to that you would not have seen people sat in groups in a pub or cafe looking at their phones. The Smartphone is now not only the font of all knowledge, through things like Wikipedia and any Google, but also the recent advent of Artificial Intelligence(AI) apps. such as Chat GPT 3.5, a Large Language Model (LLM) based system. It also is most peoples only camera and store of all their photos………..uploaded to some 'Cloud' to keep them 'safe'. It also stores all your music as well as giving access to unlimited downloadable music too. Video calling via say Facebook Messenger or WhatsApp were unknown, or very unreliable in 2012 and Wi-fi was in its infancy. Now it can be done even without Wi-fi, direct from your mobile, through 4 and 5G networks.

I joined Facebook in 2008, but only accessed it from a hard wired computer terminal or hard wired laptop computer and WhatsApp in 2023. I still haven't joined Twitter, now rebranded as 'X', or Snapchat. E-mails have been around for quite some time, maybe 20 years or so, as the internet became more available. Everybody with an account receives at least 20+ a day, mostly just 'spam'.

Certainly it's been many years now since I actually wrote a letter to anyone and put a stamp on it and posted it. Though the mail has had a rejuvenation in recent years with the advent of on-line shopping. Particularly with sites like Amazon, which give a 1-2 day delivery promise. Certainly through the recent COVID-19 pandemic, online shopping and home delivery from supermarkets such as Asda and Tesco's has boomed.

There is also technology available so you can watch your house, by camera, from your mobile. You can monitor energy use or switch on the heating, oven or washing machine while out and about. This is called the Internet of Things(IoT), or in the household Smart House or 'demotics'. While we don't have any of these things in Aunat, they are available and I feel it won't be long before they are pervasive. There are also watches which link to your smartphone, which can not only link with the internet but also keep track of your vital signs. These, like 'Alexa' described below, are all a bit intrusive for Candy and I.

In terms of an actual computer many people now rely on their mobile or pad. We have a small Sony Vaio 'laptop' which we bought for going to China, so that must have been late 2010. It does have Wi-Fi, but not Bluetooth and I did use it to write up all of my BA degree assignments(2011-17). However, though it still works, it is quite slow on the internet. To be honest there isn't much that it can do that I can't do on my pad or mobile. Even our printer/photocopier connects to our pad/mobile either through the Wi-Fi router in the house or by Bluetooth. Of course the internet itself can now be accessed by voice command if you have 'Siri, which has been about since my iPhone 4S, 2010, or 'Alexa', which is just 5 years old.

The other thing which has changed over the past 20 years has been entertainment. Personal computer games have developed from a ball and 2 bats 'tennis' to interactive games, possibly with 3D surround video glasses.

Pong, the original home computer game, played on your own TV.

Music has moved from vinyl, past cassette tapes (on 'Walkmans') and mini-discs to Compact Discs(CDs) to downloading or playing direct from the internet. TV has also changed, in 3 ways. We bought our first 'flat screen' TV in Ilkley, possibly about 2004. Throughout the late 80s and 90s it had been possible to hire films from 'Video shops', first on VHS tape cassette then by the late 90s on Digital Versatile(Video) Disc, DVD. You could also use blank cassettes to record TV programmes as they were broadcast.

By mid-naughties TV was not only available through the old aerial, but also by satellite dish and direct through optic fibre or 'cable tv'. This introduced the idea of both films and other programmes 'on demand'. Currently here in France we have a Free-sat box which delivers free French satellite TV and has about 25 channels. It is very unsophisticated, so we cannot record from it or pause.

We also have a HD TV which attaches direct to the internet and allows us to watch on demand 'Netflix', Amazon Prime and Apple TV. It also accesses other internet facilities such as YouTube......we are spoiled for choice, so much so that we often don't know what to watch.

Downstairs we also have about 100 DVDs that we have bought over the years and can watch via the DVD player attached to the TV. I am reluctant to get rid of these just yet! A far distance has been travelled since the BBC or ITV, on a black and white screen, via H shaped aerials on the rooftops of the house, of my youth!

A street of old 'H' TV aerial, possibly from the mid 1960s, with some slightly more modern UHF aerials below. Well before 'cable', 'satellite' and 'internet' TV

So it is September 2023 and I am about at the end of my story 'so far'. As I sit here typing, once again in our veranda, the weather is warmer this summer than I've ever known in France, the sky is bright. Global Warming may soon become obvious to all. Some 41 months since this writing began, we are in strange times indeed. Things have also changed with regard to COVID-19. At one point France closed its borders to all but Citizens and Resident, but it has now been open for some time. The passes needed to show vaccine status for restaurants and public events are no longer required and testing is much less rigorous. Though it may recommence this winter, as a new variant arrives.

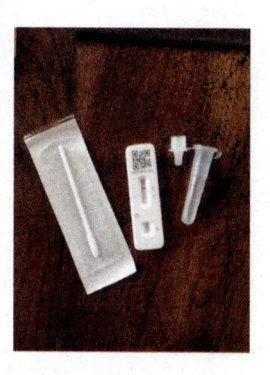

Pages from my Tous AntiCovid Pass, on my smartphone. A self administered COVID antigen test kit, showing a negative result (one, not 2, red lines). Push the cotton bud far up each nostril and twirl for 10s. Place the 'bud' in the plastic file and stir for 10s. Drop 4 drops from the file into the small square hole of the test & wait 15mins for it to develop.

Christopher Richard Martin Riley (15/04/86 - 10/03/22)

Our last trip to Skye(May 2018). A contented man, at home in his beloved mountain environment. A true mountaineer & no better companion.

This is my most difficult and unexpected chapter and it is really for Em who never got to know her dad & Toby (Jess) & Nathan who only knew him rarely at his best and for far too short a time.

The first bit is more of a blog than anything else as it is happening as I write, Tuesday 8th March 2022. Today Ruth rang us at 12:38 to say that Chris had been rushed into hospital, with severe brain damage, as he had tried, almost successfully to hang himself in Armley Jail. It had taken them 15 mins to revive him. By which time he had sustained substantial brain damage. It is now 19:00, he has been heavily sedated and Ruth, Charlotte, myself and Candy have agreed that if he dies in the night, the hospital should not attempt to revive him.

His great passion has always been in the outdoors….it is the reason he chose the jobs he has had…….I am certain he couldn't bear a life as an invalid. My feeling is that he has struggled with life for many years. Loving Charlotte, Jessica, Nathan, Emily and the rest of the family as best he could. Not always as we would have hoped, but always returning…..because he couldn't bear to be without them. Guys…..he loved us all. Don't think badly of him. Don't remember his quick temper when he was tired from a hard days work, but instead the hours he spent cuddling you all on that huge settee. You were his anchors. I strongly believe today that he could no longer bear to hurt us anymore.

Chris was in Armley Jail, Leeds. He was on remand for a series of crimes, caused I believe by a mental health problem that he has suffered from for many years. He was looking at a prison sentence. I believe the crimes he committed this last time were a result of him wanting to be taken out of society…….a last resort, to protect us all………as a result of his unstable mental health, combining badly with drink and drugs. It seems unlikely we will ever really know? We fly to the UK on Friday evening.

9th March, Chris was taken off medication today, while being kept on a ventilator. He made no recovery towards consciousness. Candy & I talked with Charlotte and Ruth in the evening about keeping him on the ventilator until we could get there. I thought it was kinder for everyone to let him pass away. A physically and mentally impaired Chris would have suffered terribly.

10th March, after tests today we were told that Chris's brain stem had died and there was no way back for him. He was pronounced dead at 16:51. As we spoke to Ruth he was being tested as an organ donor. Something which he had signed up for only a year ago, but something which Charlotte tells us he was passionate about……so typically generous even in the height of his depression. We have since learned that five recipients have been found for his organs: his heart, kidneys, pancreas and two people to share his liver.

My last words to him will live in my heart forever. Two weeks ago I spoke for a few minutes with him, by phone, in jail. The conversation ended:

"Love you bud" I said, "Love you too old man", what better last words.

So this is just a little bit about my good times with my eldest son. I recounted some of the best moments for the celebrant, to be spoken in his eulogy: "Lovely words from Wainwright, a hero for any walker. He mentions healing; there is healing needed today. As you all know, Chris struggled with his mental health through much of his life – and we must acknowledge that today. When he was at his most challenged and challenging, it is crucial to see those chapters in the light of his illness.

Yet today, we must find healing not only in being honest about his struggles, but also by remembering his strengths and his successes. Chris was a beloved partner, dad, son, grandson, brother, step-son, step-brother, fellow mountaineer and friend.

Born to his parents Ruth and Paul, Chris became an elder brother to Alasdair three years later. From a young age, and growing up in Guiseley and later Addingham, Chris was physically strong and a big lad. He loved to play rugby, first for Ilkley & Otley juniors, finally for Aireborough Senior XV at the tender age of 16. He won 3 junior Yorkshire Cup winners medals and 1 runners up medal. He also quickly proved himself to be an excellent swimmer. The day he phoned home from the pool asking for some help with some trophies he had won is a good example. Attendinga competition, he had been entered for his own age group but also that of the senior group; he won pretty much everything, and his dad watched amazed as having dropped off one armload of trophies he went back for another.

His dad also remembers Chris seeming to have it in for his cars... When Chris was only little, Paul was washing the car only to hear banging from the others side. He rushed round to find Chris, with a hammer, thumping the side of the car, 'mending 'it... Another time, when Chris was older, his dad drove down a lane to a farm in France which had barbed wire stretched across it – which of course slid up the bonnet, leaving its marks forever. Chris had put it there to 'delay 'him! "He could be a bugger", his dad says, and not least on the occasion when after trapping his fingers in the car door, told the nurse at the hospital that his dad did it! Paul, worried for his teaching career, had to do some explaining – and even then, only got away by Chris admitting he had done it himself because his dad made him rush to get in!

Chris's mischievous nature was balanced out by his good deeds though – and as a lad, he was proud to have won a green Blue Peter badge for collecting money with his friend, Joel, to help the birdlife affected by a Shetland oil slick.!

The mountains were in Chris 'blood from his parent's love of climbing – and he climbed his first Monroe at the age of 18 months! Well, at least, on his dad's back for most of it, but he toddled confidently up the last few hundred metres! He first experienced abseiling on his mum's front and tackled his first 4000 metre peak at the age of sixteen, and became a climbing partner with Paul and 'Uncle' Chris, his godfather. Spending lots of time on Skye, on the Cuillin Ridge, as well as on the glaciers and peaks of Chamonix, Chris was given the rope, known as 'the pig' to carry – he was after all, a big lad. Years later, Chris would spend time South of Geneva with his dad and Candy, where he was outstanding at helping out with Duke of Edinburgh expeditions.

Paul and Ruth will always remember with pride, Chris 'ability as a mountaineer – and as the years went by, the calm that Chris always displayed when out in the wilds. "Y'alright, old man?", he would ask his dad as the years went by…words that Paul will always hold dear - along with the big hugs his son would give him.

Combining his swimming and climbing skills, Chris, like both his parents, became an important member of the Upper Wharfedale Fell Rescue team. Over 10yrs he was both – an assistant warden and an assistant leader helping to set up the swift water rescue section. He received a Queen Elizabeth II Diamond Jubilee Medal for his services on the fell team. Today, a collection in Chris 'memory for the Fell Rescue team will be taken as we leave the chapel.

Wearing his Diamond Jubilee medal 2012

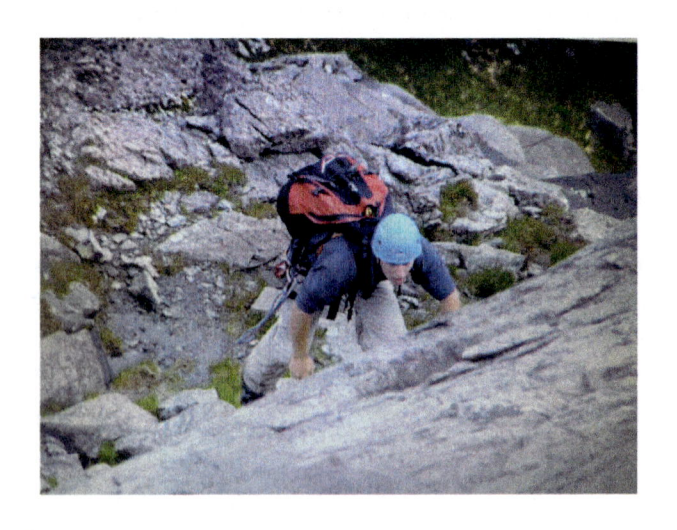

Chris, Free climbing on the Dubh Ridge, Skye, 2004.

Chris loved being outdoors. It was where he could breathe, relax and whatever it was he was doing, he did it with real skill and understanding – from climbing to kayaking; to building shelters to foraging for mushrooms. It was his environment. To many, who knew him from this outdoor context, there may be a surprise to learn of his struggles with his mental wellbeing, such was the positive effect of the outdoors on him.

Ruth, Chris's mum, recalls how he was also very helpful with his skills as a roofer. Determined to be involved, she volunteered as his labourer when he was helping renovate her house - and has lovely memories of sitting on her roof with him. He videoed her fitting the King-span, and perhaps ironically said to her, "Learn from your mistakes and move on". If only we could all do so...

Chris met Charlie in the pub where she was working behind the bar. He kept coming in, determined to ask her out. Eventually, he asked for her number, but Charlie gave him the number for the pub – which must have surprised him when the landlord answered! Anyway, he persisted, and he and Charlie became not only a couple, but soulmates. So many memories...You look back on how he took you up Jack's Raike in the Langdales – not an easy climb – and how he disappeared into a five-foot snow drift... And how, at eight months pregnant with Jess(Toby), he had you holding a bucket for fell rescue donations... And the callouts that you ended up coming along with – on at least one opportunity carrying the equipment while Chris had sprinted ahead... And that time when he collected you from work at Booths and you fancied a MacDonalds, so he drove you there – to the one in Edinburgh, and back home via Glasgow!

There are so many memories to look back on, Charlie, and while it has not been plain sailing, together you have brought three lovely children into the world – Jesse(Toby), Nathan and Emily. Jess(Toby) and Nathan, especially being older, will look back on some lovely times with daddy, and of course, little Emily more recently.There was lots of giggling and laughing, some lovely days out and holidays. The time in Wales, when he'd been fixing Candy's daughter's roof, with Paul labouring – Nathan remembers joining them on the roof – three generations of men with a head for heights!

Nathan also really enjoyed kayaking with his dad on the Wharfe at Ilkley – and looks forward to doing that again and thinking of his dad as he does. Jess(Toby) remembers baking with her daddy – making Shepherds Pie for Mother's day. It was a real success – unlike the Noodle Soup which was horrible! You also loved listening to music with your dad – he loved heavy metal and rock and was a big Evanescence fan. Jess(Toby) has been involved in helping choose music for today's service; thanks!

There were regular foraging expeditions – especially for mushrooms, which Chris was very good at identifying. Emily calling her dad 'Mushroom Daddy'. There were some you all called 'booby mushrooms 'for reasons we can all imagine! As well as mushrooms there were herbs, wild garlic and even, one day, a pheasant. As well as the more difficult times, there was a lot of fun. I heard how he loved the Rocky Horror Picture Show and was known to dress up in a basque and size ten stilettos. Charlie says he had better legs than her! Chris was a phenomenal family man; he adored his family – and the beautiful photo over the fireplace captures this love.

He loved his grandma, Joyce, too and would spend time with her, sharing his troubles, appreciating her wisdom and straight-forward approach. He will be missed by all of his family.

As Chris struggled to feel well and safe, it was necessary for him to live at Linfield Mount for a while, and even here he loved to forage. The care team recall how he'd come back with produce he'd collected outdoors – and make them fry ups and how his room was green, such was his love of nature. Very focused on the environment, he had plans to walk the Dales Way.

Back at home, he put his woodworking skills to good use and created himself a sanctuary in the loft, even making a high level bed from where he could look out at the moors. Nathan helped him with this.

The last chapter of Chris's life was difficult for him and everyone who loved him – and the sadness that is felt is only matched by the frustration that he was let down by the system, who should have taken better care of him when he was so vulnerable.

As an organ donor; Chris insisted that he should be an organ donor after he died. He was able help others: half his liver is helping a 7-year-old in Leeds and the other half has gone to Birmingham; his heart has gone to Glasgow and his kidneys and pancreas elsewhere. Helping 5 people in total. So, from a very sad story hopefully others will be able to live, which is a truly wonderful legacy, living proof of his generosity of spirit.
Chris has been so loved and has given great love in return. He will be missed always, and as his children grow, his memory will live on."
It says it all really. So many good times, but so much pain at others.

Charlotte, Jess(Toby), Nathan & Emily, he loved you especially, but in his own way. He was broken in some way we will never now know. What happened was not your fault, so feel no blame. I know we all did the best we could for him. He made some terrible life choices but I think he finally did what he thought was best for us all. ❤️

As for me, I regret we didn't have more time in the mountains bud. In all the times we did have we never had a bad day, you were always a perfect mountain buddy, I miss you and your words every day, "You OK old man?"

Not to forget Alasdair

Just a final note about Alasdair in Australia. There is a lot here about Chris, who can no longer tell his family his own story. It was never my wish to have to tell it for him, for his beautiful family.

Chris and Al turned out to be such different people. In so many ways Al has been able, from my perspective, to make much more of life's opportunities, so far. We have had numerous adventures in both cities around Europe and on our mountain bikes in the UK. I have been happy to support his Rugby too. Helping to train his team when he was at Ilkley. Unfortunately, he never managed to find a team that could reflect his own considerable talents.

After school he succeeded in completing his apprenticeship as a fitter for 'Caterpillar'. He has since moved to Australia and become a successful Supervisor in the blasting department of a very large open cast coal mine in central Queensland.

As I have said, he yet has the opportunity to lay down his own story, in his own Chronicle or here beside mine.

Part 2 - "The Unexamined Life is not Worth Living"... Socrates

"....few people on their deathbeds regret trying to achieve their dream, but many certainly regret not even making the attempt." Edith Hall

Introduction

These final chapters are a work in progress, and may be the most important to you, or of least interest. They represent a distillation of thoughts and ideas, by no means comprehensive, or correct, that I have put together, through reading, podcasts and in discussion with Candy and others, particularly over the last 10 years. Where appropriate I have used authoritative texts to help build my arguments. Though we should be clear that 'appeals to authority' or 'ad verecundiam,' where the 'opinion' of an authority, rather than 'evidence', is the primary source to support an argument, is consider by some to be a fallacy.

I begin by first looking at humans and then how they might make the most of their limited time on this Earth, but first:

Why write this & some advice from life

Up until 2012 I had spent my time trying to live my life as best I could on a somewhat ad hoc basis, feeling driven to be dutiful to myself, family and friends and working to support that ideal, but without really asking myself why! Life gave little time for thinking about the big questions, such as politics, psychology, philosophy, economics and how to live a good and fulfilling life. In short, I had a lot of doing, a lot of feeling, many pleasures but not much thinking.

Whilst living in China, a communist country, after Qatar, a Muslim benevolent dictatorship, Singapore, an autocratic 'democracy' and the U.K., a western democracy, I had a revelation. My science gave me an overview of the physical world, but I realised I was ignorant not only of the social world, but also of bigger questions; does life have a meaning and how is it best lived? To get some answers I decided, from 2012, to start a Bachelor of Arts(B.A.) degree in Politics, Philosophy and Economics. I spread it out over 6 years, working hard to see what I could achieve academically if I really went for it. I spent, and still do, a lot of time reading around the topics.

I prepared carefully for every assignment, with mountains of revision for exams. Something I'd never really done before! If you are in education at the moment I cannot, through hard learned experience, do anything other than give you four pieces of advice:

*Choose something you are passionate about & give it your absolute best!
*If you don't understand something pester your tutors, friends, parents, grand-parents until you do! Don't let things 'drift'.
*Work for every class, essay, assignment & tutorial as if it was the final exam.
*Then for your exams, there is no such thing as starting revision too early, or doing too much. Anything else is an excuse for not working!

N.B. Revision is re-learning, not understanding/learning for the first time!

Remember, you can never be over educated/qualified, that is a myth of the unqualified & the lazy. The more qualifications you have, while keeping diversity in your knowledge and understanding, the more opportunities you can access, and more importantly, the more interesting life can become. Remember, diverse experiences are as, not more, important than qualifications.

Also, if you are clever you can 'wing it' for a pass, I always did, but you will be hard pressed to achieve your dream results! I too was an arrogant youth, it took me 55 years to learn these lessons.

To ponder what we should do with our life, how we should behave towards ourselves and others, what we should aspire to and what to avoid, we might examine where humanity comes from and how we got here. We can then talk about some of the quirks of human nature, before we start to build our meaning or philosophy for living and for life. This first chapter looks at how we as humans perceive the world through a myriad of quirks.

Section I: Getting to the End.....first!

About half way through writing these last chapters it dawned on me that many of you may not get to the end of my machinations. So I decided to put the main conclusion first. If you are interested in the thinking behind how I reached these conclusion and more, then read on.

Ok, so life has no intrinsic meaning, it just is! There is no God, Santa, or Afterlife.... sorry ......there is no grand plan! Sudo-sciences such as Astrology, Homeopathy, and for me Economics, are just that, sudo!

Our mind is more powerful than we know, but it is trapped inside our brain, it cannot move objects by itself. Its 'unconscious' thoughts, though pervasive and powerful, cannot easily be interrogated 'directly', but do determine behaviours. Everything we think we know for certain has been 'hallucinated' from our perceptions by numerous parts of our brain which deliver thoughts to our 'conscious', this is the 'self' or 'me' we experience.

However, the workings of the unconscious have no awareness in the conscious 'me'! So it is very unlikely we will ever know reality as it exits outside of that 'me'! However, Sternberg maintains that we can correct the wrongs of the unconscious and the thoughts and behaviours it creates, using our conscious mind. Perhaps consciousness can also be used as a rewiring tool for behaviour?

We also know that science also make mistakes, often from lack of evidence, but sometimes when scientists allow their own biases or interests to cloud their judgments. Science is a work in progress, even 'objective' truths can sometimes turn out to be subjective, incomplete or just wrong. However, its methods give us our best understanding of the physical world at any given point in time, based on collecting 'fair' results, unbridled from opinion. Those things which depend on the unquestioned understandings of 'the ancients' or sacred books simply do not!

We must remember that science cannot easily answer questions about those things which are 'subjective'.....based on opinion. This involves many aspects of the human psyche, where there is no "objectivity'........so not based on 'fair' and verifiable facts, tested so as to remove subjectivity.

The past has gone, so is unchangeable, though its effect may influence us. Our future is often essentially unpredictable, depending on unforeseen complex* interactions, but can often be influenced, both positively and negatively, by plans we make 'now'. This makes 'the now' where we live. We are born, we live, we may reproduce though at this time this is not essential, then we die......the end! In that spec of time called life we can make the most of it and enjoy it or we can squander it and feel unhappy and unfulfilled as we head towards the inevitability of death. It makes no difference, except to you and those around you, in the here and now. It seems reasonable to assert that it is up to each one of us to search for what gives our life meaning, this can only ever be our meaning and it can only ever be subjective. This could lead you to nihilism*: a rejection of religion and morality and an acceptance that all this is meaningless, nothing matters. Personally I think that wastes what little 'now' we have. For me life is a 'once in a lifetime gift' not to be thrown to the wind, but to be built & enjoyed by everyone. As Bob McFerrin sang "Don't worry, be happy"

What is 'happiness'? For many today, enjoyment means pleasure seeking. Be warned, this can lead to a life of chasing pleasure but never being truly satisfied, always looking for the next pound, the next possession or the next thrill, but never finding fulfilment in achieving it. Happiness, through fulfilment and 'virtue', seems to me to be a better goal, Aristotle called it 'eudaimonia'**.

So, let us start in our quest by admitting we are social rather than solitary creatures, there is increasing evidence that this makes us happy and cooperation is the root of our success as a species. Doing thing for others is found to brings more sustained happiness than acts of selfish pleasure seeking. If nothing else, it certainly makes us better companions and psychologically companionship has been shown to be important to happiness and wellbeing.

*Complexity: a system where the effect is not (yet?) predictable from the factors which make up the cause or vis versa.
*Nihilism: as life is meaningless, nihilists reject all moral and religious principles.
*Eudaimonia, "virtuous activity in accordance with reason" , "flourishing" says Aristotle; " a life of happiness, where happiness coincides with virtue [which is not exclusively morality for the ancients, and may include wisdom, courage and compassion]" says Epicurus.

Cooperation is the root of our success as a species. Doing thing for others is found to brings more sustained happiness than acts of selfish pleasure seeking. If nothing else, it certainly makes us better companions and psychologically companionship has been shown to be important to happiness and wellbeing. To achieve this, in my very humble opinion, each of us needs to build 'virtuous' founding principles or 'Foundations' for our life which we can refer to when we are unclear of which behaviour to adopt. These Foundations becomes the solid basis of a Moral Code. Rocks in the quicksand of morality, something upon which we can call to live a rational existence. I use rational here in the sense of internally consistent, based on reliable evidence, so that all the behaviours we have and choices we make fit together and work towards our best interests as happy and fulfilled individuals, as a tribe and as a global society. You may not agree with me, but if you dismiss my proposal you should replace them with your own........analysed rationally!

Establishing My First Foundations

Our earth spins like an infinitesimally small spec around a tiny star, one of something like 100 million in the Milky Way galaxy alone. Which is itself a fairly insignificant galaxy among 200 billion visible others. Amongst that stellar crowd and a 14 billion year timescale, human existence let alone any one of us, is mind blowingly insignificant, yet as far as we know so far, marvellously unique. I'm a proponent of the 'big bang', an atheist and a materialist*, in a philosophical sense! In short, for me time began 13.7 billion years ago and the Universe has been expanding ever since. We are not sure how, but currently no explanation is always better than a bad one. So I don't believe god or gods made this happen, though we will never be able to 'prove' they didn't**. As an 'agnostic atheist' I have no reason, no evidence that I find credible, to believe that any gods exist or if they did would care one way or another about each of us. Religions, with sudo-sciences, for me have too many 'jokers'***.

*Materialists: all events, including those produced by the human mind are causally dependant upon physical processes
**See later, the Enlightenment
***joker: a statement which doesn't add to an argument, but gives an implausible excuse for why no argument is necessary; eg. 'God moves in mysterious ways'. Or, proposing an argument which is unfalsifiable; 'that phenomenon doesn't work under the conditions imposed by any 'fair' test. Or arguing that someone should 'prove the non-existence of something'. ie God

I have an almost lifelong aversion to any system which holds faith as proof of anything and dogma as truth. I'm a Darwinian, supporting his idea from *The Origin of Species,* for no other reason than it seems plausible and is supported by evidence from palaeontology, selective breeding and examples of actual natural selection.

We all have a long heritage, as genetically we all descended from the first life on Earth., the Last Universal Common Ancestor(LUCA). Not the fastest, not the biggest, not the strongest, but now by some measure the smartest, Homo Sapiens have been around for 2 to 300 000 years. Diverging from other apes about 8 million years ago and monkeys 25 million years ago. How did we make the journey? Certainly not alone, otherwise as Hobbs would have it in *Leviathan*, life would be "solitary, poor, nasty, brutish and short".

Cooperation seems to have been central to human development, so perhaps cooperation can underpin our moral code? However, this has to be the right sort of cooperation. We can't just cooperate with any type of behaviour and expect fulfilling outcomes. Competition seems to be the opposite to cooperation, however it has also been important in advances made by Homo Sapiens and many of our traits have developed to focus on this. In these times of plentiful resources, the question is can we do without competition? Perhaps so! My first Foundation might be:

Behave at all times in such a way as to both promote and expect reciprocal social cooperation, while actively avoiding the conflict inherent in social competition. This in itself might be where you end, but there are more Foundations to come and more to understand.

Section 2: Human Problems and Foundations

It is also crucial in my view, that we fully appreciate that life is a lottery. That much of what we are is through our luck in this draw of life. We got here through the luck of reproduction over millennia, making each one of us special because we are unique. We have inherited part of who we are through the luck of our genome (nature), which acts as a template for almost everything about us. However, there are too few genes to carry all the information about how the synapses in our brain should join up. This means that our individual experiences and encounters (nurture) form much of who we are. Again, this is the luck of parents, friends, school and the society into which we are born. Add to this that 'success' in life, whatever that is, is determined by the luck of having the right skills at the right time, JS Mill calls it "occasion & chance". Some of these skills may be less than virtuous, in fact actually vices: selfishness, hard heartedness, sycophancy, lies, tricks, gambling and knavery, are hardly admirable or virtuous qualities, in my view. This means that some people are just luckier than others but luck should be no reason to believe that any person is more valuable than any other. So, more fundamental than cooperation is treating this equality of value with respect, as a foundation of our moral code. Writings from Philosophy can help us here, with more of why I chose these two later. For now I will just use them. First the ancient Golden Rule: "....do to others as I would that they should do to me." Plato, *Laws, Book XI* which I expand to:

Treat others as you would wish to be treated, using sympathy, empathy fairness and equality of human value as your guide.

Adding this to our initial Foundation about cooperation and competition we have the building block for a more stable moral code. But what are the purposes of the Foundations?

Let's move on to the Big Questions
As I see it, we are trying to get our heads around four big questions:
#what is life?
#where does it come from?
#what might its purpose be?
#how might we live it well?

The first two of these questions can be answered quickly, as there is not much to go on. The last two I will start here then come to in more detail in later chapters.

What is life? There are many explanations for what constitutes a living thing. Nobel Prize winning geneticist Paul Nurse, says that to be alive things need, "The ability to evolve by natural selection...to do that they have to be able to grow, to reproduce and they have an hereditary system which exhibits variability". This works for even the most simple of life forms: viruses, which are at the edge of this definition, as they can only reproduce in another living cell, through to Homo Sapiens. However, because we are conscious beings, with the ability to introspect, and to story tell, life for Homo Sapiens is greater than the purely biological. In reality we really don't fully understand what life is, other than complex interacting biological systems, though the difference between life and death, for humans, seems reasonably clear.

As to where life comes from? We have no real answers to that either, and maybe never will. Current scientific theories put it as the random organisations of increasingly complex molecules over vast timescales, starting as early as 3.8 billion years ago, here on our 4.5 billion year old Earth. However, we do not, as yet, seem to be able to synthesis anything resembling life from basic chemicals in the laboratory! Maybe all we lack is time? The earth seems to have been at it for nearly 0.7 billion years before it got it right. We can tell form our DNA, the blueprint of life we carry in our cells, that current life on earth started from a single LUCA.. we are all related! So remember, 'brothers' and 'sisters', it is down to luck rather intentionality that you are here at all.

The Meaning of Life?

As it turns out this third big question is both the easiest but also the hardest for me to answer. As I see it, if there is no God, no re-birth and no afterlife, then when you are dead, that is it! So there is a semi-cycle of birth, life, death, but no 'meaning' other than perhaps to survive long enough to reproduce, which is itself somewhat random. To look at the bigger picture the entire Universe also lacks meaning, but perhaps it doesn't need one? It just is! However, maybe humanity needs its own meaning? Emil Cioran maintains that we are creatures which seek out meaning, where there is none! He goes on to claim that we adopt the stories we have for the meaning of existence to avoid this lack of meaning. However, if you accept that everything is meaningless you may not have to accept any moral responsibility: you never need to grow up! This would probably result in a society which is certainly nihilistic, probably antisocial and ultimately chaotic. These are further compounded by a lack of a morality which has no natural objective basis..........only quicksand.

The fundamental reason for meaning, to avoid anarchy, is why I feel we need a basis for a moral code, to give structure to any meaning we decide upon which will, debatably, enhance the general 'progress' of the patterns of humanity which have already placed us, again debatably, at the pinnacle of life.
If life is all we have, that brings us to question four...... how might we live it well? This is a big question, already begun above. Expanding on this, and I am sure few would disagree; I posit that happiness is better than sadness, pleasure better than pain. To achieve happiness/pleasure and avoid unnecessary sadness/pain might therefor be another key to our quest for a good life and at the same time lead us to some meaning for

which we search? I have already spoken of Aristotle, who suggested that eudaimonia is essential. But how do we get that fulfilment? Perhaps from living a 'good life', a life of virtue, and maybe this in a meaningless universe can only truly be achieved by building both meaning and purpose for ourselves & with others. This might be done initially individually, but as social creatures we need eventually to understand the power and rewards of working collectively. This is going to take time to unravel so let's dig into question four, living well, virtue & happiness, by adding more about what we know of humanity.

More about Cooperation: the bad stuff.

It is not disputed that society has largely progressed through the benefits of working together, endowed with both *Sympathy** and *Empathy** f*or each other. This for many years, was in small cooperative groups. In turn, socialisation, cooperation and adaptability have been driving forces behind our success as a species, humanities evolutionary strength, and probably integral to both speech and mental development; particularly the consciousness, the 'me', we find currently. Of course, this is not to forget that we are not angels. Pinker also believes that we are "....fitted by evolution with ......greed, lust, dominance, vengeance, and self-deception." However, I believe these are 'antediluvian'* traits, developed through competition for resources. They may be something we needed in the past but need to actively subdue now, rather than glorify, in order to allow our more co-operative traits to flourish. We should certainly not be glorifying these traits as many societies do through both their social and economic systems. Instead our system of morality should encourage, through changes in behaviour, for them to become *'vestigial**'*.

* Sympathy: for Pinker in New Enlightenment is: "....also called benevolence, pity, and commiseration."
* * Empathy: Our ability to share and understand others feelings.
* *Antediluvian: ridiculously old fashioned
* **Vestigial: forming a small remnant of something once great

David Sloan Wilson, in his article *"The Invisible Hook"* looks at it this way: "In most animal societies, dominance takes the form of the stronger individuals intimidating the weaker. These societies would be called despotic in human terms and they provide an inhospitable social environment for cooperation........... In our distant ancestors, members of groups found ways to collectively suppress disruptive self-serving behaviours, which provides a more hospitable environment for cooperation. Granted, when resources are hard won, if you exclude succeeding at the expense of those within your own group, the only alternative is to cooperate against 'others'. Rovelli adds that social structures & conflicts seem to have developed with agrarian living styles, some 50000yrs ago. While power structures, hierarchies and hereditary powers in larger societies, are only 10 000yrs old.

Alternatively, behavioural Psychologists Corr & Pagnol, in *Behavioural Economics, the basics,* posit that humans typically do not behave to maximise happiness or 'utility'. Social behaviour is governed by "fairness", cooperation and the 'warm glow' we feel when we help other people".
We have to ask, how did those feelings arise?

This may be a long-run selfish strategy because we also seek reciprocity and will go against our own self-interest to allocate punishment, when it is lacking. They also note that Emotions: moods, feelings, and attitudes; Physical states: hunger and warmth; as well as cognition or rationality can highly influence how we think, feel, judge, decide and behave towards others and in a more generally way.
It seems we are a mix of contradictory traits. Some still necessary others, as I have suggested perhaps vestigial. We are the often contradictory results of our ancestral heritage, adaptability and push to survive in changing environments. The question again is, do we still need to prize all these traits today?

Here, for me, questions three and four now start to overlap, our purpose in life being inextricably entangled with what we think, and thus with the way our minds determine both how we think and feel. As this should be an import question for all of us to consider, allow me to introduce a taster for this here, at an early stage, in case, as I fear, you don't make it to the end of this increasingly large 'exposition'!

Part 3: The Human Problem; some insights into how our brains might work

Let me set the scene, we are more than we can ever know. 'Me' is just the tip of the iceberg. From the neuroscience and psychology I have read, I believe our brains have developed in the way they have to maximise our survival, by maximising our ability to work in social groups, with other increasingly intelligent beings. Certainly consciousness in Homo Sapiens seems to have been around only 300 000 yrs(some say 50000), language 50-150 thousand years and human art dates from 45 000 years ago. Perhaps these developments were encouraged by each other and initiated by negative climactic changes in the environment of early humans in the Rift Valley of Africa. An increasing need to socialise effectively encouraging the selection/evolution of higher cerebral faculties, thus enabling us to second guess what others are thinking, and to mimic them using 'mirror neurones'. These in turn helping to develop both cooperation and empathy and use past experience to determine future opportunities outside that experience.

The modern human brain is a prediction engine, it has an 'ancient' core which looks after those things which are motor needs, including but not exclusively limited to homeostasis and general survival. Emotions or feelings evolved pragmatically in the unconscious brain, to compel evolutionary decisions , through both natural selection and experience. Then we have more recent developments such as the cerebral cortex, from the complexity of which, I believe, comes the emergence* of 'consciousness.

Consciousness is our interface to other minds. Consciousness, as opposed to just awareness of your surroundings, as humans is also self-awareness and awareness of awareness in yourself and others. The ability to introspect and plan on your own and others thoughts/behaviours from a 3rd person perspective. What it is like to be 'me'!' This definition I will use throughout.

This fits well with Kahneman's ideas of System 1 and System 2, described in *Thinking Fast and Slow*. System 1, for me, is the unconscious, Freud calls it the sub-conscious, the part of our thinking that is (mostly if not totally) hidden from us and which is the vast amount of our neural processing.

*An emergent property appears through complexity, not found in the individual things from which it is made. Eg. You can't predict the patterns of a flock of birds by looking at individual bird behaviours.

Neuroscience shows that most of our traits, decisions, actions, emotions and behaviours depend on the 95 percent of brain activity that lies beyond conscious awareness, meaning that 95 (or as much as 99%) of your life comes from the neural interactions in your unconscious mind. Patricia Churchill further warns that our "conscience* is not always a trustworthy guide" on which to base our future behavlours.

System 2 is the rest, the other 5%, for me, the conscious awareness you experience as 'me' and what most of us assume controls all we do. Surely that can't be right? We shall see, more of that later! Now lets introduce The Organ Grinder & The Monkey!

We are creatures of intellect, but introspection doesn't show us all that we are. As I have said, much of our behaviour is 'automatic'.....lets call the unconscious the Organ Grinder. The Monkey is the conscious thinking that we take to be 'me'. You can see the problem, the Organ Grinder makes decisions and takes actions to control our thoughts and behaviour, our Mind, let us call this The Music. Your conscious Monkey gets little understanding or control. Except of course a strong Monkey can perhaps, perhaps not? put on the brakes.....but it also needs some principles to guide it and it needs practice in using them! What are these principles? Well they are just the practiced and rational consequences of the 'Foundations' we have begun above!......more of the Organ Grinder, his Monkey and our Music later.

. We also need to remember that our brain is a complex array of multiple competing brain regions, not a single unified system. These being shown as neural correlate of consciousness; those things seen to be happening inside the brain, by fMRI*, in response to external & internal stimuli. Neuroscience has discovered that levels of consciousness increase as these regions interact. Thoughts and actions seem not to be taken centrally, but developed in different areas and actually compete** for implementation.
   *Conscience : a moral sense of right or wrong guiding our behaviour through feelings. Driven from the unconscious brain
   *fMRI: functional magnetic resonance spectroscopy
   **This competition will be important later when I come to discuss Free Will.

So, it would seem that there is more to the self or 'me' than a single action of the brain and certainly more than each of us know through conscious awareness. We also need to remember that the world as each of us perceives, the phenomenology, it is different for each of us, these differences can be major. This is because all sense information is interpreted by the brain, and this depends upon how the brain is set-up, which in turn depends on the nature (genetics) and nurture (feelings and experiences, including current experiences or drugs) of each individual. We experience the world through fogged spectacles, not always, as Kant said "rose coloured"!

As mentioned, we have a complex brain, with inbuilt ways to mimic and reflect others. It feels like emergent consciousness enables us to sometimes read others minds and behaviours, to enter, plan and make stories about projected futures often for better and sometimes for worse.

Remember, we are particularly good at making up stories!!! This can sometimes be problematic, when we worry about futures we have created, possibly on little or no evidence. The present is all we really have. The past is often subjective and made from often unreliable and biased memories, the future is not set. All this seems to have evolved hand in hand with our physical and social development through Darwinian selection, "principle by which each slight variation [of a trait], if useful, [might be] preserved", as the environment changes. Individuals best adapted to their environments are more likely to survive and reproduce. Variation which are hereditable, will be often selected for, promoting individuals with the most advantageous variations.

A Throw of the Dice, Nature and Nurture

Damasio, in *Descartes's Error*, tells us that the genome can set up nearly precise structures for the ancient brain, for basic life functions, this is our 'nature'. Further, these 'innate' circuits influence the development of the evolutionary more modern aspects of the brain, the cortex.

However, the precise arrangement is influenced by environmental factors and to some extent able to change throughout life through neural plasticity, the 'nurture' aspect of nature / nurture. This plasticity may allow us to attempt to make ourselves better.......or worse!

I like to think that for every aspect of our psychology and of our physiology, every trait, there is a possible continuum; ie. lets say from exceptionally musical to tone deaf. Nature, or genes, only builds an initial structure which will allow us access to only a segment of the whole continuum; say moderately musical. Then nurture dictates our place in the segment: say towards the very musical. Plasticity allows us to move, with effort, within our given segment, but not reach outside it; so we may not ever be able to achieve exceptional musical ability however much we practice, but practice moves us towards it. This applies to some of our physical make up too. Your height, weight and strength are within a segment of each genetic continuum. Each is then affected by both our environmental conditions and behaviours. Never forget, you are not a self-made child, you have had little input to either nature or nurture. Think about that the next time you pat yourself on the back for what you think 'you' have achieved, or when criticising others for being less 'successful'.

These bundles of traits are constantly being tweaked by a continual stream of perceptions, whilst interacting with each other, often in competition, in our brain. Thus, our brain can be understood as a 'probability engine", calculating the most favourable outcome, as it understands them. The traits themselves underline our personality, which determines our all important world view. This defines, for many, the favourable outcomes to be established.

So, your genes are the luck of the draw. At the very least your early environment is luck too. The circumstances you find yourself in, do people want your particular skills, are often luck? What about the choices we make? I will leave the arguments about Free Will, how much you can choose who you become, until later. For now, to make you feel more comfortable, let us assume that we have at least some ability to make some bounded choices*, lets say to reap the benefits of the luck we have had so far........or not!

*Bounded Choice: as we never know all the possibilities, we can only make choices based upon the information we have and the circumstances we find ourselves in, we never have infinite choice.

More about the Parable of the Organ Grinder and the Monkey

I mentioned above, Kahneman's System 1, which is our Organ Grinder, and System 2 our Monkey, I think its time for more details! The Organ Grinder is behind all our feelings, it 'speaks' to us in feelings, emotions and drives. We can't access it's nature or know what influenced its nurture. This means that it is difficult to analyse the veracity of its urges, which come to us quickly and directly as ideas and actions. In reality 'me', that is our Monkey, often has no real idea what it is doing, maybe until just after it has done it? Lets make no mistake, the Organ Grinder is big and powerful, has at least a massive influence on our behaviour and sometimes, particularly in moments of stress, takes total control.

The Monkey, is sat on top, we each feel it is in control, after all it is our 'me' taking all the credit. I believe most people are convinced that their Monkey rules as it is all we know. Unfortunately, for most of us most of the time, the Monkey does not bother about rationalising the feelings and consequential behaviours sent by the Organ Grinder, instead it just rubber stamps them. It does however spend a lot of time making up excuses to justify those actions, post-hoc, sometimes bending reality to make it fit to its world view and so confirm its identity. This may result in us often taking credit for our successes, while blaming our failures on others. Sometimes unhelpfully, our Monkey is an expert story teller, able to manipulate its truth. It's only when something grabs its attention that it may acts to try to control the ideas and behaviours of the whole agent, The Organ. Then the Monkey has at its disposal available memory, education, experience and most of all reason, to spot causes, analyse actions and predict sometimes novel, outcomes. With training it may be able to tame the Organ Grinder, overcoming drives and impulse to make better choices. However these are skills which for most of us need awareness of the problem that the many don't seem to have, and which have to be *practiced* in application. The actions of the Organ Grinder come quickly through System 1, the Monkey's more slowly, through System 2. Hence: "Think before you act" or "Count to 10 when you are angry".

Biases: Cognitive Biases: making decisions in an unknowingly irrational way. Often using heuristics. See later in this Chapter.

Do beware, the Monkey is often lazy and loves a short cut, the Organ Grinder is strong. For most but not all people, a good Monkey needs years of training, sometimes a lifetime, to first spot then control the biases*, bad habits and misconceptions deeply and invisibly embedded in the Organ

Grinder by both nature and nurture. I believe that the luck of the draw doesn't give everyone the same ability to wake up their Monkey. It is more of a challenge for some, being blocked by the bad luck of nature, habits and experiences of nurture and the story telling ability of the Monkey to retrospectively avoid or offload responsibility. But I do believe in most cases just an understanding of how it interacts with the Organ Grinder can help. Further, the Monkey can be taught, or less often it can teach itself, how to spot when it is needed, to stop the Organ Grinder running completely amok with the Music: thoughts/behaviours.

Through *practice* and success the Organ Grinder and the Monkey can begin to change ideas and behaviours, to better understand the Music, giving better outcomes for the Organ: the agent/us. More fulfilling outcomes at worst make behaviours more rational and less damaging, and at best re-wire the Organ Grinder, changing the feelings he pushes forward to those more inline with happy outcomes and a 'good life'. However the Monkey needs a basis for judgment, rocks in the quicksand of Morality; 'Foundations'.

The Monkey 'may' also have a large input into conscious planning, which is really important for a 'good life'. It can create and assess possible futures, looking at cost/benefit and assess risk: known unknowns. All in a brain space in which we are aware. So it is imperative that we are able to spot when the Organ Grinder is out of control and is moving contrary to virtue and the good life. Then its time to arouse the Monkey. Does this fit with Free Will, we shall see?

I must re-emphasise here understanding the role of luck. As it is central to how we might feel about what we 'deserve'. We have said, our genome is luck, our environment and thus our initial social circumstances are luck. Our instincts and drives come to us from unknowable sources, so are often formed by the luck of those circumstance. Only by using our free will, if we have one?, to make internally consistent reasoned decisions, those held to accountable 'objective' standards based on good information and careful planning, can we regard our 'self' as agent in producing a 'good life'. Otherwise we drift through life on a sea of serendipity and zemblanity (misfortune), allowing our Monkey to claim the credit for what our Organ Grinder has proposed simply by good fortune.

We may expect too much reward when we are successful, blaming others as 'lazy' or 'thick' when they are perceived to have less success, and are thus deserving of less reward. This I feel enables many of us to justify our social rewards by equating them with 'social value'. A value derived more from luck than individual efforts.

This view perhaps might give the impression that we may not be to blame for our actions, and that might actually be so, the Organ Grinder may run the show. That is not to say that by living a life according to our Organ Grinder we can escape the consequences of those actions. Currently the responsibility lies with the whole beast, as agent or Organ, to learn how to mediate The Music, combining passions with reason, as best we can. Eudaimonia is sweet Music within the grasp of most Organs, but some may need help to at least try to rewire the Organ Grinder.

Contrary to this view, David Hume(1711-1776), unaware of the Organ Grinder and his Monkey, believed that overcoming the unconscious may not actually be possible, "reason being a slave of the passions" and "moral distinctions being derived from moral sentiments: approval and blame, rather than reason". Rather he sees reason as merely an impression we feel when we knowingly give rise to an action. This difference really does hang on how much Free Will we actually have, that we shall examine much later. In some instances this may well be partly true, in my own experience the Organ Grinder can be strong.

I believe that reasoned understandings from underlying behavioural moral 'Foundations' for good and evil, right and wrong and obligation and duty can be practiced to overcome many of "the passions" or the Organ Grinder, by putting pressure on the moral sentiments through rational behavioural changes emanating from the Monkey. But, we would need the ability to acquire and accept available information, such as our Foundations, and the desire to follow them up, is this possible? Again, we will have to wait and see!

When the Organ Grinder Misreads the Input Data

There are a couple of aspect of Personality which are worth keeping in mind, especially when we believe we know what we think about the world. These are: heuristics, cognitive biases, logical fallacies and framing. Kahneman (ibid.) talks about heuristics and Thaler, in *Misbehaving,* examines biases. Both are explained quite well in Corr & Plagnol(ibid.). Theses strange phenomena distract our Organ Grinder from developing reasoned opinions. Spotting them is a key to bringing about the attention of the Monkey, rather than allowing it to 'rubber stamp' the Organ Grinder's passions. One problem with this is that smart people often make good excuses as to why the biased action or opinion was valid, rather than seeing it as a bias to be countered......the Monkey making up stories again.

Heuristics are "...simple procedures that help find adequate, though often imperfect, answers to difficult questions"........answers from the Organ Grinder! Remember, never fully trust the Organ Grinder, it has its own agenda, and your Monkey is not privy to it. Here is one example of heuristics* that are worth being aware of. Taken from Sunstein and Thaler's article in the New Yorker, *The Two Friends Who Changed How We Think about How We Think:* "For instance: ask people what they think is the ratio of gun homicides to gun suicides in the United States. Most of them will guess that gun homicides are much more common, but the truth is that gun suicides happen about twice as often.

The explanation that Kahneman and Tversky offered for this type of judgment error is based on the concept of "availability." The Availability Heuristic. That is, the easier it is for us to recall instances in which something has happened, the more likely we will assume it has. This rule of thumb works pretty well most of the time, but it can lead to big mistakes when frequency and ease of recall diverge. Since gun homicides get more media coverage than gun suicides, people wrongly think they are more likely The availability heuristic, leads people to both excessive fear and unjustified complacency— and it can lead governments astray as well." Cognitive biases are a fairly new idea, but their effects have been known for a long time.

In 1267 Roger Bacon, in *Opus Majus,* wrote: "There are indeed four chief hindrances to the understanding of truth, which stand in the way of every man [woman], however wise, and permit hardly any to arrive at the true title of wisdom; to wit, (1) the example of frail and unsuited authority, (2) the long duration of custom, (3) the opinion of the unlearned crowd, and (4) the concealment of one's own ignorance in the display of apparent wisdom...............For everyone in all the acts of life and study and every occupation uses three of the worst arguments to the same conclusion; namely, (1) this has been exemplified by our ancestors, (2) this is the custom, (3) this is the common belief: therefore, it must be held.......... the fourth is always before the eyes or on the lips of everyone to excuse his own ignorance; and although he knows nothing worth knowing, nevertheless what he knows he magnifies shamelessly so that he overwhelms and shatters the truth in the consolation of his unhappy stupidity............" still very true! Sorry, long quote, I'll try not to do that again.

Today Behavioural Scientists and Economists are more closely defining these biases, so that we can spot them, and act to counter them, in our own thoughts and behaviours. Here is a famous example: Prospect Theory, 1979, put forward by Tversky & Kahneman and can be found in the back of *Thinking Fast and Slow,* starts by looking at loss aversion; preferring to avoid loss rather than make gains, and risk aversion; preferring low uncertainty to higher uncertainty with higher possible gains.......that is me by the way! These they used to explain how, contrary to Expected Utility Theory(EUT) of rational choice, people will often *not* make the most rational choices to maximise utility. This is worrying, as Neoclassical Economics, Chapter Z, is largely based on the principle of EUT.

Psychologists & Behavioural Economists have found that many such, non rational cognitive biases exist. Unless you are aware of them, they are difficult to avoid. A common bias when looking at new information is Confirmation Bias: where we search for(Cherry Pick), interpret, favour, and recall information in a way that confirms or supports our prior beliefs or value, thus supporting our Identity. Another would be Cognitive Dissonance: where two contradictory views can be held at the same time, causing internal conflict. This internal conflict being dissipated often by blindly ignoring inconsistent facts.

My final two examples are Logical Fallacies; these can be unsubstantiated assertions that are often delivered with a conviction that makes them sound as though they are logical arguments. Informal fallacies in particular are found frequently in mass media such as television and newspaper. Eg. "The UK is in debt, it has maxed out its credit card", which is economic bollocks! Similar to Logical Fallacies is Conventional Wisdom: a generally accepted belief, opinion or judgment which need not necessarily be correct. Eg. Immigrants cost the U.K., rather than the fact which is that they add, overall, to tax and GDP.

The last is Framing; where the way something is set out, framed, influences your choice. Say if it is framed in a posited or negative way, to elicit a positive or negative outcome. Eg. Q1: should we allow more immigrants into our over full country? A1: No. Q2: Should immigrants be encouraged to come to the UK? A2:No. *Versus,* Q1: The UK has an acute labour shortage, should we employ people from overseas? A1: Yes. Q2: Should immigrants be encouraged to come to the UK? A2: Yes. Also remember when using Artificial Intelligence (AI), such ass Large Language Models (LLM) such as CHAT GPT Framing is very important!

There are many more biases, which can easily be researched on a good search engine! We have to accept that we are all susceptible to them and should be wary of them when assessing new information and making decisions. Remember there are few things nicer than finding facts which support your world view/Identity: Confirmation bias, and nothing more uncomfortable than trying to accept facts which show you were initially wrong........'Factcheck' what you are told, not only when it is uncomfortable, but particularly when it is comfortable and re-assuring too! Don't always just search for supporting evidence.

The following chart (next page) outlines some of the biases which we as humans exhibit. It is only by being aware of these biases that we can compensate in our thinking to overcome some of the effects of the Organ Grinder.

How People Actually Decide

A brief aside with Bayes, sorting the wheat from the chaff........evidence.

In many places during these last chapters, as in life, I have had to make what feel like choices. What to believe, what to dismiss and what to hold in the space between. For me, this balances on the quality and weight of evidence. Those beliefs which have no evidence or for which the evidence has little or no weight I call 'free floating ideas'. They have interest, as possibilities for a search for evidence, but are not a sound basis for a belief. Other beliefs have a weight, depending upon the quality/reliability of their source and evidence. This evidence should be as objective as possible, but sometimes subjectivity is all we have. Here sample size (larger the better) and statistics is often the key to reliability, but quality of the source should not be ignored.

The weight you give is also somewhat subjective, so very few things, are ever set in stone. Very few things, if any, should have sufficient weight to give them 100% credence, which in itself is good, as 100% confidence is dangerous as it can produce dogma. The scientific method itself, our most reliable source of objectivity, is about 'falsification' rather than 'proof'. More beliefs than we might hope turn out to be free floating ideas, others just to have surprisingly little weight, so little credence needs to be taken of them. Remember, your weighting's can be biased too!

Obtaining evidence can be done by observation or reporting of events. This is called empirical (or empiricism). It's main problems are that humans can be easily biased by their psychological viewpoint (identity) or their observational inadequacy (senses) to mis-report their observations or cherry pick their results, either consciously or unconsciously. Evidence needs to be as free as possible from other possible causes: other input 'variables' and observer biases. In other words a 'fair test'. A single persons, or even likeminded group observations should be *very* suspect.

The other type of support for a belief is through rational thought. This doesn't exclude information gained from experience, but includes reasoned interpretations to produce facts which are beyond reasonable doubt or self-evident. Montague might call these 'cognitive phenomenology' (phenomena), rather than sensory phenomenology' (phenomena), more of this in Chapter Z. In most cases good evidence is somewhat of a mixture.

When ideas clash we need some way of comparing them, to establish which has most weight. Here Bayesian probability can be useful and updated as evidence changes. Though somewhat mathematically complicated, a simple view is to to balance the weight of evidence for each case, subjectively & considering your biases, in your head. This should establish if your current belief should be given credence or exchanged for beliefs with more weighty evidence. As evidence or falsification is updated, then weight and thus credence in the belief should change. Occam's Razor or principle of parsimony is worth considering; the explanation with fewest elements is often more correct. So explanations that need multiple caveats should be viewed with suspicion.

Remember your beliefs are often tied in with your identity, making even free floating ideas difficult to let go........and yes that is a cognitive bias we all hold. Also beliefs can be both true and false. A true belief might be called a fact, but the evidence should be overwhelming.

Thoughts for moving forward

Let me pull some strands together. I have argued that life has no intrinsic meaning, but without meaning life may become intolerable. In looking for meaning I have suggested that we look at what has been helpful in the past and what could become destructive in the future. Using this and guidance from other areas of philosophy to build the way to a meaningful and fulfilling life.

We might achieve this, first by understanding and attempting to control impulses which are possibly either self-harming or harmful to others, these are often the same. We have to recognise that what I have written so far is only about the understanding of the problem. The battle for control of the Organ & it's Music is a battle between the Organ Grinder & the Monkey, deep set emotions and experience/rationality. It can, as I know from my own small encounters, be a Battle Royal. Rationalisation alone can often, as Hume predicted, may not cut the mustard! Recognition of, understanding of, and compromise with the emotional, and practices to solidify better outcomes are the keys to success.

Second, the battle between emotion and rationality is not only played out personally, but often fuels social interactions. In areas as far apart as racism and nationalism, in economics between socialism and conservatism and in politics between liberalism and authoritarianism. In understanding this we can better control the direction of our life, perhaps towards a life of fulfilment through happiness? Cooperative interactions have been central to human success, while other traits have seemed to be useful in the short term but less useful in the long run. Perhaps by enhancing these useful traits in our day to day life with others we can use them as a guide to fulfilment in our own lives. Such 'traits' as Cooperation, through Sympathy, Fairness and Empathy would seem to make a good starting point, perhaps towards definite principles of Morality.

Where does this leave us?

Up Front, My Aim is to;

Achieve 'flourishing' through a 'good life' by promoting the propagation of humanity as a single whole.

My First Foundation is:

Behave at all times in such a way as to both promote and expect reciprocal social cooperation, while actively avoiding the conflict inherent in social competition.

My Second Foundation is:

Treat others as you would wish to be treated, using sympathy, empathy, fairness and equality of human value as your guides

The Golden Mean, everything in moderation.

Aristotle used the Golden Mean to determine 'good' patterns of behaviour. In this 'virtue' always lies between two extremes: bravery falls between recklessness and cowardice, love falls between hate and obsession, moderation between sobriety and over-indulgence. This has to be achieved within the setting of society, so interacting in a positive way with society is central. However, it also means that we have to assume that much of what we take as good is based on existing social constructs and norms, or does it? Understanding this helps us to understand how to spot what is going on in our own mind, so we can wake up the Monkey and get her 'onboard'.

First the Philosophers

Whether or not our mind is all nature, all nurture or a combination it has to take on board knowledge. How it acquires that has been a long standing philosophical debate. Philosophers come in two 'flavours':

Rationalists claim that there are significant ways in which our concepts and knowledge are gained independently of sense experience. They begin from a stance of self-evident truths, epistemologically these are truths which are so obvious they need no proof...Plato, Descartes and to some extent Kant are examples of rationalists.

For example Kant believed that it was possible to create a set of morals or "categorical imperatives", from first principles, based on the belief in Natural Morals: morals based on human behaviour rather than social norms, much as I have. These he thought were "Universalisable"; applicable in every case. This 'Formula for Humanity' which I will use as part of the support for My Foundations is the second formulation of this principle: This is for me a cornerstone of any forms of human cooperation and social interaction, you may disagree? So, from Kant we get:

The Golden Rule shows us how best to be social. Treat others as you might wish to be treated, never using yourself or others merely as means, to which we can add, *while remaining empathetic & acting fairly and with sympathy, respecting equality of human value as your guide.*

Further, but less essential here, remember, it was Kant who also believed that we could only ever see the world through 'rose tinted spectacles'. These spectacles are the filter of the Human Mind; shaped not only by genetics but by untold numbers of perceptions. This shapes the way future perceptions are interpreted. Thus he believed that we can't experience the world directly as it is. We only experience the world through our mind, this he called the *phenomenal* world; the world as we perceive it. He felt 'time' and 'space', was where one thing follows another and cause and effect are innate, with everything being processed through that. Kant claimed that the mind conforms to the world, but the world also conforms to the mind.

This understanding of our relationship with the actual or *noumenal* world; the world as it actually is, is called Metaphysics; the study of the fundamental nature of reality, which Kant wrote about in his *Critique of Pure Reason*.......a difficult book to read! My view is that the phenomenal world is all we can experience, the rest will always be conjecture, so let us focus on explanations of phenomena. Kant falls somewhere between rationalism and empiricism. I am more of an empiricist, looking for 'objective'* evidence. However, there is room for the Rationalist in terms of the social world, where self-evident truths as a basis for thinking must by their very nature be more 'subjective'**. Hegel was an *Idealist,* for him ideas shape the real world, rather than a materialist for whom matter, the phenominal world, it all that exists.

Thus what we perceive is not fixed for either Rationalists or Idealists, but changed in different ways. For Idealists as humans become increasingly more self-aware. So that humanity was going somewhere and wisdom would only come towards the end of its history as it hit its goal of self understanding and looked back at all its actions. I believe Hegel puts too much emphasis on the effect, that human consciousness can have on the material world.

Hegel also supported the *dialectic method,* where advance is made by a clash of *thesis* versus *antithesis* leading to a new idea by *synthesis,* where the process starts again; this is not unlike the Bayesian approach to evidence, mentioned earlier. This eventually leads to a full self-understanding by the Spirit: Mind or Geist of humanity, leading to freedom for individuals in a political state that lets everyone contribute to society. For me this is all a bit too far away from the material world in which, I believe, we exist!

Alternatively, *Empiricist* believe that Analytic or *a priori* (self-evident) knowledge is not possible. For them knowledge is all *synthetic*, it all comes from experience and observation. Hume's understanding of morality comes from his observations, believing some virtues are natural while others are by social convention. He believed that we were both selfish and humane, much like my competition between 'good' and 'antediluvian' traits. He also believed that 'the passions': desire, hope, fear, grief and joy........do we recognise the Organ Grinder here?.....create intentional actions. You will remember Hume also said "reason alone can never be motive to an action of the will" and "can never oppose passion in direction of will".

Also, Hume's Law or Guillotine, reasoned that if you only have non-moral premises you cannot logically reason your way to inferring the truth of moral statements. This is true of logic, but perhaps not helpful in life. Closely linked to Hume's Guillotine is the fact-value distinction of epistemology. Here it is impossible to derive or defend ethical claims or statements of values using statements of fact from empirical evidence based on reason or physical observations. Here, the question for us is, what other ways do we have to produce a way of living, in order to achieve a fulfilling and virtuous life?

Moving On, Thoughts From Some Other Philosophical Schools On How We Should Live

First, I would like to remind you of my difference between pleasure and happiness. I wonder if you remember, because it could make an important difference to the way you look at life. It has for me!

"Plaisir et bonheur se confondent souvent".
                              Françoise Hardy

One of my favourite 'chanteuse', Hardy sings, 'Pleasure and happiness are often confused.' A life of pleasure doesn't necessarily mean a life of happiness or fulfilment. As I have said in the last chapter, for me pleasure is something which often lasts for a short time and when the event is over it is rare that happiness results, just a lack of long term contentment and a longing for the next pleasure or 'fix'........and beware, pleasure can lead to addiction! Consumerism, alcohol, gambling, food, creating wealth are example which rarely lead to happiness, they are simple short term pleasure fixes, which need the next fix.

Happiness, for me, leads to more long term contentment and doesn't even need to be pleasurable of itself, though long term it often becomes so! I've got pleasure nailed, 'a short term fix', but I'm struggling to show you happiness more succinctly. So my example is: I hated reading as a child, it brought no pleasure, just hard work. When I went to college I sometimes had a dull bus ride of 1.5hrs. I picked up a book at the bus station, which had an interesting cover. While I found the task of reading it hard, I enjoyed the book enough to finish it. I was part of a series, which I bought and read. As I read more I stopped noticing I was reading and just enjoyed the stories and pictures they built in my head. Even though we have video on smartphones and e-books I still read a lot……….it makes me happy. Happiness is a long term investment, it often needs to be earned through practice, time, effort and right emotion (virtue)! But remember 'bad luck' can seriously affect your happiness, watch out!

For yourself, try to achieve long term happiness through fulfilment in what you do, rather than being reliant upon a string of pleasures.

Victor Frankl in the last century, somewhat like Cioran mentioned earlier, believed that humans are motivated by, or need, a "will to live"; a desire to find meaning in life. He went on to predict that "When a person can't find a deep sense of meaning they distract themselves with pleasure." I think this links together well the ideas we have been building. Perhaps achieving happiness and/or eudaimonia and achieving a good life become interdependent in forming both the purpose and meaning of our existence? As the 'good life' seems to requires us to act in particular ways let us examine what previous scholars have thought about how we should onduct ourselves, for an overview of what is possible.

Choose your own favourites. For the detail on 'Philosophers' in this chapter I have drawn on my own reading and Warburton's 'A Little History of Philosophy'.

The *Sceptics* can be exemplified by Pyrrho: for him nothing is certain, because no one knows anything. In essence don't commit and be open minded about everything, nothing matters. You only have your own beliefs to go on. While often a positive initial approach to new information, being sceptical can be a bit difficult at times, as you can easily walk off a cliff, eat poisonous stuff (or not eat) or get savaged by a wild dog.

The next Sceptic we have is Epicurus (often mistakenly taken for a hedonist!): he was a materialist who maintained that a fear of death is a waste of time, you won't be there when it happens! You need to be moderate in all things such as greed and excess, what I have term pleasures, which lead to unfulfillable cravings. He also maintained that one way to endure physical pain was by re-living past pain. I agree about pleasures, but I'm more 'sceptical' about practicing for pain. I would move more towards using happiness or pain killers as your analgesics!

There were three famous *Stoics*: Epictetus, Cicero & Seneca. For them mental control is important. It is controlled by not worrying about

the things you cannot change. Instead come to terms with them. If you lose a leg you can stay in bed, use a wheel chair, crutches or a prosthetic. Some choices give you a better life than others. This is an idea well worth remembering! However, they go on to say, only attempt to change those things you can. It is only our attitude to what happens which is within our control, what has happened isn't. Don't worry about the event, only about your reaction to it, remember you can't change the past, but we are responsible for what we feel and think. The future is not yet written and we can influence it with actions now. However, constructing outcomes on limited information is dangerous, and often causes unnecessary worry.

Seneca didn't think our lives were short, but rather worried how badly most people use the time, which they regret as they get old. Something we should all be aware of...when we think should I play another video game or go out into the world and grab an opportunity? Seneca would sleep on the floor one night a week to prepare himself for discomforts to come.....this seems Sceptically and a bit excessive!

There are more aspects to Stoicisim, with some of which I don't agree. However, overall, I think Stoicism is my favourite philosophical approach. With practice it helps you to stop worrying about things you can't control. I try to be Stoic in adversity.

Live in the moment, not worrying about those things you cannot change, or your ideas of their consequences, but instead being passionate about those things you can influence now.....be Stoic!

A Bit About The Enlightenment

Earlier I dismissed religion without talking much about why. Before I can go further with my reasoning of how to live a good life we need to take a side step. After all, it could be claimed that following the teachings of 'A Church' will bring you there. My first question would be which religion? The one you are born into, as most people do? Most Catholics, Muslims, Protestants, Hindus, Jews and Buddhists are just following the guidelines of their 'local' book of rules. Why should any be more correct than any other? You need to ask yourself, do these stories of meaning of existence just provide an easy 'off the shelf' gap filler to replace a meaningless existence. While providing a useful power structure for the senior adherents to control society? After all, religious 'dogma' has many varied interpretations, who makes those?

My religious scepticism stems both from experience and reason, but a lot of it can be found in The Enlightenment or Age of Reason which began in the early part of the 17th Century. It is based on David Hume's statement that "A wise man proportions his belief to the evidence". To appreciate religious 'jokers' read Thomas Pain's *An Age of Reason*. As an example he points out that Christianity is a religion of faith based on revelation. Yet if you are not the one to which it has been revealed, by a deity, it is just hearsay! I personally find it interesting that there is a vastly different outcome for you, between hearing voices in your head telling you what to do, if you say they are God or Hitler! The difference being canonisation or incarceration! Having said all that, if faith brings you happiness it may be for you. Just be aware, at every turn, of its power structures, dogma and intolerance.

Immanuel Kant in his, *What is Enlightenment?* said, "Enlightenment is man's emergence from his self-imposed nonage. Nonage is the inability to use one's own understanding without another's guidance [eg doctrine]. This nonage is self-imposed if its cause lies not in lack of understanding but in indecision and lack of courage to use one's own mind without another's guidance, *Sapere aude (Dare to know!)*..... If I have a book that thinks for me, a pastor who acts as my conscience, a physician who prescribes my diet, and so on, then I have no need to exert myself. I have no need to think, if only I can pay[or pray]; others will take care of that disagreeable business for me..........". Security, but at what price?

However, discrediting or eroding religion and superstition, as both Science and the Enlightenment implicitly do, can lead to a moral vacuum. Max Weber, in a 1918 lecture popularised for this the term 'Disenchantment'. This concept shows science and religion to have opposing roles in society. For Weber the scientific method* rendered gods and spirits implausible. Instead, one put one's faith in the ability of science to eventually explain everything in rational terms. For him the disenchantment of the world was alienating, societal values/morals are eroded and people would seek pleasure in private relations.......[and perhaps in having power and owning stuff.] However, The Scientific Method inadequately replaces religion, as it is incapable of answering subjective questions of values and morals. Our problem is that with only a scant look at modern society, my society of the early 21st Century, it looks as if Weber had a point. So if not religion and superstition, where do we go for morality, a good life and a reason to exist?

Thomas Hobbs, in *Leviathan* believed that to live in harmony people needed to give up some freedoms. Otherwise life would be 'in a state of nature': without political authority......and as I have said: solitary, poor, nasty, brutish and short. As people, for him, were born selfish we need to be kept in check by laws created by a powerful individual or parliament. Each person agreeing to this 'social contract'. Though pushing for monarchy, at his time in history, I believe he had a point in the idea of a social contract.

* Scientific method: careful sceptical observations, taking into account how cognitive assumptions and distorted sense perceptions could affect observations, resulting in a fair test. Then using inductive reasoning on those observations to formulate an hypotheses which can be further tested by experimental and measurement-based testing of deductions made from the hypotheses; to refine or 'falsify' them.

John Locke, in *Two Treaties of Government* believed that we are all born with a mind empty of selfishness, a 'tabula rasa' or empty slate, which I don't believe is the case. This meant therefore, all knowledge comes from experience or perception.....remember he was, like Hume, an Empiricist: experiences of the senses is the source of all knowledge. He also believed in 'Natural Rights', that everyone had a right to 'life, freedom, happiness and for me strangely, he added without qualification "property". I believe that property rights are essential, but we will need to look very carefully, later, about the rules we use to allocate and re-allocate property in a way which recognises both equity of opportunity and value of individuals.

Locke supported a trust-conception of government. Here the trustee (government) has duties , but not rights, towards the beneficiaries (community). This is perhaps better for the community than a social contract, as that would give rights to the government. In Locke's view government exists in, through and for the community. This was heavily influential on the US Bill of Rights (1791-today).

Rousseau, like Descartes, was a Rationalist: knowledge is based on reason and derived from self-evident truths. Rousseau wrote "Man was born free and everywhere he is in chains". He felt that people were naturally good and when living in the wild were 'noble savages', but the state of nature was unstable and intolerable. In society they needed to follow not Natural Rights but the 'General Will', more akin to Plato's *Republic* and pre-dating Hegel, so as not to be restricted and enslaved by that society. The General Will is *not* the 'Will of All', but instead based on how people *ought* to live together; what is best for the whole community, is to establish a contract for self-preservation. The General Will ignores self-interest, instead promoting the common good of the whole society. Justice and a higher morality, from self-conscious rationality. So freedom for Rousseau was achieved by following the rules of a society developed for the benefit of all. Possibly developed by a benevolent 'sovereign. Unfortunately he also believed that those who would not follow the General Will should be forced to do so; being forced to be free sounds like something of an oxymoron!

Interestingly, Rousseau was critical of the English parliament, saying, "The people of England regards itself as free; but it is grossly mistaken; it is free only during the election of members of parliament"[sic]. Something which our recent history (2022) has suitably confirmed. Thus he preached a doctrine of a primary legislative, sovereign or benevolent dictator over an executive serving as a commissaire........a totalitarian view not unlike the Philosopher-Kings of Plato's *The Republic:* who have intelligence, wisdom, reliability and a love of the simple life. This contrasts somewhat with the famous thoughts of John Dalbeg-Acton who said "Power tends to corrupt, and absolute power corrupts absolutely. Great men are almost always bad men, even when they exercise influence and not authority........"

Perhaps I follow Rousseau, my General Will being obtained from both empirical observations and rationalist thought, rather than sovereigns, benevolent dictators or philosopher kings?

More recently I read this and rather like it, as it brings together much of our investigation so far. It is by Steven Pinker, *Enlightenment Now*, 2018. In answer to the question "Why should I live?"

"In the very act of asking the question, you are seeking reasons........so you are committed to reason as a means to discover and justify what is important to you......As a sentient being, you have the potential to flourish. You can refine your faculty of reason itself by learning and debating. You can seek explanations of the natural world through science, and insight into the human condition through the arts and humanities. You can make the most of your capacity for pleasure [though I prefer 'happiness' here] and satisfaction, which allowed your ancestors to thrive and thereby allow you to exist. You can appreciate the beauty and richness of the natural and cultural world. As heir to billions of years of life perpetuating itself, you can perpetuate life in turn. You have been endowed with a sense of sympathy - the ability to like, love, respect, help, and show kindness - and you can enjoy the gift of mutual benevolence with friends, family, and colleagues.

And because reason tells you that none of this is particular to you - you have the responsibility to provide to others what you expect for yourself. You can foster the welfare of other sentient beings by enhancing life, health, knowledge, freedom, abundance, safety, beauty, and peace. History shows that when we apply our ingenuity to improving the human condition, we can make progress in doing so, and you can help to continue that progress"

This last part echoes the ancient's version of the 'Golden Rule', based on an idea of reciprocity, which I have used in my initial Foundations. Reciprocity itself being something of a trait which many feel strongly if they perceive something as unfair. The earliest version of the Golden Rule dates from 2000 BCE, but the version from a later papyrus (664-323 BCE) is more common: "That which you hate to be done to you, do not do to another". For most of us, that would result in very equitable relationships............cooperation!

To Conclude

In this chapter I have developed some ideas on which I can now attempt more fully expound My Moral Foundations, necessary for our 'good life, building not only on purpose but also meaning. All based on the ways, historically, humans have progressed and some of its best thinkers have argued, blending Rationalism with Empiricism:

My Foundations: Aim to achieve 'flourishing' through a 'good life' by promoting the propagation of humanity as a single whole.
1) *For yourself, try to achieve long term happiness through fulfilment in what you do, rather than being reliant upon a string of pleasures. The Golden Mean, everything in moderation.*
2) *Behave at all times in such a way as to both promote and expect reciprocal social cooperation, while actively avoiding the conflicts inherent in social competition.*
3) *The Golden Rule shows us how best to be social. Treat others as you might wish to be treated, never using yourself or others merely as means, while remaining empathetic & acting fairly and with sympathy, respecting equality of human value as your guide.*
4) *Live in the moment, not worrying about those things you cannot change, or your ideas of their consequences, but instead being passionate about those things you can influence…..be Stoic when you can't!*

My conclusion here, while not quite finished, is also indisputably subjective and not remarkably new, but I hope it gives the rock we are looking for in what is otherwise a sea of behavioural sand. In always measuring our behaviours against these Foundations I hope I have created an overarching principles on which to build a good life and achieve meaning through the rewards of future thoughts and actions.

There are, of course, always the alternatives that I mentioned much earlier. These are a choice for you! Though I don't agree with religion and the ideas around spirituality they often come with moral codes that can help you through life. I would recommend that you avoid four things: those things that demonstrably harm others, those things that come enmeshed in giving the dominant part of the 'sect' power and control, those things that promote bigotry and finally those things that encourage tribalism of any sort. And remember you are in search of happiness and the 'good life' so do not be totally satisfied with 'serial pleasures'.

The next stage then is to looking more explicitly towards Ethics and Morals. Here, we can continue to take from both the Rationalists and Empiricists, while being as open minded as the Sceptics but not accepting nihilism and that 'nothing matters'. The mental control of the Stoics is important as the idea that we should only worry about those things within our sphere of control, but perhaps leave behind their ideas of practicing for the worst scenarios!

However, before we leave this chapter let me ask a couple of questions:

>Have you identified the things you are good at?
>Usually these things are often things you enjoy.
>Remember the difference between pleasures & happiness!
>This should give you a clue to your potential.
>How and where might you use/develop your potential? Hobbies? Career? Family life?
>Now your life has direction 😊

A final a warning quote, to remind you of how difficult this all is: "Ken Lanning (Behavioural Science Unit, FBI) wrote, "Regardless of intelligence and education and often despite common sense and evidence to the contrary adults tend to believe what they want or need to believe [in order to maintain their Identity]. Perhaps most important, the greater the need the greater the tendency".

Strangely.......It frequently coincided with our World View! 😊

Ethics & Morals

*"Uncertainty is an uncomfortable position,
certainty is an absurd one"* Voltaire

A Basis for Morality

"Morality exists, in part, because of human needs and through recognition of the importance of living together in a cooperative and significant way. It may not be the case that all human beings can be convinced of what is moral or that they should be moral, or even that it will be in each individual's self-interest to be moral. However, the question "Why should human beings be moral?" generally can best be answered by the statement that adhering to moral principles enables human beings to live their lives as peacefully, happily, creatively, and meaningfully as is possible.

Having established some 'Foundations', which is essentially the bedrock of my morality, I now turn to looking at the good life through Morals and Ethics. There are several 'schools' of Morals that we need to consider:

Moral Realists, who believe that morality has objectively true 'codes' which are discoverable facts. I am sceptical as to how these can exist on a metaphysical* level, outside facts in nature. Epistemologically** it is doubtful that we gain access to these truths objectively. What is, may not help us find what ought to be? (the 'is' 'ought' dilemma we met as Hume's Law or Guillotine).

Anti-Realists, try, as I have done, to deduce moral 'codes' from natural ones, such as achieving happiness. The downside to this being Moor's 'open question' .... "Is happiness good?". Moral Constructivists, such as Kant who I have also used in my Foundation, builds principles based on normative values***. Universalities of what ought to be.
*metaphysics: looking philosophically at abstract concepts such as those behind being, knowing, identity, space & time.
** epistemology: philosophical theory's regarding knowledge & the distinctions between opinion and justified belief.
***In both Social Sciences and Philosophy 'what ought to be' are called 'norms' or normative............which can be confusing, as norms seems to refer to 'what is' happening under normal circumstances. These are referred to as outcomes or behaviours!

With Moral Relativism, essentially there is no universal code, so each person needs to develop their own. Plato, in the *Republic* states that Moral Philosophy is inquiring 'how we ought to live'. In fact Moral Philosophy is often as good at helping us find reasons for rejecting beliefs which are internally inconsistent, or built on false assumptions or premises, as it is in providing positive reinforcement for holding a belief. As I work through these final chapters, as I did with the last, I will try to give information/ideas on both sides of an argument, then draw MY conclusions. Again, if you don't like my conclusions look at the evidence, then use your own rational thought to determine your own answers. Remember, if you just disagree with something it may be because it clashes with your world view or cognitive biases……….the ones the Organ Grinder won't let you see! That is when you need to rationalise for yourself, from your 'Foundations', to your own outcomes.

The words ethics and morals are often used interchangeably. Though strictly speaking morals are our individual appreciation of which behaviours are right and wrong. Ethics is the set of principles or rules that govern a persons behaviour: what is right & wrong, good or bad. We are mostly interested in an individuals Morals here, but its difficult not to stray into Ethics from time to time.

At once it must be appreciated that neither morals nor ethics are, unless you follow a religious code, set in tablets of stone. They are geo-temporal, a moveable feast which changes over time and place, according to those in society who hold influence/power. As Socrates says, Moral wisdom must admit our ignorance and imperfection, while phoney wisdom has the look of dogmatic conviction.

Ethics are social constructs, sometimes supported by laws and other times by social pressures via social norms and social conventions. For example: stealing is both against the law and mostly disapproved of by society, while eating with your fingers in a good restaurant is only a social faux pas! What we see as morally 'good' or 'bad' behaviour are often based on these same social constructs. However, there is a view that aspects of morality need to consider those things which are innate to us as humans, our genetic traits. Some of these can be used as evidence to build a moral code, while other may need ethical constraints. We have already found that not all of human nature, through vestigial traits, is necessarily supportive of our aim of a good life for everyone!

While it is usually prudent to observe both the law and many social norms I am interested in perhaps a structure on which we can hang our own ethics. A number of people have put their minds to this over the millennia. Several are worth mentioning.

Plato thought that only Philosopher-kings understood enough to organise society and decide what is moral. While Aristotle and later Aquinas were interested in 'Virtue ethics'. This focuses on a person's character or traits, rather than on specific actions. The truly virtuous person always has the right feelings, developed through practice of the right actions under the guidance of an expert. Socrates argued that virtue is knowledge, which suggests that there is really only one virtue. The Stoics concurred, claiming the four cardinal virtues were only aspects of true virtue. Stoic perception of cardinal virtues are wisdom, justice, courage and temperance. Here again, I am bent towards Stoicism.

Aristotle never laid down an actual 'code'. In other words, for him, you become virtuous by practice. Modern Behavioural Scientists would certainly agree with Aristotle, in so far as behavioural modifications can be achieved by repeated behavioural changes. The more you practice the behaviours, good or bad, the more they become ingrained. You may have spotted a problem here, who says what is good, bad and virtuous, how do we define words like: wisdom, justice, courage and temperance? This chasing of definitions is common is philosophy and worth remembering, as it can be the crux of an argument.

'Deontology' is different, it puts forward the argument for decisions made out of duty, obligation and rights. This presents immediate problems, who decides what is duty, obligation and rights? Kant, in his *Groundwork on the Metaphysics of Morals* attempted to established, as we have mentioned, what he called *categorical imperatives*. A categorical imperative is an absolute, unconditional requirement that should always be obeyed. Kant laid down that you should "act only according to the 'maxim of universalisability' whereby you can, at the same time, will that it should become universal law.

Kant's categorical imperatives included an absolute moral duty to tell the truth, don't steal and don't deceive others. A moral duty was absolute in every case, despite the consequences! Kant also had *hypothetical imperatives,* these often have self-interested motives, such as, 'don't cheat, because you may go to prison. To find categorical imperatives Kant asked the question "what would it be like if everyone broke them" universally?

As quoted earlier, Kant thought you should never use people for your ends, but respect their autonomy and their capacity to make their own rational decisions. Kant, for me, does run into problems. For example, there are no circumstances, for him, whereby the best result for everyone concerned might be a small 'white lie'? "Yes my love, the tea you cooked was wonderful". The other problem that Kant has is to not address what to do in the case of a clash of morals. For example, if someone is shooting people is it morally acceptable to shoot them? The thought experiments* of Judith Jarvis and Philippa Foot, see later, explore these ideas. In short sometimes any *imperative* can come into conflict with any other. If you understand what your personal moral code is founded upon, for example we might want to keep harm to others at its lowest level, by "........*remaining empathetic & acting fairly and with sympathy'......*, then you are better armed to determine the right path when these clashes arise.

Consequentialism (teleology; explaining by purpose not cause) allows that the morality of an action is determined by its outcome. Various forms of consequentialism differ on what is valuable. The main philosophy is that 'the end justifies the means', something with which I'm not entirely comfortable. For example 'Utilitarianism', promoted by Bentham, and later Mill, has the maxim of "an action being right if it holds the most happiness (called 'Utility') for the greatest number of people." Bentham originally described happiness as the gaining of pleasure and the avoidance of pain. He believed that we are all motivated to seek things from which we can derive pleasure and avoid things which give us pain. In maximising happiness he hoped that bringing about the most pleasure would produce the greatest benefit for society. He also believed that each person's (and animal's) pleasure was as valuable as everyone else's, a great promoter of equality. Later happiness was amended to 'maximising utility 'or maximising usefulness, by Anscombe. Economists, even today, often use utility as a measure of how people will behave. Believing that people will behave in such a way to maximise their own utility, called Expected Utility Theory(EUT)....something which Tversky & Kahneman's Prospect Theory would dispute.

* A thought experiment is usually a 'story' with specific guidelines, sometimes unrealistically ridged, constructed to intellectually deliberate the potential consequences of a specific problem or domain.........at first it is usual to be critical of the experiment, using 'yes but what if?' but with practice useful ideas can often be extracted. For best effect concentrate on

the moral dilemma rather than trying to punch holes in the shortcomings of the Thought Experiment itself!

My own personal slant on the Utilitarian maxim would be 'The least harm for the most people gives the greatest social benefit!' This fits better with My Foundation, *"Behave at all times in such a way as to both promote and expect reciprocal social cooperation, while actively avoiding the conflicts inherent in social competition."* However, I'm not convinced that the ends justifying the means can work in all cases. For example people are often uncomfortable thinking about a couple of well known thought experiments:

Judith Jarvis Thompson's *Trolly Problem:* A trolly is travelling down a track. It will hit 5 workmen and certainly kill them. However there is a very fat man next to you, if you push him onto the track it will certainly derail the train (you are too small to derail it), killing him but saving 5 other lives.........should you push him? Consequentialism would say yes!

And Philippa Foot's *Transplant Surgeon Objection:* Five people are certain to dye if they do not get transplant surgery. One needs a pair of kidneys, another a spleen, another a heart, another lungs and another a liver. The surgeon is good enough to guarantee success if the healthy parts were available. A healthy person arrives on the ward with a bad splinter, should they be used for the spare parts, certainly dying in the process of saving 5 others. Again Consequentialism says yes!

Both these do not, *"Treat others as you might wish to be treated, never using yourself or others merely as means,......".*

John Stuart Mill 'improved' on Bentham by introducing 'values' to utility calculations. In his system not all pleasures were equally valuable. For example going out for a drink was not as valuable as higher pleasures such as going to see Shakespeare, reading a well written book or reading your fathers/grandfathers ideas on morality! But who decides the relative values?

Trying to keep chronological, another and later Deontologist that I admire is Rawls. In *Theory of Justice* he believed that moral acts would be those that we would all agree upon, from 'The Original Position', where we were unbiased by our own situation, behind a "veil of ignorance".

From his veil Rawls established that we would all agree on three principles: The Liberty Principle; everyone has the right to basic liberties, including property (but not excessive), the right to vote etc. Fair Equality of Opportunity; opportunities in education & work should not be discriminated by race, religion, social status, disability/appearance, sexual preference, gender or the ability to pay. The Difference Principle; where any unequal distribution of social or economic goods must be such that the least-advantaged members of society would be better off under that distribution than they would be under any other distribution. It is interesting that Michael Sandel, another interesting thinker, thought in 'Liberalism and Limits of Justice', that the veil of ignorance was psychologically impossible. However, I feel that Rawls made some significant deductions, however subjective they may seem. Deductions which I believe, sit quite nicely with my 'Foundations'

There are others, like Nozick, who would disagree about our duty and obligation to others, saying that our first duty is to ourselves, through rational self-interest. People who hold these views can often not understand the arguments I have given to establish my 'Foundations' in Chapter W. I will try to address, if not solve, this dichotomy with a bit of psychology from Haidt and De Wit, later in this chapter. Another example is Ayn Rand, with her 'Objectivism'. She has this to say, with my replies, in *The Virtue of Selfishness:*

1. "Is the concept of *value* of "good or evil" an arbitrary human invention.......?".
I would reply it is subjective, but not arbitrary if built from the correct 'Foundations'
2. "Is ethics a subjective luxury or an *objective* necessity? Should it be the "province of personal emotion, social edicts and mystic revelation - or is it the province of reason?"
For me Ethics it is a province of reason, built from subjectively reasoned, yet empirically obtained evidence rather than emotion, social edicts or revelation.
3. "Happiness and desires should not be of the hedonistic type, as it might have been for Bentham, as this can be driven by emotional whims."
Agreed!

Rand goes on to argue that the highest value is life, for without life there is no value, no good or evil. Continuing that *choosing* to develop rational thought, through consciousness, is the only way to achieve life and value. Objectivist ethics thus judges good and evil as "that which is required for man's survival" and is "proper to the life of a rational being"' exemplified for Rand by thinking and productive work. These should be achieved by reason, not brute force, fraud, looting, robbing, cheating or enslaving those who produce.

I agree without survival of 'man' nothing matters and it should be achieved as she stipulates, by reason. However, there is an enormous gap between survival and flourishing. I believe this gap to be bridged by cooperation, not competition forced by shortage of resources. However, though thinking and productive work is to some extent necessary I'm not sure how their antithesis is necessarily 'evil'? I would also add that from my previous arguments on the virtues of society that I fall more in line with Star Trek's Spock when he says "Logic dictates that the needs of the many outweigh the needs of the few", *Wrath of Khan,* rather than the so-called virtue of selfishness, as is often interpreted by Neoclassical Economics, based on a poor interpretation of Adam Smith's "Invisible hand of the market". Of which more later. Life is, as I hope I have shown, mostly luck rather than desert and a social activity, remember Hobbs!

Rand also sees altruism as against self-interest, causing resignation, denial, self suffering and self destruction. I believe it to be an essential, if perhaps recently downtrodden human trait. I think Spock, with impeccable logic, might agree. We all seem to have altruism instinctively, possibly for a reason, I suggest group preservation. At a more basic level, nature has made it feel good for the giver. Implanting a reward for 'I'll scratch your back now as an insurance of me needing my back scratched later'. I believe those who don't have it, have had it dulled by a competitive society or are sociopaths! Interestingly, according to De-Wit in *What's Your Bias?,* we also have 'altruistic punishment' as a trait. This is where we are inclined to punish others who break what we take to be a moral code, even at our own expense.

This is best seen in discussions on Universal Basic Income*, where people will disagree with it because some recipients don't earn/deserve it. While, as a consequence, missing out themselves! Obviously both Nozick and Rand run foul of 'My Foundations' laid down in the previous chapter. To recap, for me, without a moral obligation to cooperate with others and ethical and legal rules to codify those behaviours, we resort to a society pre-set for competition above cooperation, leading to winners and losers, in a zero sum game.

Damning us to a devil takes the hindmost society. Which I suggest is aptly where we are now. So without social contracts to establish egalitarianism, equity and a sort of fraternity, then justice in liberty and equity in property, we are alone and should not expect others willingness to co-operate in our endeavours when luck has failed us. The selfish have few friends and fewer loyal accomplices. The best they can hope for is the zero-sum game*

So, we either have off the shelf Ethics from religion/creed, follow the heard through the minefield of the socially constructed zeitgeist, or a rationalised approach of the types offered by Kant, Rawls or Rand, all have their problems! We learn what others; our parents, friends, idols, politicians & teachers think is right & wrong. Then we have to apply these rules ourselves to each new decision we make. Sometimes this leads us to make mistakes, because we have no baseline to which we can retreat. On other occasions we let the Organ Grinder go to work, while the Monkey spends its time fabricating excuses to keep the triumvirate of the identity, self-image and world view in tact.

A glimmer of hope?

There is some glimmer of hope if we take a general overview of societies around the world. Raphael maintains that we find moral codes may be different, but they have some commonality. Even in those societies which in the past have kill their elderly or abandon sickly children, their is a high value given to the preservation of the social group. However some societies give more importance to the individual than the whole. This is a major difference between Western, who favour freedoms of the individual over the State and Eastern cultures, which favour the well being of the State. This may have originated due to different 'economic' circumstances, where the lack of survival of the social group is/was a real possibility. It is an ongoing source of political friction between East and West, when it comes to human rights.

Commonalities, rather than levels of application shows us that all societies tend to think that within the group: hurting others is wrong, trust is important, the needy should be helped, rule breakers should be punished. While: forgiving enemies and applying your group code to 'the other'* is less well established even in modern societies.(Raphael).

Patricia Churchland and *Conscience*

We met Churchland earlier. She is a cofounder of neurophilosophy and believes we are wired to care, having both empathy and sympathy. These express themselves in our conscience: a moral sense of right and wrong guiding one's behaviour. You should remember she believes that in terms of morality our conscience is not an infallible guide, as there are often clashes between "what your conscience tells you and what mine tells me.." from *Conscience, The Origins of Moral Intuition*. Not only that, but on a variety of issues our conscience can changes over time. Churchland also issues the warning that moral arrogance can also be a cover for manipulative intent, often via power, sex, money or increased self-esteem. Once again the spectre of the Organ Grinder raise its head.

Matthew Taylor and human 'Core Motivations'

Taylor suggests that Morality is a part of our social system, Hilary Lawson adds 'a cloak for power' or 'I'm right, you are wrong'. Taylor pins morality on three, often conflicting 'Core Motivations' for a moral code: Authority, Belonging/Values & Self-interest. He believes that society can only be successful when these three are aligned. Yet each is internally conflicted, causing tensions.

Authority: essentially doing what you are told by state institutions or religion; the conflict here arises because the 'rules' should be in the interest of everyone. Often their interest is balanced towards those in power. So society needs effective democracy.

Belonging/Values: essentially being a part of a group and living by its values; this can lead to compassion and 'other centred-ness'. However, it can cause tension between groups, such as racism & tribalism.
The current Popularist politics is about the morality of tribes, it is vibrant but antagonistic. Causing polarisation and lack of moral responsibility for other tribes.

Self-interest: essentially getting what you want from life; the tension here is between the freedom of the individual and the dignity of every other individual to express their freedom. Essentially asserting certain freedoms creates inequality if not checked. Homo Economicus and neoliberalism, where you can take what you want with minimal interference are now being seen as creating massive social and economic inequalities.

Haidt & De-Wit: Psychological Foundations of the Moral Mind: political choices

Earlier in the chapter I said that I would return to the work by two psychologists Jonathan Haidt and Lee De-Wit. This is to try to better understand the unresolved, possibly unresolvable, dichotomy between 'liberals 'such as Rawls 'and 'conservatives 'such as Rand's standpoints. Both Haidt and De Wit posit psychological causes of Morality, from innate foundations, I'm not so sure, believing some morality is earned from experience. They then relate these traits* to Political standpoints centred around, but not exclusive to, differing interpretations of fairness.

This is not unlike the way My Foundations came about, so is more about analysis of 'what is' rather than 'what should be'. I have already put my arguments against Rand, who bases her morality around selfishness. This is an undoubted human trait, but perhaps as I have said a 'vestigial trait', a hangover from a less abundant time. A time when selfish and aggressive behaviours were necessary to obtain the necessary wherewithal for mere existence. We could consider these as outdated trait, or animal instincts, not suitable to still be used as building bricks of morality in this age of relative abundance.*

Trait: a characteristic of someone which can be determined by their genes(nature/genotype), or by their environment(nurture). How this comes across in the world is called the phenotype.

Haidt calls this application of traits, to produce a moral framework, the Moral Foundations Theory, found in his book *The Righteous Mind*. In this theory Haidt doesn't try to lay down a moral code, but rather examine what he considers to be innate foundations of peoples morality, much as I have with 'My Foundations'. John Alford et al, in *Are Political Orientations Genetically Transmitted,* supported this by asserting '...genetic make-up is in fact more important than environmental factors...'.

Alford proposed two distinctive groups, two genotypes, which he called *contextuals* (liberals) and *absolutes* (conservatives). Absolute, which I will call *purists,* thinking results from a partisan application of right vs wrong, where contextuals, which I like to think of as *'compromists'*, allowed more nuanced divisions to determine behaviour.

* *I label this age, the early 21st. Century, as a time of abundance.*

However the current political and economic systems which govern our world of Nation States greatly skew the availability of this abundance. Not only between competing States, but also within individual States. The ancient trait of selfishness still has a huge hold over distribution of resources.

If Alford is correct then removing the purist approach from society, if possible at all, would be an extremely long process. Traits run deep in our psyche and are difficult to dislodge in short timespans. We would need to change our approach to what is moral and even then we may end up still having the opinions and factions we do today. Only by moving the Overton Window* can we hope to make a start on this.

Haidt himself proposes five categories of innate behaviours or traits: Care/Harm, Fairness/Cheating, Loyalty/Betrayal, Authority/Subversion and Liberty/Oppression. Each of these is a continuum which between them can describe how an individual might ascribe their own moral standpoint. Interestingly De Wit uses this same framework to describe how people arrive at their political, and perhaps economic, views. Of these traits apparently Fairness is the one most shared by humans. It could be that appealing to fairness is the inroad to changing the effect of some vestigial traits? Thus moving the Overton Window. [*Overton Window: the range of political policies acceptable by the general population. This window, influenced by politicians and the media can enable the policies it covers to changes over time.*]

So we have 'My Foundation' in Chapter W and it looks as if we may be close to establishing their usability, rather than the rusty beams of Nozick and Rand, incompatible with those foundations. These have been extractable from: the virtue ethics of the Stoics & Aristotle, the Deontology of Kant and Rawls, the Teleological Consequentialism of Bentham and Mill, the norms of Commonalities expounded by Raphael, and Pinker's Blank Slate, on whose bedrock we can support a superstructure for a Moral Code. If you are lucky, you may be able to find enough material to bulk out this superstructure into the full-blown Edifice of Ethics of your own, which can be extrapolated, with the aid of Haidt's Moral Mind, to guide many if not all of your actions as well as the Political and Economic choices set out next in Chapter Y.

Where does this leave us?

My Foundations, on which you can build a moral Superstructure tries to use those aspects of morality that seem to be taken from our history as humans and a distillation of best practice from Philosophy. It has deselects those 'animal instincts' as best it can, to look at what makes us truly humans and such a successful species. For me it comes down to two factors; our intelligence, or more precisely our ability to call on our Monkey or re-direct conscious Free Will to guide us thoughtfully and rational. Secondly it uses our natural, genetic abilities to work cooperatively to achieve remarkable goals. Without those things we are truly in a state of nature and life becomes, if not short or poor then: solitary, nasty and brutish. We also need to remember that there are other genetic, what we might call antisocial behaviours, which come as part of the package of our inherited animal/human genome. We need to bear in mind that some of these trait: for example violence & jealousy, may be socially destructive and so not morally useful at a time when our sophisticated society could choose to make all essential resources non-competitive. Thus making Haidt's political traits: Harm, Cheating, Betrayal, Subversion and Oppression, not only ethically, but eventually morally wrong. While promoting Care, Fairness, Loyalty(to larger society), Authority (within larger society) and Liberty.

In conclusion to this section, I think I can sum up simply with:

"Do your best & don't be a dick"
Russell Howard, comedian.

Politics, Economics and the Existential Life

The opportunity of a lifetime lasts only for the lifetime of the opportunity!

Post-Truth, Popularism, Polarisation and the 21st. Century

Before we attack the Ethics of Political and Economic life let us say a word about the elephant.....not that Elephant......in the room, truth. A major problem of our time is the existence or not of 'truth' and the apparent fact that since 2016; Brexit in the U.K., the election of Donald Trump as US President and the burgeoning of Internet search engines and Social and Main Stream Media(MSM), we are in the early stages, at least in the West, of a 'post-truth' Political world. Where alternative truths can be taken as 'alternative facts', often with high emotional content, and without evidence in the real world. These are often classed as Conspiracy Theories, but still have an increasingly wide audience.

Truth, when possible, should be internally consistent and subject to verifiable objective evidence. Though this is always true of 'scientific' truths, social truths are often more slippery and subjective, containing emotion and opinion. Themselves depending upon perspective and interpretation; self-identity preservation and an authoritarian trait, being main influencers in these.

When it comes to 'truth' I sit on the horns of a dilemma being "........epistemological committed to be sceptical towards the existence of truth but morally committed towards it" says Hannah Dawson, in Philosophy for our Time podcast. Our main lesson from this being......beware!! Always ask yourself "is this true? Or is it just something which I uncritically accept because it makes me feel good, as it supports what I want to believe?" Aka a Cognitive bias.

Fake news, or Post-Truth on MSM and social websites is a huge problem. Helping to create Popularism, which seeks to move the Overton Window of socially acceptable speech & behaviour, and intentionally cause Polarisation of the electorate. It tends to result in increasingly more authoritarian governments and dictatorships. There are currently a number of governments worldwide who are sliding in this direction: UK under Johnson & The US under Trump are mild examples. More extreme recent changes would be Hungary, Poland, Turkey, Russia, India & Israel, to mention but a few.

We have had access to the Internet, at home, since the late '90s. Becoming more sophisticated as we moved into the 2000s. It's rise from academic platforms to the public domain expanded with Desktop computers being reasonably priced for home use. Then further rising with Smartphones. The advent of social media, which is actively accessed by 57 million (84%) of people in the UK, has not only created more information but also sources of political disinformation (and conspiracy theories). With the use of 'Trolls' & 'Bots' disseminating post truths to selected audiences, particularly near elections & in autocracies. It has expanded to such a state that 'Fact Checking' is now central to any information gathering exercise.

The latest worry is the burgeoning of Artificial Intelligence(AI). At this time AI is about, unnoticed, in numerous aspects of our lives. The one everyone seems to be interested in at the moment is a large language model transformer called Chat GPT 3.5. It seems to be able to give human like responses from the training it has received with large amounts of data from the Internet. To the extent that it can make a passable effort at writing answers to kids homework and possibly undergraduate essays? The problem is that it can only interpret the data that it finds, and can NOT analyse its veracity. So it is susceptible to disinformation and simply can be incorrect. It's answers are also susceptible to the framing of the question. Meaning that it will try to give you what you want to find. When asked directly it said: "I don't have the ability to independently verify the accuracy of information."........ "It is important to consult reliable sources and exercise critical thinking to determine the most reliable data" ...... "It's always a good idea to cross reference sources to ensure accuracy." .... "... the framing of a question can influence the emphasis or direction of my response"....and finally..... "I do not have the capability to determine which piece of information is more reliable or accurate. Fact-checking and consulting with trusted sources or expert opinion is always recommended." We'd can see how a hacked site or biased algorithms could easily be use for disinformation and conspiracy. But on the positive side lets look at what Chat GPT 3.5 can do in 2023, I asked it for "What makes a good life?" It seems I could have saved myself a lot of time! (Appendix 12)

The next sections are not a tutorial on Economics or Politics, but just to give a flavour of each and show why they may be faulty.

Politics & Economics which can dictate Morality and Ethics: Price & Value

Over the past forty or fifty years there has been a move to put economic factors, prices, on things which before had been seen as the sort of thing you can't put a price on. Morals, ethics and social norms had seen these things as un-priceable. Such things included; having babies to sell them or putting a price on spoiling a beautiful view. However, there was always a market somewhere for such un-ethical things as selling sex or finding an assassin. Selling babies and assassins are still frowned upon in most societies, but prostitution and paying to spoil someone's view are now within the norms of some societies as thus objects of economic study.

In *The Economic Approach to Human Behaviour,* Gray Becker rejects the idea that economics is just "the study of the allocation of material goods". He believes that there is a "reluctance to submit certain kinds of human behaviour to the 'fridge' calculus of economics". Instead he believes that we act to maximise our welfare, economists call it utility, in everything we do. This does not assume that we can calculate, or even know we are calculating decisions in an 'economic' way, but that all behaviours can be explained by cost benefit rational calculations. He maintains that otherwise behaviour is unpredictable and based on "ignorance and irrationality". So for Becker price effects and income should be our focus and monetary incentives backed by suitable legislation, can solve any problem with scant recourse to a moral code. Economists do not learn about or apply morality to their prognostications.

Becker's view has become a potent idea. Even a life has a price, depending on age and 'potential', if someone dies in an accident the family may be awarded monetary compensation if some one is culpable; "the U.S. Office of Management and Budget puts the price of a human life in the range of $7 million to $9 million. But could it be that economists and now a lot of the western world know all about price, but nothing at all about value. To expand the idea of value we could look at remuneration for work and this I will do later when I look at what has happened to our society by valuing most everything by its price or monetary reward. These two conjoined ideas; everything has a price & that price denotes its value in a broad sense of the word, is changing the way not only economists but also politicians and ordinary people look at the world. Value and even morality itself are becoming sub-sets of price. For now we need to get a brief overview of Economics, I will return to value in due course.

Economics which follow the Ethics of Politics I: Neoliberals and neoclassical economics

I should perhaps start this section by outlining my view on Economics. Sometimes called Economic Science, it really is no so thing. Having studied it up to first degree level I feel confident in asserting that there is a lot wrong with its basic foundations. Also, often 'truths' spouted by economists do not stand up to objective enquiry and tend to support belief and opinion than fact. Factually, economic predictions are susceptible to many changeable factors, often dominated by economic beliefs, so are closer to weather forecasting than actual science. Mistakes in predictions, and in future strategies often turn out to be incorrect or biased towards a particular outcome. The outcome being to the benefit of those currently with influence and political and/or economic power. It is for this reason that I will focus on Political Economy, rather than the nuts and bolts of Political Science. It is good to see that we are moving through a time where both students and some economists are trying to promote more heterogeneity in economics (Heterodox Economics), making it a more interdisciplinary subject.

Essentially there are two views on the way in which economics should work, when it comes to free markets and government; three if you include no free markets! The first is that government should interfere in the 'free-market' and 'personal responsibility' only to uphold the rules and laws. Taxation and regulation should be minimal and the market will sort out the rest. Effectively this is Neoliberal Economics, based on 'neoclassical' economic models, itself being based on the idea of 'rational choice'*. Their hero is Adam Smith, who in *The Wealth of Nations(1760)* outlines the idea of *'the invisible hand of the market'*. It is interesting that after the 2008 crash even adherents such as Alan Greenspan (Chair of the US Federal reserve) said "I have found a flaw" and that his view of the world, his free market ideology was not working.

Others, such as the Nobel Laureate Joseph Stiglitz, and of course myself, argue that "relying solely on business self-interest as the means of achieving the well-being of society and economic efficiency is misleading, and that instead "What is needed is stronger norms, clearer understandings of what is acceptable – and what is not – and stronger laws and regulations to ensure that those that do not behave in ways that are consistent with these norms are held accountable". The free market has many failings. The government should be there to search them out and correct them for the benefit of the public.

As I discussed in Chapter W, I believe that neoclassical models are built on false axioms and that we shall find that Behavioural and Heterodox Economics will push their way to the fore in years to come. Obviously one example is that of Cognitive Biases and Heuristics already discussed, which don't exist for 'Econs' (neoliberal economists, such as Becker). The second is that of non-selfish behaviours. These are demonstrated by experimental psychologists who use Game Theory. They illustrate how, in general, people make choices which are less self-regarding, less efficient, than the neoclassical 'Econ' should be expected to make. Economic games were developed by Von Neumann and Morganstern as early as 1944. John Nash, of *A Beautiful Mind(film)* fame, win a Nobel Prize in 1994 for his contribution to non co-operative games involving two or more players. Introducing the idea of the Nash Equilibrium*. The experimental psychologists have found that many players will not take the Nash Equilibrium, selfish, position. Instead preferring a position reliant on trust, fairness and reciprocity. This has been found also as the initial standpoint in repeat games. It is soon lost however, when opponents are seen to favour competition, for their own self-interest, when retaliation and 'tit-for-tat', becomes the norm.

This century writers such as Nozick, who we met in the last chapter, in *Anarchy, State and Utopia,* followed in the extreme Locke and Smith, believing that we all have natural rights, such as Locke's "life, liberty and estate(property)". For Locke when a person mixes their labour to anything he removes from the state of nature (unowned by anyone else); rocks, fruit, wood etc, then that becomes their property. However, a lot of people forget that he adds "......*at least, so long as there is enough, and as good left in common for others."* This suggest some equity of opportunity of acquisition. Could we establish a position where we could say: a) with land and it's resources (minerals, water, arable), simply by being mostly now enclosed there is no longer ".......sufficient and as good as...." for the rest. So taxation of the 'owners', the 'rentier 'class, redistributes the profits made above what is legitimately earned from labour and return on investment made. b) taxation of wealth should provide "......sufficient and as good as....." from those who have obtained wealth either through the plethora of market failures and asymmetries across time (which also call into question legitimacy of ownership), allowing redistribution to society from these inequities. For me, this all says you can have as your property no more than your fair share. For someone like Nozick, this is often forgotten, for him even taxation by government is theft, irrespective of the excesses you may own. For him, everyone has the right to do as they wish with wealth that has come to them according to the law. But what is legal is not always moral. I must point out that people who make laws may well have their own motives. Also this in no way takes into account those things which are run for the benefit of everyone........social goods! These might include defence by an army, roads, the legal system & law enforcement. It could be extended to environmental protection and suitable health and social care for those who are unlucky enough to need it, but can't afford it.

We must remember that Adam Smith, so revered by Neoliberals such as Nozick, didn't trust those who made the laws on finance. In *The Wealth of Nations(1760)* he wrote: "The proposal of any new law or regulation of commerce which comes from this order [those who profit from stock] ought always to be listened to with great precaution, and ought never to be adopted till after having been long and carefully examined, not only with the most scrupulous, but with the most suspicious attention. It comes from an order of men whose interest is never exactly the same with that of the public, who have generally an interest to deceive and even to oppress the public, and who accordingly have, upon many occasions, both deceived and oppressed it."

Modern Neoliberals such as Nozick would have us reduce government, ostensibly to give power to individuals. I suspect that it is centred around reducing both taxes collected and stopping legislation which demands equity and long term responsibility for social goods and externalities*.

This was spotted by David Hume in *A Treatise on Human Nature*, as far back as 1739: "The origin of civil government"..........[is predicated upon the fact that]......... "men are not able radically to cure, either in themselves or others, that narrowness o soul, which makes them prefer the present to the remote."

Externalities: a consequence of a commercial activity which is not captured in the market price. Eg. Fossil fuels creating carbon dioxide pollution in the atmosphere.

Bailouts for banks/ supporting private business in the COVID-19 pandemic..............privatising profits/socialising losses.

Ecomonics which follow the Ethics of Politics II: Behavioural & Hetrodox Economics

There is quite a lot wrong with society at the time I am writing, there probably always has been? I hope it is better for you, the reader, in your time. It seems to me that a great part of the problem is created through greed, which creates dreadful inequalities around the world. Neoliberal ideology and its associated capitalist self-interest, supported by Neo-classical economic models, morals and legislation would seem to be at the crux of the perpetuation of this problem.

The Existentially Good Life: The Tyranny of Merit, Michael Sandel

"The meritocratic conviction that people deserve whatever riches the market bestows on their talents makes solidarity an almost impossible project. For why do the successful owe anything to the less-advantaged members of society? The answer to this question depends on recognising that, for all our striving, we are not self-made and self-sufficient; finding ourselves in a society that prizes our talent is our good fortune, not our due. A lively sense of our own contingency of our lot can inspire a certain humility. There but for the grace of God, or accident of birth, or mystery of fate, go I. Such humility is the beginning of the way back from the harsh ethic of success that drives us apart. It points beyond the tyranny of merit towards a less rancorous, more generous public life"

Personality traits and political choices!!!

Philosophical Thoughts: Causation, Consciousness, Free Will

I think, therefore I can..choose....or can I?

To end, for which you must be grateful after all this, a couple of topics that I have spent considerable time thinking about........and leave for posterity!

Section 1 Consciousness

Consciousness, for me is not just being 'awake' and 'aware' it is the content of that awareness. In humans, the world which is created for us, at a second level, as we interpret the sense information from our surroundings and re-create what we believe is 'out there' inside our brains. The trouble is, that this interpretation is to some extent determined by our brain structure and the influences of our experiences to date, so is a subjective rather than than an objective view of the world. Some might even say an illusion? I don't believe this is so, I believe the 'phenomena', sometimes called 'qualia', that we experience are mostly decent representations of the real world.....remember Kant called the things in the real world, noumena.......in sufficient detail to best navigate the world safely. Illusions, or delusions, do exist, from physical deceptions such as light bent in water to mental illusion such as visions. While not everything gets represented, ie infra red radiation, simply because they are not needed.

Central to my view of consciousness in humans, I define as not only as a subjective awareness of one's own and the worlds existence, but also a 'third eye', 'an awareness of that awareness' on what it is like to be me and what it might be like to be you; now, in the past & in some possible futures. Perhaps Thomas Reid and John Locke were right, and it is a continuing thread of memory [of what it is like to be you] connecting the different stages of your life that makes you the same person, the self you call 'me'? Thus limiting it to 'higher' organisms.

Mine is a *physicalist or materialist* approach, I believe consciousness, as we experience it, is a product of vast complexity, and so can be found only in the most complex physical systems, currently biological brains. For me, conscious experience is an emergent property; it does not exist below the level of the system as a whole. This would make me also an *'eliminativist'*: as I would deny the existence of any suggestion of a dualist non-physical consciousness. This consciousness is best exemplified by, but not exclusive to humans. Meaning that the more complex the brain, the 'higher' the level of consciousness. Which suggests that there is an 'animal 'hierarchy.

Michelle Montague talks about other sorts of consciousness, something different to the subjective 'phenomena'* or 'qualia'** we experience from sensory inputs; "sensory experiences". She believes, and I tend to give it some weight though it is not a popular theory, that we also have conscious thoughts not directly produced by sensory experiences. Feelings such as sadness she terms "evaluative experiences". While thought processes which allow you to add   1 + 1 = 2 are " cognitive experiences".

*Phenomena: an event, a sense experience.
**Qualia: a subjective conscious experience

In terms of other sorts of consciousness, there is always the question of could computers become conscious? It may be that what is important here is what John Searle called the difference between *syntax:* computers operate on the level of a formal syntax, they read computer code without any understanding, and *semantics:* in sentient beings, being the understanding of the meaning of the information being processed. To support this Searle used the "Chinese Room Argument'*.

Chinese Room: To Searle the Turing Test, where a human evaluator would judge the natural language conversation between a human and a computer, was wrong. The Chinese room illustrates this, when 'played' empirically. Here a Chinese person is in a room and passes questions in Chinese under the door to a non Chinese speaker. This second person has reference books that allow them to locate appropriate responses in Chinese and pass the responses back They understand neither the question or the answer.....syntax. But the Chinese person would believe the response is from another human, who is using semantics because they are conscious.

Functionalism disagrees with Searle, for it, the complexity of the system is all important, not the substrate. A Mind occurs for Functionalists with sufficient complexity. For the moment, I tend to agree with Searle. Maybe as AI, using machine learning, will prove him wrong. However, Chomsky believes it may not. He believes that the Mind is not a probability correlation engine of mass data, syntax, but instead uses relatively small amounts of data, used in novel ways, through semantics.

My recent exploration of the newly launched ChatGPT 3.5, a version of AI using a Large Language Model(LLM) makes me think that Chomsky may be right. Though the full power of ChatGPT to use machine learning does not seem to have been released yet. It doesn't learn from interactions after its initial data input.......perhaps through fear of its negative potential?

Back to brains, brain states(Neural Correlates of Consciousness), observable to fMRI, seem to be the closest thing we can get to, in seeing how the brain works, at the moment. I subscribe to the idea that consciousness is dependant on the structure and function of these brain states. How those brain states become phenomena in consciousness is unknown, this is Chalmers "Hard Problem of consciousness". Perhaps, as Identity Theory of Mind suggests, brain states are not correlated to mental states, but 'just are' mental states These being viewed from two different perspectives, externally; fMRI, or internally; though other, perhaps older, brain mechanisms such as sight and sound & memory, thus appearing in conscious awareness as phenomena or qualia

So, why do we have consciousness? I will endeavour to suggest it may be the complicated nature of the brains arrangement, through its long history of evolution by trial and error, alongside its relatively recent development of cortical complexity which has 'unwittingly' created a glitch, a loophole to what I will call 'secondary determinism'.....What Harry Frankish may describe as 'secondary desires' dare I say, a type of Compatibalism?

Section 2.1: How might the illusion of Free Will actually influence determinism?

"In the mind there is no absolute or free will, but the mind is determined to this or that volition by cause, which is also determined by another cause, and this again by another, and so on ad infinitum" Spinoza, Ethics, 1674.
A hypothesis on consciousness, how it might simulate a 'secondary' type of free will, and the consequences for moral responsibility.

The metaphysics of Philosophy of Mind needs to be at the vanguard of the associated science, not in the baggage train chasing flights of fancy through First Philosophy and 'god of the gaps'. I hope that in some small way this article might stimulate such conversations?

Do conscious entities actually have 'free will'? In other words can they choose what they do, within the bounds of possibility? This is an important question which both science and philosophy have struggled to answer for over 2500yrs. It has many implications, particularly for how we look at moral responsibility and its consequential praise or punishment, but also in the area of social recognition and financial reward. My views here rest on accepting two debatable yet essential precepts: that there is a weight of evidence which suggests the physical universe at a macro level is deterministic; and that consciousness is a relatively new emergent property of extreme brain complexity, probably due to brain cortex development, and occurs at different levels in different animals.

First determinism: causation claims that each effect or outcome, at least at a macro level is pre-determined by prior cause(s). David Hume, debatably, showed that cause and effect have no logical connection, but agreed that life would be impossible without assuming it to be so. In my view, all events are determined by what has gone before. At least at a macro level, there seem to be no contrary examples to this. Chaos theory, the "butterfly's wings effect" is sometimes held as evidence against determinism, but this is really just a small cause eventually ending in a large effect, causing 'apparent' randomness.

Another fly in the ointment might be seen at the micro level. Down at the quantum level Heisenberg, with his Uncertainty Principle, which is managed in the context of Quantum Mechanics, suggests a fundamental inability to predict causes at an individual level. However, this quantum randomness effect may eventually be found to have a cause? Nevertheless, the world renowned quantum physicist Carlo Rovelli maintains that the small fluctuations caused by this randomness cancel with regard to choice. To support this, Quantum indeterminacy has not been, as yet, found to have an effect on our macro-world. Remember that randomness is no indicator of choice or 'free will'! Laplace's Demon, determinism incarnate, where "We may regard the present state of the universe as the effect of its past and the cause of its future" might indeed have some validity.

As an ex-chemist, I have no evidence to suspect our brains are anything other than determined chemical/electrochemical systems and thus follow the deterministic pattern of cause and effect. Reactants, concentrations & conditions determine the outcomes, which do not have to be just a switch like mechanism, yes or no, but can move towards a balance point, an equilibrium, all of which might be changed by future events. In short, it seems to me, our immediate thoughts and actions, including what we feel are choices, are determined by our past, sometimes our very immediate past, controlled by a myriad of chemical environments, determined by previous chemical and physical environments within and without our brain. These include 'plastic' changes to the brain structure from internal and external factors and those things established by our DNA. I know of no mechanisms for choice, only balance and influence, that could explain 'free will'. As Martin Luther said, "Here I stand, I can do no other"

Second Consciousness: Neuroscience tells us that conscious thought occupies less than 5% of brain activity. However it is the 'me' each of us lives with. Thomas Nagel describes it as, "something that it is like [internally] to be....". I would add, having not only attention and awareness but also, Montague's "awareness of awareness" or a 'third eye' with which to look at not only ourselves and our thoughts and experiences but also others and their experiences in the second and third person. I have already said that I believe it is an emergent product of extreme brain complexity in the recently acquired cortex, found only, as yet, in animals with such brain complexity. I believe it's development gives Darwinian advantages particularly in terms of empathy, planning and decision making. Possibly co-evolving with language and availability of, a sometimes inconsistent, conscious memory. Could it be that this is the source of 'free will'?

It is perhaps time to propose a fairly simple definition of 'free will'(*see endnote), though many might disagree; "the ability of an agent, at the instant before a decision, to consciously CHOOSE between 'events', where other possibilities were within their bounded choice". In short, this definition excludes the apparent determinism of the macro-physical world described above, which seems to have no mechanism for 'choice', outside possible randomness.

Notice, I have included consciousness into my definition.

Let's peruse some, but by no means all, alternatives to determinism: Compatiblism, a sort of soft determinism allowed to exist alongside free will, which Kant described as "petty word jugglery". It seems to me, that Compatiblism has a need to deny causality, or re-engineer the meaning most of us would take by 'free will'? The most reasonable of Compatibalist explanations, though outside my definition, seems to be to allow that free will is satisfied by being the determined will of the 'autonomous agent', with regard to all the weighted experiences, ideas and cerebral hardware it has available. We shall see!

Cartesian Dualism, involves the invention of 'mind' stuff, something without physicality, for which a few currently still have hope, and belief, but not much in the way of evidence! What I would describe as an idea with no weight or epistemic warrant, a "free floating idea".

Another view of living in a deterministic universe could consider consciousness as an epiphenomenon. From this perspective consciousness creates only an illusion of free will, as it passively observes our internal and external world, without the actual advantage of influencing thought and behaviour; an unavoidable curiosity, a side effect of complexity maintained by other requirements of brain function. However, epiphenomena must exist in the brains chemistry, so can have an effect. Also, if Darwin was correct about the environmental inertia of natural selection then accidental consciousness as a side-product of neural complexity sits uncomfortably as a very energy expensive luxury. Without giving environmental advantage, would it not have vanished or at least stalled rather than expanded and blossomed as has become so evident to us?

Finally but not exhaustively, Panpsychism. Here even basic particles such as quarks contain 'consciousness'. This falls well outside my definition for consciousness and has no evidence and currently no method of either refutation or proof. Another "free floating idea". Feelings, may now become the secondary determined option. The effect is it both inwardly and outwardly feels and looks like choice/ free will. Returning to the psychology for a moment, we can recognise in secondary determinism aspects of Hume's "Will" and Freud's "Ego", Kahneman's "System 2", Haidt's "Mahout" and Frankish's "secondary desires".

Behaviour modification may be able to influence changes here. Second, and perhaps more important, if we live in a deterministic universe where does this leave blame and praise, punishment and reward? These are huge questions for another time.

*Endnote: Stephan Cave looks at the definition of Free Will in a different way. I think it is worth a mention here. He asks the question 'what do we mean by making a free choice?'

He first asks if we have an Intelligence Quotient(IQ) and Emotional Quotient(EQ), should we also try to measure levels of free will using a Freedom Quotient(FQ)? This fits with my idea of our differing abilities (including between species) to utilise the effect of consciousness to influence the primary determined path into a secondary determined path. Should there be a scientific method to determine this, particularly in cases of , say, blame?
Cave proposes that free will has three constituent parts: first, the ability to generate options for one's self......from my perspective this is the selection of different options created in the brains 'control area' as it weighs bundles of considerations, these are of course bounded by nature and nurture; second, the ability to choose, which runs contrary to my view on competition between possible determined outcomes; third, the ability to pursue one or more of these options after choosing. Again, for me, the only restriction here is by unforeseen determined influences, both natural and nurturing, which make the ability to pursue a chosen option either internally or externally bounded.

Section 2.2: Consequences for moral responsibility: blame & retribution.

Aquinas, in *Summa Theologise* wrote of determinism that," counsels, exhortations, commands, prohibitions, rewards, and punishments would be in vain"; an inconceivable state for society. However, let us accept for the moment, that determinism may be so, then where does this leave humanity? After all, don't ethics rest on a bed of responsibility?

If it is not given to everyone to have the same level (weight) of conscious belief in their ability to act against their feelings, then perhaps we could say that not everyone has the same ability to influence their primary determined actions. I submit actions instigated by the unconscious without the ability to be effectively re-aligned by secondary determined factors are less likely to evolve. Some people are determined to be impulsive, driven by the unconscious with its own internal and unknowable flaws: genetic, environmental or even chemical. Their Organ Grinder does its own thing; the Monkey is effectively an observer, spending its time justifying the Music, which hardly changes. Others seem to be determined in a way that makes them more flexible, their consciousnesses more open to new information, secondary determinism more influential. In others still there behaviours suggest that neural systems are perhaps broken or unduly influenced by poor experiences or drugs. If we accept that these are all determined outcomes, rather than choices, then our reaction to each of them needs to fundamentally change.

If we are not able to choose, we have no responsibility for our actions, so some might contend we should receive no blame or praise, no punishment or reward for our actions, leading perhaps to anarchy. I don't precisely hold to this view. However, what is required is a long term and perhaps uncomfortable transition from the current zeitgeist. We live as social creatures & have evolved, by determinism, rules to facilitate this. Largely accepted codes of morals & ethics, backed where necessary with laws. When an agent transgresses these behaviours for whatever reason, there needs to be consequences, society needs to have mechanisms to address these. Courts are needed try to prove the veracity, or not, of the transgression by the agent, this is not unreasonable. However, causes of behaviour are often scaled to determine what is often a punitive outcome. If determinism is correct then there is no scale. The cause needs to be more closely examined, psychiatrically & psychologically, followed not by punishment but by remedial treatment. This may involve things from behaviour modification strategies at weekly clinics for a set period all the way to undetermined detention in a psychiatric hospital.

Praise and reward are more difficult to address. As both are seen as beneficial to both maintaining and changing behaviours, as perhaps less reliably is the blame and punishment examined above.

Thus determinism has taken me to a re-assessment of our legal structure and it's consequences: from Veracity(proof) to Cause(s)(Diagnosis) to detention if necessary(safety) & finally above all things treatment(rehabilitation).

Not easy!

Part 3: Was David Hume Wrong when he questioned Causation & the Inductive Effect?

Having listened to the *In Our Time* podcast, *Hume,* again recently I remembered that I always struggled with Hume's explanation of causation. As you may recall, in his theory he has 3 components for Cause & Effect: cause precedes effect, spacial contiguity and necessary connection. He goes on to show that we are lacking evidence of 'necessary connection' between causal events. This does seem a bit counter intuitive and at first I wondered if there was a problem with his 3 components?

I re-looked at his Billiard Ball 'thought experiment': perhaps he was correct that cause needs to 'precede effect' and there needs to be spacial contiguity, but perhaps spacial contiguity IS also the 'necessary cause'? QED, job done!

But then I started to wonder if there were other cases of Cause & Effect where actual contiguity was not that important, and in fact the problem was with the thought experiment and not the original thesis? At first I thought about two people on a telephone call, how one could make the other unhappy through a series of words: cause preceding effect, contiguity being a 'connexion' and necessary connexion being an exchange of information. This sort of worked, but 'thought experiments' which include people are always distracting IMHO!.....people do odd things which complicate the pureness of the idea under examination and introduce a plethora of 'what ifs'.

I needed a physical system where contiguity was replaced by connection. Luckily I've been reading a bit about Quantum Entanglement and come across Einstein's 'spooky action at a distance' and the fact that there is some experimental evidence to suggest that it exists........so, lets use that.

Two quantum entangled particles, act as if somehow joined. Even separated by light years, changing the conditions of one particle in one place, will instantly change the properties of the other, connected particle(effect). Some mysterious communication channel must exist and some instruction must pass between the two. So we have Cause and Effect; where cause precedes effect, contiguity becomes a 'connexion' (in this case the quantum entanglement) and necessary connexion becomes an exchange of something which we could label as 'information'..........looking good so far? Hidalgo, 2015 helps by telling us that "The universe is made of matter, energy and information."

Now lets go back to the billiard balls and apply our post-Humean terms. We can see cause precedes effect and there is a connexion, in this case a contiguity, but what about exchange of information? Then Candy added the idea of the thing we are missing, movement of energy! And all of a sudden the problem seems to disappear. We can't see the exchange of energy, but we know that it must occur as *ceteris paribus* the second billiard ball can't move on with the energy it holds before the collision, this is the source of our information. QED?
So we now have an explanation, if not a proof, of causality.....or at least I think we do.
I've never read anything else about disproving Hume's ideas, so I have no idea if anything like this exists ....it just came out of the podcast and Candy and I chewing the fat over breakfast.

Notes from stanford Encyclopedia of Philosophy
".......although Kant does not explicitly refer to Hume in the essay on *Negative Magnitudes*, he proceeds to illustrate his problem with an example (among others) of the causal connection in the communication of motion by impact (2, 202; 240):

A body *A* is in motion, another *B* is at rest in the straight line [of this motion]. The motion of *A* is something, that of *B* is something else, and, nevertheless, the latter is posited through the former.

Hume famously uses this example (among others) in the *Enquiry* to illustrate his thesis that cause and effect are entirely distinct events, where the idea of the latter is in no way contained in the idea of the former (EHU 4.9; SBN 29):

The mind can never possibly find the effect in the supposed cause, by the most accurate scrutiny and examination. For the effect is totally different from the cause, and consequently can never be discovered in it. Motion in the second billiard-ball is a quite distinct event from motion in the first; nor is there anything in the one to suggest the smallest hint of the other.

A few lines later Hume describes this example as follows (EHU 4.10; SBN 29): When I see, for instance, a billiard-ball moving in a straight line towards another; even suppose motion in the second ball should by accident be suggested to me, as the result of their contact or impulse; may I not conceive, that a hundred different events might as well follow from the cause? ... All these suppositions are consistent and conceivable."(https://plato.stanford.edu/entries/kant-hume-causality/. Accessed 12/04/20)

"Section 4 of the *Enquiry* is entitled "Sceptical Doubts Concerning the Operations of the Understanding". In part 1 of this section (as we have already seen) Hume maintains that the idea of the effect is never contained in the idea of the cause (in Kant's terminology, the relation is not analytic), and thus, according to Hume, it is never knowable a priori. We therefore need experience in the Humean sense in order to make any causal claims—that is, the observation of an event of one type *A* constantly followed by an event of another type *B*. Otherwise (as we have also seen) any event could follow any other (EHU 4.10; SBN 29):

And as the first imagination or invention of a particular effect, in all natural operations, is arbitrary, where we consult not experience; so must we also esteem the supposed tye or connexion between the cause and effect, which binds them together, and renders it impossible that any other effect could result from the operation of that cause.

Note that Hume is here supposing that, in our idea of the relation between cause and effect, the "tye or connexion ... which binds them together" is necessary ("it is impossible that any other effect could result"). In the corresponding section of the *Treatise*, Book 1, part 3, section 2 ("Of probability; and of the idea of cause and effect"), Hume makes this completely explicit (T 1.3.2.11; SBN 77):

Shall we then rest contented with these two relations of contiguity and succession, as affording a compleat idea of causation? By no means. An object may be continuous and prior to another, without being consider'd as its cause. There is a NECESSARY CONNEXION to be taken into consideration; and that relation is of much greater importance, than any of the other two above-mention'd.

In the *Enquiry*, section 4, part 2, Hume presents his famous skeptical argument concerning causation and induction. Since we need "experience" (i.e., the observation of constant conjunctions) to make any causal claims, Hume now asks (EHU 4.14; SBN 32): "*What is the foundation of all conclusions from experience?*" The conclusion from an experience of constant conjunction is an inference to what has not yet been observed from what has already been observed, and Hume finds an unbridgeable gap between the premise (summarising what we have observed so far) nd the (not yet observed) conclusion of this inference (EHU 4.16; SBN 34): These two propositions are far from being the same, *I have found that such an object has always been attended with such an effect*, and *I foresee that other objects, which are, in appearance, similar, will be attended with similar effects.*

Hume concludes that this inference has no foundation in the understanding—that is, no foundation in what he calls "reasoning".[5] How does Hume arrive at this position?

All our inductive inferences—our "conclusions from experience"—are founded on the supposition that the course of nature is sufficiently uniform so that the future will be conformable to the past (EHU 4.21; SBN 37–38):

For all inferences from experience suppose, as their foundation, that the future will resemble the past …. If there be any suspicion, that the course of nature may change, and that the past may be no rule for the future, all experience becomes useless, and can give rise to no inference or conclusion.

Therefore, what Hume is now seeking, in turn, is the foundation in our reasoning for the supposition that nature is sufficiently uniform.

Section 4, part 1 of the *Enquiry* distinguishes (as we have seen) between reasoning concerning relations of ideas and reasoning concerning matters of fact and existence. Demonstrative reasoning (concerning relations of ideas) cannot establish the supposition in question, since it implies no contradiction, that the course of nature may change, and that an object, seemingly like those which we have experienced, may be attended with different or contrary effects. (EHU 4.18; SBN 35)

Moreover, reasoning concerning matters of fact and existence cannot establish it either, since such reasoning is always founded on the relation of cause and effect, the very relation we are now attempting to found in reasoning (EHU 4.19; SBN 35–36):

We have said, that all arguments concerning existence are founded on the relation of cause and effect; that our knowledge of that relation is derived entirely from experience; and that all our experimental conclusions proceed upon the supposition, that the future will be conformable to the past. To endeavour, therefore, the proof of this last proposition by probable arguments, or arguments regarding existence, must be evidently going in a circle, and taking that for granted, which is the very point in question.[6]

Although Hume has now shown that there is no foundation for the supposition that nature is sufficiently uniform in reasoning or the understanding, he goes on, in the following section 5 of the *Enquiry* ("Skeptical Solution of these Doubts"), to insist that we are nonetheless always determined to proceed in accordance with this supposition. There is a natural basis or "principle" for all our arguments from experience, even if there is no ultimate foundation in reasoning (EHU 5.4–5; SBN 42–43):

And though [one] should be convinced, that his understanding has no part in the operation, he would nonetheless continue in the same course of thinking There is some other principle, which determines him to form such a conclusion. This principle is CUSTOM or HABIT. For wherever the repetition of any particular act or operation produces a propensity to renew the same act or operation, without being impelled by any reasoning or process of the understanding; we always say, that this propensity is the effect of *Custom*. By employing that word, we pretend not to have given the ultimate reason of such a propensity. We only point out a principle of human nature, which is universally acknowledged, and which is well known by its effects.[7]

In section 7 of the *Enquiry* ("On the Idea of Necessary Connexion"), after rejecting the received views of causal necessity, Hume explains that precisely this custom or habit also produces our idea of necessary connection (EHU 7.28; SBN 75):

It appears, then, that this idea of a necessary connexion among events arises from a number of similar instances which occur of the constant conjunction of these events; nor can that idea ever be suggested by any one of these instances, surveyed in all possible lights and positions. But there is nothing in a number of instances, different from every single instance, which is supposed to be exactly similar; except only, that after a repetition of similar instances, the mind is carried by habit, upon the appearance of one event, to expect its usual attendant, and to believe that it will exist. This connexion, therefore, which we *feel* in the mind, this customary transition of the imagination from one object to its usual attendant, is the sentiment or impression, from which we form the idea of power or necessary connexion. Thus, the custom or habit to make the inductive inference not only gives rise to a new idea of not yet observed instances resembling the instances we have already observed, it also produces a feeling of determination to make the very inductive inference in question. This feeling of determination, in turn, gives rise to a further new idea, the idea of necessary connexion, which has no resemblance whatsoever with anything we have observed.

It is derived from an "impression of reflection" (an internal feeling or sentiment), not from an "impression of sensation" (an observed instance before the mind), and it is in precisely this sense, for Hume, that the idea of necessary connection is merely subjective. Hume emphasizes that this is a "discovery" both "new and extraordinary", and that it is skeptical in character (EHU 7.28–29; SBN 76):

No conclusions can be more agreeable to scepticism than such as make discoveries concerning the weakness and narrow limits of human reason and capacity. And what stronger instance can be produced of the surprising ignorance and weakness of the understanding, than the present? For surely, if there be any relation among objects, which it imports to us to know perfectly, it is that of cause and effect.

Kant agrees with Hume that neither the relation of cause and effect nor the idea of necessary connection is given in our sensory perceptions; both, in an important sense, are contributed by our mind. For Kant, however, the concepts of both causality and necessity arise from precisely the operations of our understanding— and, indeed, they arise entirely a priori as pure concepts or categories of the understanding. It is in precisely this way that Kant thinks that he has an answer to Hume's skeptical problem of induction: the problem, in Kant's terms, of grounding the transition from merely "comparative" to "strict universality" (A91–92/B123–124). Thus in § 29 of the *Prolegomena*, as we have seen, Kant begins from a merely subjective "empirical rule" of constant conjunction or association among our perceptions (of heat following illumination by the sun), which is then transformed into a "necessary and universally valid law" by adding the a priori concept of cause.

At the end of our discussion in section 1 above we saw that there is a serious difficulty in understanding what Kant intends here—a difficulty to which he himself explicitly calls attention. Kant does not think that the particular causal law that "the sun is through its light the cause of heat" is itself a synthetic a priori truth.
Indeed, the very same difficulty is present in our discussion at the beginning of this section. For, what Kant is saying in § II of the second edition of the Introduction to the *Critique* is that necessity and strict universality are "secure criteria of an *a priori* cognition" (B4; emphasis added). More specifically (B3):

Experience in fact teaches us that something is constituted thus and so, but not that it cannot be otherwise. Hence, if ... a proposition is thought together with its *necessity*, then it is an a priori judgment.

Yet, once again, Kant does not think that particular causal laws relating specific causes to specific effects are all (synthetic) a priori. Accordingly, when Kant provides examples of (synthetic) a priori cognitions in the immediately following paragraph, he cites the synthetic a priori principle of the Second Analogy of Experience ("All alterations take place in accordance with the law of the connection of cause and effect" [B232]) rather than any particular causal law (B4–5):

Now it is easy to show that there actually are such judgments in human cognition which are necessary and in the strictest sense universal, and therefore purely a priori. If one wants an example from the sciences, then one need only take a look at any of the propositions of mathematics. If one wants such an example from the most common use of the understanding, then the proposition that every alteration must have a cause can serve.

On the basis of this important passage, among others, the majority of twentieth-century English-language commentators have rejected the idea that Kant has a genuine disagreement with Hume over the status of particular causal laws. One must sharply distinguish between the general principle of causality of the Second Analogy—the principle that every event b must have a cause a—and particular causal laws: particular instantiations of the claim that all events of type A must always be followed by events of type B. The former is in fact a synthetic a priori necessary truth holding as a transcendental principle of nature in general, and this principle is explicitly established in the Second Analogy.

But the Second Analogy does not establish, on this view, that particular causal laws are themselves necessary. Indeed, as far as particular causal laws are concerned, the Second Analogy is in basic agreement with Hume: they (as synthetic *a posteriori*) are established by induction and by induction alone.

It is indeed crucially important to distinguish between the general principle of causality Kant establishes in the Second Analogy and particular causal laws. It is equally important that particular causal laws, for Kant, are (at least for the most part) synthetic a posteriori rather than synthetic a priori. It does not follow, however, that Kant agrees with Hume about the status of synthetic a posteriori causal laws. On the contrary, Kant (as we have seen) clearly states, in § 29 of the *Prolegomena* (the very passage where he gives his official "answer to Hume"), that there is a fundamental difference between a mere "empirical rule" (heat always follows illumination by the sun) and a genuine objective law (the sun is through its light the cause of heat) arrived at by adding the a priori concept of cause to the merely inductive rule. Any law thus obtained is "necessary and universally valid", or, as Kant also puts it, we are now in possession of "completely and thus necessarily valid rules". In such cases (A91/B124):

The succession is *necessary*; ... the effect does not merely follow upon the cause but is posited *through* it and follows *from* it. The strict universality of the rule is certainly not a property of empirical rules, which, through induction, can acquire nothing but comparative universality: i.e., extensive utility.

Therefore, it is by no means the case that Kant simply agrees with Hume that particular causal laws are grounded solely on induction and, accordingly, that the necessity we attribute to particular causal connections is merely subjective."(StanfordE of P)

    Yes I wondered about the use of the word 'information', but it does fit nicely into both the telephone message and quantum entanglement scenarios. At a pinch I could steal a wider definition for information as being "Information is any type of pattern that influences the formation or transformation of other patterns" (Shannon C.(1949)*The Mathematical Theory of Communication,)*. So, the 'pattern' of energy in the first ball being the 'information' which the second ball needs to transform its behaviour in space?

Wouldn't you agree that replacing 'necessary connexion' with 'information transfer' moves us on from just making sense of an experience for expediency to establishing process for a causal link. Suceeded in moving to the other side of the world, acquire a beautiful family of his own, becoming an exceptional father and acquiring a well paid career in Australia. I am so proud of his achievements to date. So proud of his high moral standards and the way he is choosing to live his life. Closer to me in some aspect of life, more than he perhaps realises or I could ever hope.

One example of his courage is that he has taken an opportunity to give his family the experience of living with the indigenous people on an aboriginal island for a whole year....brilliant.

Hopefully his kids, Hemmi, Toby and Remmi will have many years to get to know him......and if he wishes he can eventually tell them his own story, better than I ever could. Good luck Al, there is space below....... 🥲

The Blog Posts

Things can only get better?
   Or so you would think!

That was meant to be the close, but 2022/23 still had some kicking to do.

In the first week of June I flew out to Morocco from Toulouse, leaving Candy behind with Bea and Brigid. I met my long time mountain buddy Chris Ainsworth in Marrakesh to go on a guided walk up North Africa's highest mountain, Toubkal(4167m). This was my first time in Africa and my visits to all seven continents complete: Europe, Asia, Oceania, N. America, S. America & Antarctica being the others. I have written the adventure itself up in a previous chapter.

I had lost 5kg since Chris died and put this down to stress. It made going up hill easier, so it was a 2022 win, or so I thought. On my return I had severe diarrhoea, losing a further 5kg. I was also suffering from an aching back when I tried to sleep. The doctor thought I might have a back problem and sent me for an x-ray and physiotherapy, but this was inconclusive. I also started to lose my appetite and a further 2kg.

The next stage was blood tests and what is called in France a Radio Scanner (CT scan). The blood test showed a risk of cancer and the Scanner a 4cm lump on the head of my pancreas, I was referred to a surgeon in Toulouse for an Endoscopy and biopsy. This was top down and thankfully under a general anaesthetic. The biopsy showed the lump was a cancer and the endoscopy showed the cancer had not yet spread. By the time I got to see the Oncologist at Toulouse the cancer had blocked my bile duct and I was going yellow. Another endoscopy at Toulouse put a stent in my bile duct and the yellow started to fade over a number of weeks. Meanwhile, I chose to move my treatment to Foix as it is an hour each way closer to home. There they fitted a 'port' into my chest for what seems is going to be a long term treatment by Chemotherapy.

An interesting note for those of you genetically related to me. My mum died at my age now 66yrs, of the same Pancreatic cancer in 1997 after a 2yr illness. Her cancer had spread, metastasised (spread to her liver), by the time she was diagnosed. Her father, my grandad Joe, died in about 1972, at about 66yrs, of an illness which made him lose weight and unable to keep down food.....the cause was never found, but it could easily have been a similar thing.
Currently the hospital is looking into a possible genetic marker....As of 2023, they didn't find any!

Interestingly my old mate Kevin Boyle was diagnosed with bowel cancer a few months ago. The same thing his mum, Christine, died from. We are, to some extent, living the journey together!

My chemo stated on 5th Sept. 3 months after summiting Toubkal. The Chemo. is once every 2 weeks. It takes 8hrs of drips in a nice room in Foix hospital, with Candy. Followed by 48hrs on a portable drip, through an internal chest plug, at home. We get a free taxi there and back, 1.15hr each way, and the nurse visits me at home for the next 2 days. As I write I've just finished session 5. It makes me feel sick for 7 days and very weak. A walk round the garden is tough! The second week sees improvement, we go shopping or out for a meal. I can manage some gym, stretching and a 1hr walk. The first week on this last session has been much better, so I'm hoping it gets easier as it goes along. We shall see.

December has arrived and I've had 6 long chemo sessions. The effects are less severe and following the chemo I get 4 goodish days, four with no energy or appetite at all, then 5 improving days, before we are off again. I had a scan last week & the results look promising. The cancer has shrunk back a bit and there is no evidence it has spread. I will see the consultant on 22nd to find out what comes next!

Meanwhile, we are taking advantage of 6 weeks off Chemo. Meals out and trips to the coast. To start I managed a couple of flat bike rides along the coast, of 2hrs each & a 3hr walk over the Bois de Linas. We regularly do the Pic de l'Orte(1109m), which is a 3.5km round trip and 150m of ascent..... it takes me about 1.25hrs, lol! More recently we did 3 days biking from a base in Torreille, with a final day of 32km. I do feel so much better.

The Consultant was quite encouraging, though he had noticed another small unidentified lump in my chest, he suggested no investigation was needed yet. My liver & kidneys are clear, but there is some evidence of smaller growths towards my spleen. Apparently these have shrunk back somewhat, so the overall view is positive, with regard to progress.

He was a bit keen to get me back on treatment after 6 weeks, so I'm having 2 x full Chemo sessions, starting on the 29th. This will be followed by 6 reduced doses, taking 3 more months. We are just starting our 'Réveillon' or Christmas Eve meal….so it's going to be a quiet Christmas. Just as things seem to be improving!

    A good X-mas with an afternoon HVR walk, an Ourtiset ascent and a Crêt de Camurac walk. Seven weeks off chemo needed for me to have a 'full fat' session before 6 lighter doses, once a fortnight. 'Full fat' was 'harsh, but next 'semi-skimmed seemed to go well and I recovered ok. 4 times out on the snowshoes in good snow from the door. Mostly up to Telephone Hill, taking about 1.5hrs. Wed. 25th was another semi-skimmed, but before the end I was cold and a bit shaky. They sent me for an échographie on my heart which found the beginnings of a blockage. So I'm going up to Toulouse on Thursday for more tests. The new tablets they gave me have made me feel very sleepy this week. Snow is still here & night time temp is between -4 and -9……..brrrr!

Thursday 2nd Feb. Had a cardiograph. Injected with a fluid and the cardiologist stuck a probe in my wrist. This appeared on a real time x-ray screen like a piece of wire. He played about for a bit, it was really difficult to know what was happening, then it was over. The result it that I have a 'lesion' causing a bit of a blockage in a vein on the left, which needs a stent. I also have a chronic calcareous blockage on the right, which need 'drilling out'. Have to take care for 2 weeks, no exercise…… back on the 15th for 2 nights.

9 th Feb, woke up yellow this morning!! After 9 hours in Emergency at Foix it was decided my stent was blocked & needed to be replaced. Kept in for 8 nights until the op. could be done in Toulouse. It happened on the 15th & seems to be a success. The Cardio was postponed until 23rd and I ended up with a stent in the left artery and 3 in the right…..wow. The op was 1.5hrs, without a general anaesthetic. Chemo for 8 th March at Foix was postponed until I have been signed off by the Cardio. Hopefully this will be at a meeting on 29th March……we shall see! I'm keen to get going, as I don't want to lose the progress I've gained.

5th May, so my cardio exam went fine in March. I am making slow progress, but still find more than a couple of hours of biking very tiring. I enjoy it by the coast as it is very flat. Back on the light Chemo, every other week now. Just had my third. The doc. said that the main cancer has grown a bit and has metastasised a very small amount into my spleen. So it's Chemo every other week for the next 3 to 4 months..........and fight it back, with little hope of an actual cure. Still feel quite tired & nauseous for a couple of days after chemo. Hope this only lasts for 3 to 4 days as it did in the last 2week cycle. Where I got 2x20 Km rides by the coast & a meal out with Candy & Lob. It could all be so much worse!

13th July: signed off until Jan. by the cardiologist, who says my heart is making good progress. The bi-monthly Chemo has settled to 3-4 days of nausea an tiredness, followed by 10 days of relative OK. get tired quickly, but it varies from day to day. Ending up at about 72kg by the time my nausea has ended, I eat as much as I can to try to get back to 75-76kg by the next chemo. My body mass is now 'normal' for my age. Which is strange for me as I have been on the close to obese side all my life and so feel freakishly thin. On the up side Candy likes my new look and it's an excuse for a new wardrobe!

19th August so CT scan early August, with the overall conclusion of 'stabalised' was a good result. This followed by a meeting with my consultant in Toulouse raised the possibility of some radiotherapy. Before this I need a PET scan, which requires 3 weeks off Chemo. I have felt recently that 3 months of chemo is wearing down my body. I get very tired in heat or after 1 hour of any activity. So whoopee, next Chemo 6th Sept. The consultant also cleared me of genetically linked cancer. Good news for Alasdair and the six grandchildren!

Its two weeks now since my last chemo and I'm starting to get a bit of 'get up and go'. Let's hope it continues........Crête du Camurac, here I come. However today was a bit of a sad day, Candy took it quite hard. I decided to sort clothes and ditch those which don't fit, for charity & the bin. These included quite a few lovely Rohan trousers, some shirts & fleeces.

Later this week I'm going to do the same with suits & t & rugby shirts in the loft! Yesterday I was 71 kg, with a waist of 32 inches........from 92kg and 36 inch waste 18 months ago.......I'm not getting back to that, but Candy seems to like my sleeker look, so all good.

Get a bit down sometimes from lack of energy, but it never lasts. The practice of Stoicism through Chris' problems has helped me with that, the thought of "you alright old man?" still brings a tear to my eye.

On the upside I can't describe how pleased I am that Al is doing so well in Aus. Its just the way I hoped my boys would turn out. Not only is he a much better dad than I was, he is upright, principled and smart. Earning lots of money from a job he seems to enjoy & turning down advancement, as I did, for more family time. My admiration for him is unbounded. I can only hope that I have had some small influence? We are more alike than you might wish bud 😉

6th Sept, debrief from PET scan in Toulouse 2 weeks ago. Really pleased, there is no metastasis so I am cleared to start radiotherapy on the main cancer. My first meeting is at Oncopol in Toulouse on the 27th Sept. One more chemo before then. The oncologist has given me some stronger pain killers for my back pain, which worked well until yesterday afternoon, when I became very nauseous..........once again, we shall see!

Appendix 1, Horsforth

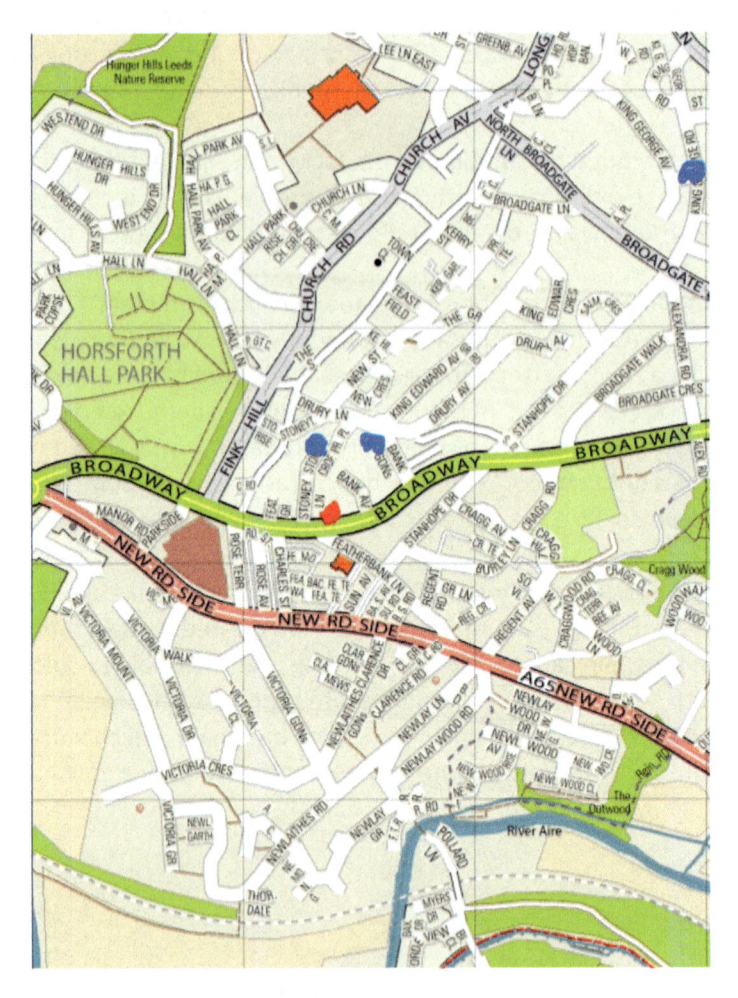

*Blue: Stoney Croft, Bank Gardens and King George Road.
     Stanhope Drive unmarked.
Red: Featherbank School and Broadway Hall (on Broadway)
     Also on the map is Clarence Road (off New Road Side), which had on it Four Gables nursing home & Stanhope Drive is on the right.*

Appendix 2, 12 Stoney Croft, (Right)

The ground is sloping so there is a garage under the kitchen window, but a lawn below the main room window. My bedroom was in the roof above the kitchen window, its roof sloped. it had a window looking east, towards Arthur and Linda's house.

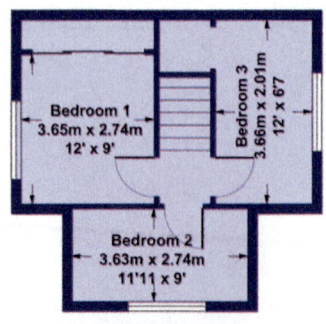

FIRST FLOOR

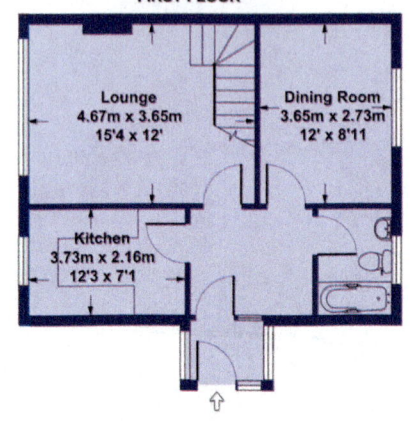

- Bedroom 1: 3.65m x 2.74m (12' x 9')
- Bedroom 2: 3.63m x 2.74m (11'11 x 9')
- Bedroom 3: 3.66m x 2.01m (12' x 6'7)

GROUND FLOOR
STONEY CROFT

- Lounge: 4.67m x 3.65m (15'4 x 12')
- Dining Room: 3.65m x 2.73m (12' x 8'11)
- Kitchen: 3.73m x 2.16m (12'3 x 7'1)

APPROX. GROSS INTERNAL FLOOR AREA 807 SQ FT / 75 SQ M

Appendix 3, AGS Letter [4 was meant to be a class photo of 1967]

COUNTY COUNCIL OF THE WEST RIDING OF YORKSHIRE
EDUCATION DEPARTMENT

AIREDALE AND WHARFEDALE DIVISIONS
EDUCATION OFFICES
BARCROFT
NEW ROAD
YEADON

E. J. DUCKER, M.A.
Divisional Education Officer
Tel.: Rawdon 2261 (4 lines)
In reply please quote:—

2nd June, 1967.

Secondary Education

To the Parent or Guardian of ___Paul David Riley___

Your child has been allocated a place at AIREBOROUGH GRAMMAR SCHOOL and should commence attendance there when the School re-opens on Monday, 4th September, 1967.

The School has a five year course and you have already given an undertaking that if admitted to this school your child will remain in attendance for the full period.

No fees will be payable. All books will be provided through the school and approved travelling expenses, where the distance is over two miles, will be paid in accordance with the Authority's Transport Regulations. Where such travelling is involved the enclosed FORM G.56. should be completed and returned to me at the above address without delay. It should be understood that where a pupil is admitted to a Grammar School other than that regarded as serving the area of residence the approved travelling allowance will not necessarily cover the full cost of travelling.

Subject to the provisions of the Education Act, 1944, the Authority will consider applications for free dinners and/or an allowance in respect of certain approved articles of _distinctive_ _clothing_, to be determined in accordance with an income scale. Applications for such aid should be made on Form G.7. a copy of which may be had from me on request.

Details of school uniform and the Suppliers from which it is available, together with other relevant information concerning the School are enclosed.

Please note that admission to the School is provisional, and if at a later stage it becomes clear that another course is more suitable, transfer will be considered.

If you do not wish to accept this place, please let me know _within seven days_.

If this School is not the one you originally chose it is because there were more applicants than places available, but if any vacancies do arise before September, you will be considered.

Your reference number is D.W. 1708, and this should be quoted in all correspondence.

Yours faithfully,

Appendix 5, a selection of autographs

What is left of the 1967 England Cricket Team, after my dog 'Tiger' got hold of it!

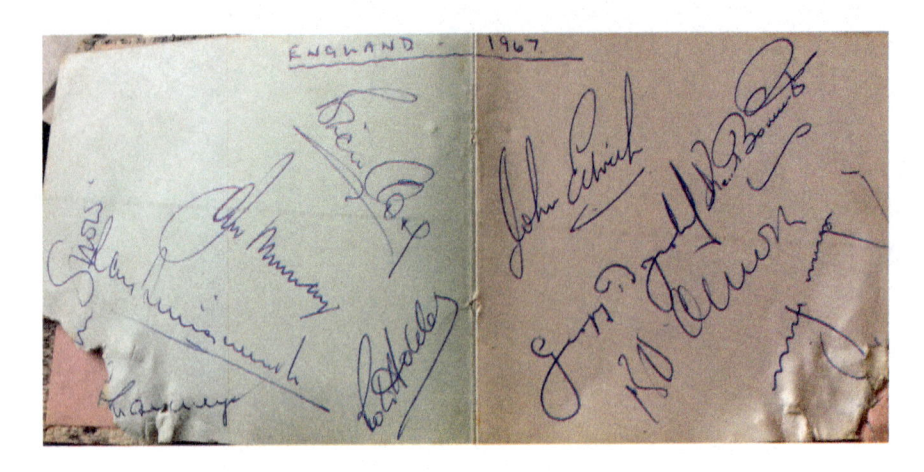

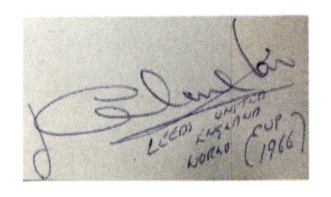

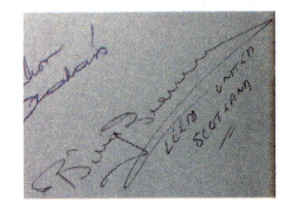

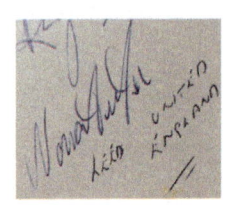

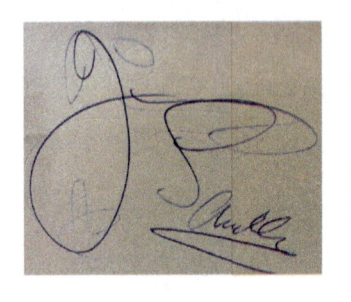

Jack Charlton, Billy Bremner and Norman Hunter from Leeds United

The infamous Jimmy Savile........I sat on his knee in my mum's chair in the office!

Appendix 6 [unfinished] some of the coins I still have

1937-1967 (except 1950 which are quite rare)

1936-1918, including 1926ME

My authority letter from the Bank of England to deal in gold coins. As it turned out I only ever had two Sovereigns and two half Sovereigns.

I sold one Sovereign to buy some other coins, gave one to a girl friend for xmas(Gillian) and lost one at rugby training. The remaining one is below.

My half Sovereigns were similar to this, just a little bigger than a 1p coin.

Appendix 7, Grant Award for 1977/78

```
                                              DATE  19/09/77
LEEDS CITY COUNCIL
DEPARTMENT OF EDUCATION
AID TO STUDENTS

LEEDS AWARD - NOTIFICATION OF VALUE
FINAL REASSESSMENT


AWARD NUMBER  3850 75 13473   ACADEMIC YEAR  77/78

NAME OF STUDENT      MR PAUL D RILEY

INSTITUTION          COLL OF RIPON AND YORKSTJOHN
                     LORD MAYORS WALK
                     YORK
                     YO3 7EX

COURSE               B ED HONS

(A) GROSS VALUE:                                £
    STANDARD MAINTENANCE GRANT              785.00
    ADDITIONAL PAYMENTS
        ADDITIONAL DAYS                       0.00
        DEPENDANTS: SPOUSE                    0.00
                    CHILDREN                  0.00
                    TWO HOMES                 0.00
    MATURE STUDENT GRANT                      0.00
                                          --------
                            TOTAL          785.00
                                          --------
(B) DEDUCTIONS:                                 £
    PARENT'S/SPOUSE'S CONTRIBUTION          346.00
    STUDENTS INCOME                           0.00
                                          --------
                                           346.00
                                          --------
(C) NET VALUE:
    PAYMENT BY LEEDS AUTHORITY              439.00
    PLUS ANY APPROVED FEES.                --------

    NOTE: PREVIOUSLY PAID                     0.00

          AMOUNT DUE                        439.00

    THE FIRST INSTALMENT OF THE GRANT WILL CONTAIN
    THE VACATION ELEMENT. FOR DETAILS SEE THE ENCLOSED
    NOTES

STUDENT

MR PAUL D RILEY
142 HARROGATE ROAD
RAWDON
NR LEEDS
                                   FOR STUDENT
                                   FOR REGISTRAR
```

I was living at home this year, so mum and dad's contribution was board and lodging. It worked out about £14 a week, term time. Most weeks I spent £5 on petrol (50p a gallon) and £7 on living expenses. The rest went on college materials.

Appendix 8, Student Union Cards

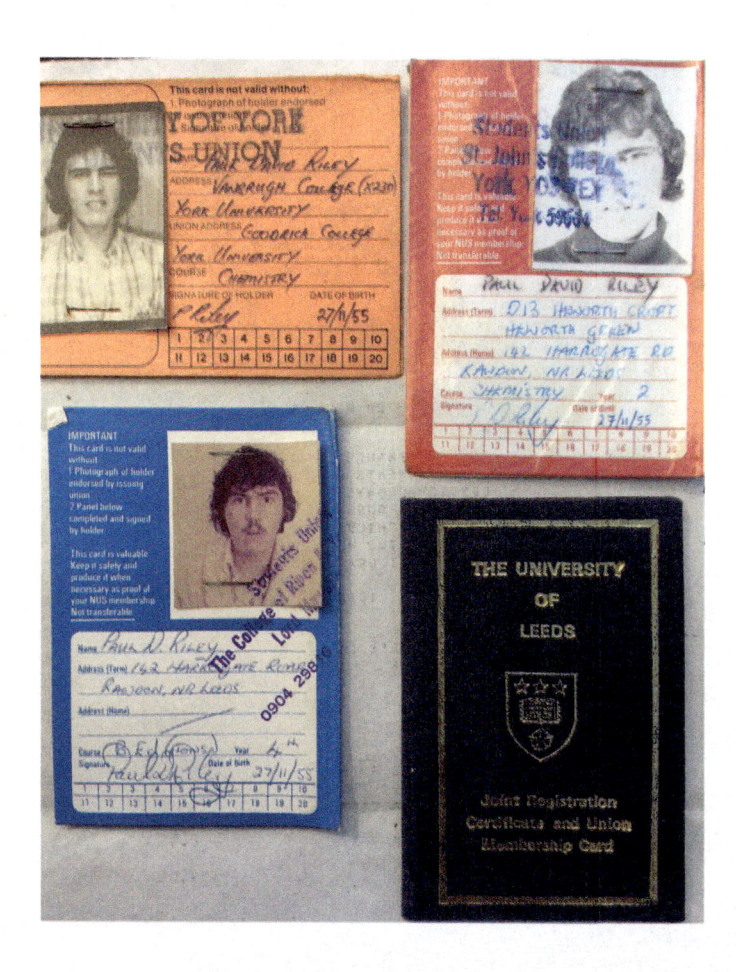

Appendix 9 [Missing] Lesson Observation, final TP, King's Pontefract.

Appendix 10, Cars

These are pictures from the internet, not the actual cars, except for the last two. I've tried to get the colours as close as possible.

Ford Escort Mk 1 Van. Mine was also red and 'H' (1970) reg. It did have large side windows fitted.

Vauxhall Victor Estate. Mine was dark blue and again a 'H' reg. I bought it from my dad, it was the only car he ever owned from new.

Triumph Spitfire Mk. IV. Possibly my favourite car. It was a 'J'reg. so 1971.

Morris 1800 'Roadcrab', Auto. The Spitfire stopped running and I needed a vehicle for work. It was automatic, had a steering gearshift and a bench front seat. Ruth christened it 'Herc'.

Ford Fiesta Mk 1. Something reliable and cheap to run to get Ruth and I to work.

Vauxhall Chevette. Without a doubt my least favourite car. Bought cheap to get me to work, when we moved to Menston.

Vauxhall's Astra Mk II. My first brand new car, bought in 1986, just before Chris was born, from Menston Garage.

Renault Espace Mk II. Another brand new car. A people carrier to get the family around and on Continental camping holidays. It had a roof box and trailer, for the bikes and frame tent.

Renault Laguna Estate. When it came time to changing the Espace the new model Espace was not ready. So we chose a new one of these to fill the gap.

Renault Espace Mk III. This Espace was two years old when we bought it.

Mk 1 Landrover Freelander. Bought after my divorce. The Espace was too big, meant for family holidays. Alasdair and I took it to a Landrover show.

Mk 1 Landrover Freelander(2002). This was a joint purchase with Candy. It was a newer version of the first one above. We had it 2004-2020, it did   178 000 miles.......on one clutch!

Nissan Pathfinder 4.0 lt. L.H.D, Auto. We bought a new car in Qatar. With its 4 wheel drive and leather seats it was the poshest car I will ever own.

Dacia Duster Prestige Blue dCi 115 4x4
LHD, bought new in France(2020) I rather like this car, with all its technology.

Appendix 11 - Mountains and Caves
Mountains Above 3000m

Table 1

Number	Name	Region	Height(m)	Date	Partner(s)	
1	Domes des Miages	Alps/Mont Blanc	3564/3633/3666	21/8/91	Chris Ainsworth	
2	Aig. du Tour	Alps/Mont Blanc	3542	24/8/91	Chris Ainsworth	
3	Aig. du Goûter	Alps/Mont Blanc	3863	27/8/91	Chris Ainsworth	
4	Dome du Goûter	Alps/Mont Blanc	4304	27/8/91	Chris Ainsworth	
5	Mont Blanc	Alps/Mont Blanc	4808	27/8/91	Chris Ainsworth	
6	Gaspaltenhorn(col)	Alps/Bernese	3224	18/8/93	Chris Ainsworth	
7	Tschinglhorn	Alps/Bernese	3576	21/8/93	Chris Ainsworth	
8	Quintino Sella Refuge	Alps/Aosta	3585	16/8/99	Chris Ainsworth	
9	Punta Castor	Alps/Aosta	4221	18/8/99	Chris Ainsworth	
10	Gnifetti refuge	Alps/Aosta	3647	21/8/99	Chris Ainsworth	
11	Signalkuppe (Margarita Refuge)	Alps/Aosta	4554	22/8/99	Chris Ainsworth	
12	Parrotspitze	Alps/Aosta	4432	23/8/99	Chris Ainsworth	
13	Ludwigshohe	Alps/Aosta	4314	23/8/99	Chris Ainsworth	
14	Corno Nero	Alps/Aosta	4321	23/8/99	Chris Ainsworth	
15	Balmenhorn	Alps/Aosta	4167	23/8/99	Chris Ainsworth	
16	Pyramide Vincent	Alps/Aosta	4215	23/8/99	Chris Ainsworth	
17	Tete Sud du Replat	Alps/Dauphine	3442	29/7/02	Chris Riley	Chris Ainsworth
18	Pic du Râteau	Alps/Dauphine	3809	30/7/02	Chris Riley	Chris Ainsworth
19	Pic de Neige Cordier	Alps/Dauphine	3614	4/8/02	Chris Riley	Chris Ainsworth
20	Barre des Ecrins, Dôme de neige	Alps/Dauphine	4012	5/8/02	Chris Riley	Chris Ainsworth
21	Col du Tour Noir	Alps/Mont Blanc	3553	21/7/04	Chris Riley	Chris Ainsworth
22	Grand Montet	Alps/Mont Blanc	3293	22/7/04	Chris Riley	Chris Ainsworth
23	Trient Refuge	Alps/Mont Blanc	3180	27/7/02	Chris Riley	Chris Ainsworth
24	Fenêtre de Saleina	Alps/Mont Blanc	3200	28/7/04	Chris Riley	Chris Ainsworth
25	Col Sup.du Tour	Alps/Mont Blanc	3289	29/7/04	Chris Riley	Chris Ainsworth
26	Pisang Gompa	Nepal/Annapurna	3300	15/10/07	Monkman, Ogden	Stone
27	Manang	Nepal/Annapurna	3519	16/10/07	Monkman, Ogden	Stone
28	Yak Karta	Nepal/Annapurna	4000	18/10/07	Monkman, Ogden	Stone
29	Leder	Nepal/Annapurna	4150	19/10/07	Monkman, Ogden	Stone
30	Ban Thanti	Nepal/Annapurna	3180	15/2/10	AKIS, DofE expéd.	Candy Giaquinto
31	Breche du Replat	Alps/Dauphine	3286	14/8/13	Chris Ainsworth	Mark Bonner
32	Refuge Des Ecrins	Alps/Dauphine	3173	18/8/13	Chris Ainsworth	Mark Bonner
33	Britannia Hutte	Alps/SasFee	3030	13/8/15	Chris Ainsworth	Mark Bonner
34	Freejoc	Alps/ Sas Fee	3826	17/8/15	Chris Ainsworth	Mark Bonner
35	Allalinhorn	Alps/Sas Fee	4027	18/8/15	Chris Ainsworth	Mark Bonner
36	Mittaghorn	Alps/Sas Fee	3143	20/8/15	Chris Ainsworth	Mark Bonner
37	Weismeis (col)	Alps/Sas Fee	3800	22/8/15	Chris Ainsworth	Mark Bonner
38	Pic d'Aneto	Pyrenees/Aragon	3404	17/8/17	Chris Ainsworth	Mark Bonner
39	Pic de Maupas	Pyrenees/Luchon	3109	20/8/17	Chris Ainsworth	Mark Bonner
40	Pic du Montcalm	Pyrenees/Ariege	3077	17/9/18	Candy Giaquinto	Mari-Jo Daingneaux
41	Pique d'Estats	Pyrenees/Catalonia	3143	17/9/18	Mari-Jo Daingneaux	
42	Pic de Verdaguer	Pyrenees/Catalonia	3131	17/9/18	Mari-Jo Daingneaux	
43	Mont Perdu	Pyrenees/Odessa	3352	15/8/19	Chris Ainsworth	Mark Bonner

The tour de MONT BLANC

Words & pictures: Paul Riley

With only a couple of years experience at fellwalking in the English Lakes and the Yorkshire Dales it was a big decision to attempt the Tour of Mont Blanc. It turned out to be an excellent first taste of Alpine walking and a trek we shall remember for many years. Just right for the Alpine beginner and no more difficult than a tour of the Lake District. Our preparation was simple; to read the English T.M.B. guidebook and to obtain rather expensive maps. We also booked cheap return coach travel from London through the B.M.C.

Non-stop travel by coach from Leeds to Chamonix is not to be recommended for those who like luxury travel. Especially as the night coffee stops through France seem to involve the drivers in putting on all the coach lights and making lots of noise. The advantage was the cheapness and we did get to Chamonix in one piece, though rather bedraggled. It was good to have friends in Chamonix and have a good night's sleep after 29 hours travel.

Our first morning was a great disappointment, from our bed we had a splendid view of the plastic bubbles of the telepherique vanishing into the mist on their way to Planpraz. It was with a certain lethargy we left our sweaty pit and, missing an Alpine start by some six hours, made our way to the plastic bubble stop. From Chamonix this gives the most direct start to the T.M.B. route and also provides an easy finish.

Once at Planpraz we were off. My pack seemed very heavy as we toiled up the well marked path to our first summit, the Brevent (8,284 ft). In fact at 24 and 30 pounds per pack we had cut our kit to the bare minimum as we intended to use small hotels, refuges and dortoirs for beds. We also decided to dine in whatever style we could afford, or find, each evening. Breakfast and lunch was to be taken "on the hoof", needing two days supplies to be carried at the most. The rest of our kit comprised only a change of clothes, light footwear, waterproofs, first aid, water container, wash kit and light sleeping bag. We also carried one cooking pot and a small Camping Gaz stove with a 190g cartridge. The gas lasted the whole tour and an emergency dehydrated chilli made a round trip from Leeds.

The view from the Brevent in mist was not memorable. The cafe, complete with a mass of teenage tourists and fizzy pop cans, was something of a shock. We were happy to be on our way, into the mist, towards Les Houches. As the mist cleared we were able to see the long white fingers across the valley of the Bossons and Taconnaz Glaciers stretching deep into the Chamonix valley.

A cup of tea in Les Houches was splendid preparation for the ascent to the Col de Voza. As we made the Col the improved weather turned to torrential rain. We were pleased to see a single unshaded light showing a sign of life at the Belvue Hotel. Though rather quaint and quite run down the food was good and the wine very welcome. Better weather later that evening provided excellent views of our day's labours and the promise of things to come.

Starting to walk by 6.30 a.m. became the status quo for the rest of the tour and by 7.15 a.m. we were making precarious progress over the bridge at the foot of the Bionnassay glacier. The Co de Tricot and the steep pull to the Chalets du Truc went without too much pain and we reached Tontamines by 2.00 p.m. More progress could have been made but we needed to stock up with food and lire for our journey towards Italy. Shops and Banks which close in the afternoon can be a problem.

The long walk south slowly climbing the Val Montjoie was made easy by a cool wind. Through woodland and fields of clanking cows the path stretched out to the Col du Bonhomme. Just as we arrived at the rather windy col, over patchy snow, we had our first and only light snowfall. This seemed to me very strange for July. Around from the Col is the refuge which is a must for all T.M.B.ers. The food, brought from the valley by foot, is excellent. This also gave us our first experience of sharing a room with 25 others, five of them in our bed! For those with more base interests

Mont Blanc from the Grand Balcon

Glacier de Trient & Aiguille de Tour

20

The Tour de Mont Blanc

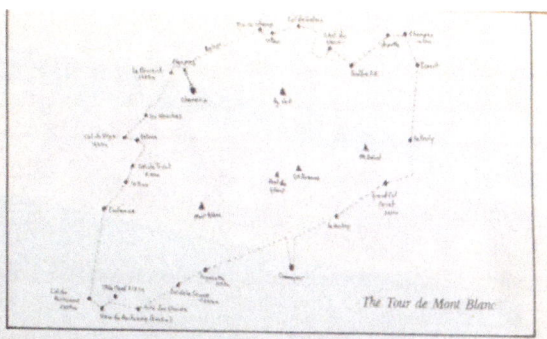

the outside toilet has a hole in the door which gives a fantastic view of the Les Chapieux valley 3,000ft below.

Day four saw us at 9,000ft with a short return walk to the Tete Nord des Fours followed closely by a 1km glissade over a rather large patch of snow. This was the warmest day of our tour and made the walk up to the Franco/Italo border at Col de la Seigne go on forever. Frequent stops, to take photographs of course, were rewarded with superb views of the Glacier des Glaciers and Aiguilles des Glaciers. Once at the Col Mont Blanc came into sight, but just as spectacular was the view down the Val Veny, the sight of our next day's struggle.

The Elizabetha Refuge was rather full. However, a room with a view and good food more than made up for the noise. For purists this refuge is too easy to reach by road. We met four Frenchmen, over dinner, doing the tour in four days. In return for a needle and cotton for their blisters(??) they introduced Ruth, my wife, to the local spirit.

The next day was our longest walk. We decided to push on to Cormayeur and up the Italian Val Ferret to La Vachey. The road walking was easy and lunch in Cormayeur was had at the Red Lion. Well, we all know a pie and a pint is traditional English tourist fayre. The dortoir at La Vachey is rather like an outhouse next to the small hotel. Real spaghetti bolognese was on the menu.

Mist again clogged our ascent to the Grand Col Ferret. Just like a blanket being lifted it vanished as soon as we were over the Col. Once in the Swiss Val Ferret most of the walking is along narrow roads but the views of the Mont Dolent mountains take your mind off the tarmac below your feet. In La Fouley we had a cheap night in a good ski lodge. The night was broken by a severe storm which had, we heard later, taken lives near Chamonix.

As we set out down the road to Issert we had a feeling of being on our way back. Once again we were walking in light mist but luck was with us and it did not rain. Champex was passed quickly and the night was spent in a dortoir, Arpette. Before dinner we walked by the stream and Ruth made a delicate crossing of a ladder bridge. Never try to follow your wife over a ladder bridge!!

The Fenetre d'Arpette was the highlight of the tour. A notch on the skyline at first opens to a small Col as the steep ascent is made. Once at the Col, which is very narrow, there is a superb view of the morning's endeavours and the prospect of an almost precipitous descent towards Trient. Most spectacular though is the proximity of the Trient glacier and a feeling of real altitude. Pressing on down the valley we were surprised to meet some friends from home. They walked with us for some time but we had become quite fit over the past few days and soon left them behind as we headed for the Franco/Swiss border at Col de Balme. Feeling very much in the mood for celebration our evening meal was a fondue and a couple of bottles of wine in la Tour.

Although we only had a short distance to cover on the last half day things did not start well. Confusion over paying our hotel bill in Swiss francs to a receptionist who spoke no English was only resolved by getting the manager from his bed. This was soon left behind and after a short pull onto the 'Grand Balcon' all seemed right with the world. The route here is very impressive with its not so dangerous 'passage dangereuse'. There were good views over the valley to the Aig Vert, Mont Blanc and the Mer de Glace. It was here, on a particularly narrow stretch, we met a lone Frenchman clung to the rockface. There was no need for words to be exchanged as his eyes pleaded with us to step out and let him slide past, hands and face to the rock. We really shouldn't have but we fell about with laughter as the apparition rounded the next bend.

Finishing at Planpraz after 8½ days, about 100 miles and 30,000ft of ascent, into tourists and the smell of frying chips was a bit of an anti-climax. The return to Chamonix, or Cham as we alpinists call it!, was rather good. Once again in the plastic bubble of the telepherique we were launched into the valley. A magnificent end to a truly memorable walk.

INFORMATION
Tour of Mont Blanc, Walking Guide, Andrew Harper, Cicerone Press.
Carte touristique 231 and 232, Massif du Mont Blanc 1:25,000.
British Mountaineering Council, Crawford House, Precinct Centre Booth St. East, Manchester.

21

Printed in Great Britain
by Amazon